# Crowned with Immortal Glory

# Princeton Theological Monograph Series

K. C. Hanson, Charles M. Collier, D. Christopher Spinks,
and Robin A. Parry, Series Editors

*Recent volumes in the series:*

Robert A. Hand
*Theological Epistemology in Immanuel Kant's Transcendental Idealism and Karl Barth's Theology*

Scott P. Rice
*Trinity and History: The God-World Relation in the Theology of Dorner, Barth, Pannenberg, and Jenson*

Hakbong Kim
*Person, Personhood, and the Humanity of Christ: Christocentric Anthropology and Ethics in Thomas F. Torrance*

Lisanne Winslow
*A Trinitarian Theology of Nature*

Matthew T. Prior
*Confronting Technology: The Theology of Jacques Ellul*

Edmund Fong
*Obedience from First to Last: The Obedience of Jesus Christ in Karl Barth's Doctrine of Reconciliation*

Chad Michael Rimmer
*Greening the Children of God: Thomas Traherne and Nature's Role in the Ecological Formation of Children*

Steven Schafer
*Marriage, Sex, and Procreation: Contemporary Revisions to Augustine's Theology of Marriage*

# Crowned with Immortal Glory
*Eschatological Hope in the Spirituality of William Perkins*

MATTHEW HUTTON HARTLINE

*Foreword by Donald K. McKim*

☙PICKWICK *Publications* · Eugene, Oregon

CROWNED WITH IMMORTAL GLORY
Eschatological Hope in the Spirituality of William Perkins

Princeton Theological Monograph Series

Copyright © 2024 Matthew Hutton Hartline. All rights reserved. Except for brief quotations in critical publications or reviews, no part of this book may be reproduced in any manner without prior written permission from the publisher. Write: Permissions, Wipf and Stock Publishers, 199 W. 8th Ave., Suite 3, Eugene, OR 97401.

Pickwick Publications
An Imprint of Wipf and Stock Publishers
199 W. 8th Ave., Suite 3
Eugene, OR 97401

www.wipfandstock.com

PAPERBACK ISBN: 978-1-6667-8850-1
HARDCOVER ISBN: 978-1-6667-8851-8
EBOOK ISBN: 978-1-6667-8852-5

*Cataloguing-in-Publication data:*

Names: Hartline, Matthew Hutton, author. | McKim, Donald K., foreword.

Title: Crowned with immortal glory : eschatological hope in the spirituality of William Perkins / Matthew Hutton Hartline ; foreword by Donald K. McKim.

Description: Eugene, OR : Pickwick Publications, 2024 | Series: Princeton Theological Monograph Series | Includes bibliographical references and index.

Identifiers: ISBN 978-1-6667-8850-1 (paperback) | ISBN 978-1-6667-8851-8 (hardcover) | ISBN 978-1-6667-8852-5 (ebook)

Subjects: LCSH: Perkins, William, 1558–1602. | Theology. | England—Church history—16th century.

Classification: BX9339.P43 .H47 2024 (paperback) | BX9339.P43 .H47 (ebook)

03/11/24

*Scripture quotations from The Authorized (King James) Version. Rights in the Authorized Version in the United Kingdom are vested in the Crown. Reproduced by permission of the Crown's patentee, Cambridge University Press*

"The price and crown for which we run is everlasting glory."
WILLIAM PERKINS

# Contents

*Foreword by Donald K. McKim* | ix

*Preface* | xi

1. Introduction | 1
2. A Perfect Vision of God | 10
3. God to Us: Eternal Union with Christ | 28
4. God with Us: Historical Union with Christ | 53
5. God in Us: The Mystical Union with Christ | 70
6. The Hope of Glory | 93
7. Conclusion | 135

*Appendix 1: The Book of Revelation* | 139

*Appendix 2: Robert Hill* | 150

*Appendix 3: George Gifford* | 152

*Appendix 4: Thomas Brightman* | 155

*Appendix 5: William Perkins's Ocular Catechism* | 158

*Bibliography* | 161

*Index* | 173

# Foreword

WILLIAM PERKINS (1558–1602) WAS a premier English theologian whose writings were important and had long-lasting influence for English and American Puritanism. Perkins was devoted to Reformed theology and used theologians such as John Calvin, Theodore Beza, and Franciscus Gomarus and other Reformed writers throughout his three-volume collected *Works*. The effects of Perkins' theology were significant for generations of Reformed Christians.

Perkins was committed to showing how theological concepts can impact the lives of Christians in the church. He advocated a unity of "theology" and "ethics"—what one believes should be expressed in how one lives. Perkins' rigorous theology was coupled with a concern for "piety," or the living Christian faith of those who read his works. This emerged from Perkins' understanding of theology itself. He wrote in his major book, *A Golden Chaine: or, The Description of Theologie*, that "Theology is the science of living blessedly forever."[1] Theology provides right teaching about who God is and what God has done; but it also impacts one's personal life so one may live "blessedly forever"!

This blending of doctrine and Christian living is seen in Perkins' use of a "Doctrine/Uses" pattern in which he discusses a Christian doctrine and then goes on to expound the "Uses" or benefits of this doctrine for Christian living. This signals Perkins' concern for readers to understand that Christian theology impacts life and—indeed!—provides insights that enable Christians to be those who will be "living blessedly forever."

These emphases are found clearly in this fine book by Matthew Hartline. This splendid work treats Perkins' eschatology—his views, based on Scripture, of the future of the world and the future for Christian believers. Hartline's, *Crowned with Immortal Glory: Eschatological Hope in the*

---

1. Perkins, *Golden Chain*, 6:11.

FOREWORD

*Spirituality of William Perkins* shows us that Perkins' views of the glorious, eternal future in immortal glory that awaits those who believe in Jesus Christ are grounded in his understandings of important Christian theological doctrines and themes. What one believes now has eternal consequences—and glorious benefits! Also, the "eschatological hope"—the hope Christians have for their ultimate future—affects their lives of the Christian faith in the present, in the here and now. Theology helps us "live blessedly forever" while our great hope for the future shapes and directs the lives we live by faith throughout all our days.

This interplay of present and future; future and present was a basic feature of William Perkins' theology. Now, Hartline helps us see how this is developed throughout Perkins' writings and the impact this approach can have for contemporary Christian believers. Hartline's rich explication of Perkins' theology, including eschatology, enables us to appreciate even more deeply what Perkins described as being "ravished" with "the meditation of the glorious estate of the kingdom of heaven."[2]

Perkins' eschatological perspectives are pervasive through his many works. By focusing on the "eschatological hope" of which Perkins wrote, Hartline's book can be seen as an effective introduction to William Perkins' whole theology. The eschatological focus sheds light on major elements of Perkins' entire theological thought. The great benefit is that we can read Hartline's book and have a clarity on many of Perkins' key theological commitments. At the same time, Hartline's presentation of Perkins' eschatology fills a lacuna in Perkins studies. This full treatment will be a helpful guide for scholars who will read this work with interest.

The flavor of Perkins' approach to Christian faith and life comes through in the language of Perkins himself. Perkins is quoted plentifully. Hartline admirably organizes this study and shows how various categories relate to each other. This book is a compelling, theologically-grounded presentation of Perkins' eschatology.

We receive this work with gratitude to the author for his scholarly labors. Here we receive insights from the great William Perkins who continues to bless us with his theological writings. Perkins reminds us that "blessed life arises from the knowledge of God."[3]

Donald K. McKim
Germantown, Tennessee

2 Perkins, *Estate of Damnation or in the Estate of Grace*, 8:496.
3 Perkins, *Golden Chain*, 6:11.

# Preface

For most of my Christian life, I have greatly profited from the writings and teachings of the Puritans. Their pursuit of, and devotion to, the glory of God in all of life has been inspiring––something to be admired, respected, and imitated. It has been said that Puritan spirituality "seeks a deeper awareness of God's presence as defined by the Christian faith according to the Bible."[1] As Leland Ryken remarks, "The Puritan movement was populated by a God-obsessed people."[2] This God-obsession is on full display in the writings of William Perkins. I thank God for raising up a man like Perkins, and for continuing to use his writings today.

I owe a great debt to those who have gifted me the time and resources to pursue my study of William Perkins's doctrine of eschatological glory. I am grateful for their prayers, encouragement, and support. While these are but words on paper, it is important for me to acknowledge them and thank them.

First, I want to thank First Baptist Church of Cobden. I have been privileged to pastor this wonderful congregation for the past ten years, seven of which I have spent pursuing part-time my MDiv and PhD at The Southern Baptist Theological Seminary. I thank God for the love and encouragement they have shown to me and my family. Their financial support and continual prayers have been a great encouragement. I must make special mention of Mrs. Peggy Dent, who proofread every paper I have written. I am amazed by her patience, guidance, and assistance. Hopefully, I have by now made her a fan of the Puritans. I also want to thank my pastor, mentor, and close friend, Dr. Ed Falgout. I have seen in him what it means to be a faithful pastor. He has shown me how to lead God's people biblically and lovingly in the truth. I do not have the words to describe my gratitude to him for his leadership, pastoral care, and most importantly his friendship.

---

[1] Gleason and Kapic, *Devoted Life*, 24.
[2] Ryken, *Worldly Saints*, 11.

Second, I want to thank Dr. J. Stephen Yuille. From the beginning of my MDiv course work to my last PhD seminar, Dr. Yuille has taught, advised, and mentored me beyond all expectations of a seminary professor. He has instilled in me a greater love and passion for teaching, and the necessity for having an informed biblical spirituality. As advisor for my dissertation, I want to thank him for his encouragement and guidance in pursuing this specific project. He led me in the direction I needed to go and gave me the freedom to pursue avenues I wanted to take. I am thankful he always took the time to respond promptly and exhaustively to all my questions (and there were many). His supervision and direction have been indispensable throughout my time at The Southern Baptist Theological Seminary. As for the rest of the advisory committee, Drs. Donald Whitney and Shawn Wright, both of whom I was privileged to have as seminary professors, I am thankful for their time, input, and instruction. Their love for God and his word, and their faithfulness in following it and teaching it have set a tremendous standard for me to follow. Lastly, I want thank Dr. Donald K. McKim for serving as my external reader. I consider it a great privilege that he willingly took the time to engage with my work. To all these men, I am humbled and honored for your time, insight, and critique.

Third, I want to thank my parents (Steve and Lisa) for their continuous love. I am beyond grateful that they gave me Christ and his gospel from the moment I was born. Their support in all my endeavors has been unwavering. I am blessed to have them as my father and mother, and I thank God for his faithfulness to their home.

Lastly, I am so thankful for Carrie, my best friend, co-laborer in Christ, and the wife of my youth. She merits recognition more than anyone else. Words cannot express the love and gratitude I have for her. Were it not for her encouragement, support, and patience, I would not have started, let alone finished, this work. She has expressed a love toward me that I could never repay. I want to convey my love and gratitude to her for picking up where I have lacked, fixing what I have broken, and stepping in where I have been absent. She has shown grace and mercy over the years that only comes from an ultimate love for Christ. I can only wish to give her the love that she has shown me. She is a gift to me, an excellent wife, a loving mother to Lillie and Judah, and a keeper of her home. "She is far more precious than jewels."

I am honored to have written this book, and I pray it serves to edify the church of the Lord Jesus Christ to the glory of his great name.

MATTHEW HARTLINE

# Introduction

## Biographical Sketch

WILLIAM PERKINS WAS BORN in 1558 in Marston Jabbett, Warwickshire, located in central England, to Thomas and Hannah Perkins.[1] It was a significant year, as it marked the beginning of the reign of Elizabeth I. Perkins died in 1602, making Elizabeth the only sovereign he ever knew.[2] Unfortunately, very little is recorded of Perkins's childhood. In 1577, at the age of nineteen, he enrolled in Christ's College, Cambridge. An early biographer records, "No sooner was he admitted in Christ's college . . . but quickly the wildfire of his youth began to break out."[3] He indulged in "recklessness, profanity, and drunkenness."[4] He was also "much addicted to the study of natural magic."[5] His curiosity in the "black art" was such that "he bordered on hell itself."[6] Years later, Perkins reflected, "I have long studied this art [of astrology], and [I] was never quiet until I had seen all the secrets of the

---

1. Beeke and Pederson, *Meet the Puritans*, 469.
2. For a fuller understanding of the historical significance of the Elizabethan reign and William Perkins, see Beeke and Yuille, "Biographical Preface," 1:ix–xxxii. For a more thorough analysis, Paterson, *William Perkins*; Paterson, "William Perkins," 252–69; Sisson, "Apologist," 495–502; Wright, "William Perkins," 171–96. Additionally, see Yuille, *Living Blessedly Forever*; Beeke and Yuille, *William Perkins*.
3. Fuller, *Abel Redevius*, 432.
4. Beeke and Pederson, *Meet the Puritans*, 469.
5. Fuller, *Abel Redevius*, 432.
6. Fuller, *Abel Redevius*, 432.

same. But at length it pleased God to lay before me the profaneness of it, nay, I dare boldly say, idolatry, although it is covered with fair and golden shows."[7]

While a student, Perkins allegedly overheard a mother scolding her son for behaving poorly. As a punishment, she threatened to hand him over to "drunken Perkins."[8] Although the details of the story are impossible to corroborate, the change that occurred in Perkins is beyond dispute. Burdened by his sin, he fled to Christ for refuge. "The happy hour was now come," writes Thomas Fuller, "wherein the straggling sheep was brought home to the fold, and his vanity and mildness corrected into temperance and gravity."[9] Samuel Clarke remarks, "The Lord in mercie was pleased to reclaim him, that hee might bee an eminent instrument of good in his Church."[10]

Under the tutelage of Laurence Chaderton, considered by many to be "the pope of Cambridge Puritanism,"[11] Perkins began to devote himself to his studies. He was formally trained in Reformed theology "within a scholastic framework," for Cambridge was the "leading Puritan[12] center of the day."[13] He possessed "a rare felicity in speedy reading of books, and as it were but turning them over would give an exact account of all considerables therein.... He took strict notice of all passages, as if he had dwelt on them particularly; perusing books so speedily, one would think he read nothing; so accurately, one would think he read all."[14] Perkins received his

---

7. Perkins, *Resolution to the Country Man*, 9:409.

8. This story is recorded in Beeke and Pederson, *Meet the Puritans*, 469; Beeke and Yuille, "Biographical Preface," 1:xi. However, both admit that the details might be "apocryphal." Beeke and Yuille, "Biographical Preface," l:xi. Paul R. Schaefer Jr. also quotes this story in "Spiritual Brotherhood," 65–66. Schaefer, Beeke, and Yuille quote from Brook, *Lives of the Puritans*, 2:129.

9. Fuller, *Abel Redevius*, 432–33.

10. Clarke, *Marrow of Ecclesiastical History*, 414–15.

11. Beeke and Yuille, "Biographical Preface," l:xi.

12. The term *Puritan* (or *Puritanism*) is difficult to define due to its broad range of usage. For an introduction to the historical, sociological, political, ecclesiastical, theological, and spiritual use of this term, see Yuille, *Puritan Spirituality*. See also Yuille, *Great Spoil*; Packer, *Quest for Godliness*. I adopt the definition of Beeke and Yuille who use the term *Puritan* to describe "those who desired to reform the Church of England and promote a life of godliness consistent with the Reformed theology of grace." Beeke and Yuille, "Biographical Preface," l:x.

13. Beeke and Pederson, *Meet the Puritans*, 469.

14. Beeke and Yuille, "Biographical Preface," l:xii.

bachelor's degree in 1581, and master's degree in 1584. Upon receiving the latter, he was ordained into the ministry and appointed as fellow at Christ's College.[15]

From the time of his ordination, Perkins began to preach to prisoners at Cambridge Castle.[16] Following "Christ's example," he preached "'deliverance to the captives,' whose bodies were in prison, and souls in a dungeon.... Here, though free himself, he begot sons to God in fetters: many an Onesimus in bonds was converted to Christ."[17] From 1584 until the time of his death, Perkins also ministered as a lecturer at Great St. Andrew's Church, Cambridge.[18] He was also a fellow at Christ's College from 1584 to 1595, serving as dean from 1590 to 1591. During this time, he preached, lectured, and tutored students. He served in this role at Christ's College until 1595, when he left the position to marry a widow, named Timothye Cradock.[19]

In addition to his prison ministry, lecturing and pastoring at St. Andrew's Church, and serving as fellow at Christ's College, Perkins catechized "students at Corpus Christi College on Thursday afternoons, lecturing on the Ten Commandments in a manner that deeply affected them. He also worked as an adviser on Sunday afternoons, counseling the spiritually distressed."[20] What made Perkins stand out, and what made his preaching and lecturing so effective, was his tremendous ability to take the rich truths of Scripture and apply them in the most effectual and practical ways to his listeners. "His sermons were not so plain, but the piously learned did admire them; nor so learned, but the plain did understand them," writes

15. Beeke and Yuille, *William Perkins*, 8.

16. Several biographical sketches tell the story of Perkins proclaiming the gospel to a convict right before his execution by hanging. The convict went from being fearful of death and hell to being comforted and taking "his death with such patience and alacritie, as if hee actually saw himself delivered from the hell which hee feared before, and heaven opened for the receiving of his soul, to the great rejoicing of the beholders." Clarke, *Marrow of Ecclesiastical History*, 418. For a vivid description of this incident, see Moore, "Predestination and Evangelism."

17. Fuller, *Abel Redevius*, 433.

18. Beeke and Yuille write, "The regular pastor assumed all other church responsibilities, thereby freeing the lecturer to focus exclusively on expounding God's Word." Beeke and Yuille, *William Perkins*, 15.

19. Beeke and Yuille explain, "During their seven years of marriage, they conceived seven children—three of whom died in infancy." Beeke and Yuille, "Biographical Preface," l:xv.

20. Beeke and Yuille, "Biographical Preface," l:xiii.

Clarke. "Hee brought the Schools into the Pulpit, and unshelling their controversies out of their hard School-tearms, made thereof plain and wholsom meat for his people."[21] Joel Beeke points out, "Perkins aimed to wed predestinarian preaching with practical, experiential living."[22] As a result, Perkins had a great influence upon the common people of his day, as well as great divines such as Richard Sibbes, John Cotton, John Preston, and William Ames.[23]

Perkins was not only a wise counselor and powerful orator, but he was a prolific writer. Even in his earliest work "did that blessed Spirit begin to show itself which afterwards was so mighty and powerful in his tongue and pen."[24] Harry C. Porter records that between 1590 and 1618, there were nearly 210 books printed and published in Cambridge, and of these, "over fifty were works by Perkins."[25] Jonathan Moore notes, "Given the relatively small number of publishing houses in England at that time, this is the rough equivalent of Perkins' theology today being published in one out of every ten books across all subjects."[26] While living, he published twenty-one books and became "the first of the Cambridge best-selling authors."[27] As a result of the editorial work of students and friends, an additional twenty-seven books appeared after his death. All of his works were gathered into three-volumes in 1608.[28] Subsequently, they were translated into Spanish, Welsh, Irish, French, Italian, Hungarian, and Czech. Regarding Colonial America, historian Samuel Morison notes, "The New England Puritans quoted their revered Ames and Perkins and the church fathers much more than they did Calvin. . . . Ames and Perkins, Preston and Chaderton, were

---

21. Clarke, *Marrow of Ecclesiastical History*, 415.

22. Beeke and Pederson, *Meet the Puritans*, 473.

23. Beeke and Yuille, "Biographical Preface," 1:xiii. The impact of Perkins's ministry "is what [John] Cotton considered the 'one good reason why there came so many excellent preachers out of Cambridge in England, more than out of Oxford.'" Beeke, "William Perkins on Predestination," 185. J. Stephen Yuille quotes Thomas Goodwin, who in 1613 writes, "The town was then filled with the discourse of the power of Master Perkins's ministry, still fresh in most men's memories." Yuille, "Simple Method," 230.

24. Crashawe, "Dedication Epistle," in Perkins, *Fruitful Dialogue*, 449.

25. Porter, *Reformation and Reaction*, 264.

26. Moore, "Predestination and Evangelism," 27. Moore adds, "So that's not just one in ten books in every bookshop, but one in ten books of any and every bookshop in the land!" Moore, "Predestination and Evangelism," 27–28.

27. Spinks, *Two Faces*, 3.

28. Yuille, "William Perkins."

often on their lips, and always in their hearts."[29] Morison records that a "typical Plymouth Colony library comprised a large and small Bible, Ainsworth's translation of the Psalms, and the works of William ('Painful') Perkins, a favorite theologian."[30] His writings greatly influenced divines such as William Brewster, Thomas Hooker, John Winthrop, Roger Williams, Richard Mather, and Jonathan Edwards. It is due to this widespread influence that Perkins became a "pillar of protestant orthodoxy"[31] and "the father of Puritanism."[32]

## Summary of Research

By 1635, eleven posthumous editions of Perkins's writings were printed, containing nearly fifty books.[33] In 1970, Ian Breward collected and published several of Perkins's treatises in one volume.[34] In 2020, Reformation Heritage Books completed its publication of Perkins's *Works* in ten volumes. The Reformation Heritage Books series is the primary resource for this project.

Approximately thirty academic dissertations and theses related to Perkins were completed between 1961 and 2021.[35] In addition, several

---

29. Morison, *Intellectual Life*, 11, 20.

30. Morison, *Intellectual Life*, 134.

31. Moore, "Predestination and Evangelism," 25. He is also included, along with John Calvin and Theodore Beza, in "the trinity of the orthodox." Yuille, "Simple Method," 217.

32. Beeke and Yuille, "Biographical Preface," l:x.

33. Beeke and Yuille, "Biographical Preface," l:xvi. Joel Beeke and Derek Thomas state, "It is puzzling why his full *Works* have not been in print since the early seventeenth century." Beeke and Thomas, "General Preface," 1:vii.

34. Breward, *Work of William Perkins*.

35. Baarsel, *William Perkins*; Ballitch, "Scripture Is Both the Glosse and the Text"; Barbee, "Reformed Catholike"; Breward, "Life and Theology"; Chalker, "Calvin and Some Seventeenth Century English Calvinists"; Cushing, "Inspiration of Scripture"; Ditzenberger, "William Perkins and Seventeenth-Century Conception"; Greve, "Freedom and Discipline"; Grimes, "God's Imposition"; Kendall, "Nature of Saving Faith"; Lee, "Trinitarian Theology and Piety"; Letham, "Saving Faith and Assurance"; Lightfoot, "William Perkins' View of Sanctification"; Markham, "William Perkins' Understanding of the Function of Conscience"; McKim, "Ramism in William Perkins"; Muller, "Predestination and Christology"; Munson, "William Perkins"; Op't Hof, *Engelse Piëtistische Geschriften*; Pipa, "William Perkins and the Development of Puritan Preaching"; Priebe, "Covenant Theology of William Perkins"; Shaw, "Marrow of Practical Divinity"; Schaefer, "Spiritual Brotherhood"; Sisson, "William Perkins"; Sommerville, "Conversion, Sacrament and Assurance"; Song, "Theology and Piety"; Tipson, "Development of a Puritan

published books deal with aspects of his theology, and there are numerous journal articles addressing Perkins's views on a variety of subjects such as preaching, predestination, covenant theology, the conscience, the family, medical ethics, demonology, and covenant theology. Most of these works focus on Perkins's more popular treatises such as *A Golden Chain*; *An Exposition of the Creed*; *Commentary on Galatians*; *Cases of Conscience*; and *An Exposition on the Sermon of the Mount*.

## Research Methodology

This book focuses on a particular aspect of cosmic eschatology.[36] That being the final state of man in glory. Consequently, this work has three chief ends. The first is to define Perkins's eschatological hope; that is, what it means to be "crowned with immortal glory." To date, there has been no major study of Perkins's eschatology. The second end is to demonstrate how Perkins's eschatological hope is dependent upon his formulation of seven theological truths: (1) the divine decrees, (2) the creation, (3) the covenant, (4) the incarnation, (5) the order of salvation, (6) the end times, and (7) the eternal state. Perkins recognized the connection between these truths, writing, "Election, vocation, faith, adoption, justification, sanctification, and eternal glorification, are never separated in the salvation of any man, but as inseparable companions go hand in hand."[37] The third end is to demonstrate how Perkins's eschatological hope shapes his approach to the Christian life, his spirituality. There is a direct relationship between the above seven theological truths and Perkins's pursuit of holiness. His application of eschatological glory falls into four broad categories: (1) meditation, (2)

---

Understanding of Conversion"; Tufft, "William Perkins"; Wilcox, "New England Covenant Theology"; Williams, "Evaluation of William Perkins' Doctrine of Predestination"; Woolsey, *Unity and Continuity in Covenantal Thought*.

36. Theologians distinguish between "cosmic eschatology" and "personal eschatology." Kenneth Gentry identifies cosmic eschatology as "the providentially governed flow of history as it develops toward its foreordained consummation, . . . the unfolding of God's kingdom in history, the second advent of Christ, the resurrection of the dead, the final judgment, and the eternal state." Personal eschatology, he states, deals with "the destiny of the *individual* at death, . . . a study of physical death, the immortality of the soul, and the intermediate state." Gentry, *He Shall Have Dominion*, 5. See Berkhof, *Systematic Theology*, 666–67. See also Vos, *Pauline Eschatology*, 5. While ideas within cosmic eschatology will overlap in this work, the primary focus and development will be man's final and glorified state.

37. Perkins, *Whole Treatise of the Cases of Conscience*, 8:153.

ministry, (3), holiness, and (4) suffering. Naturally, as a Protestant, much of his application deals with the errors of Rome and includes warnings against its teaching and doctrine. As a pastor/teacher, he wanted to see his fellow believers walking in holiness in accordance with the gospel to which they had been called (Eph 4:1). Therefore, he emphasizes the relationship between future and present realities. Biblical promises are to be made real at present, in that they ought to create in believers a sense of urgency to (1) love Christ with all their heart, soul, mind, and strength, (2) obey all he has commanded, and (3) endure to the end with a fullness of joy and confidence.

This study of Perkins's eschatological hope begins with a broad analysis of his eschatology, including his insights on the history of the church, the nature of the millennium, the signs of Christ's return, the final judgment, and the beatific vision. It then proceeds to look at his "order of salvation" laid out in his *Golden Chain*, particularly his understanding of the doctrines of predestination, creation, covenant, union with Christ, justification, and sanctification. With this foundation in place, the work turns to Perkins's thoughts on glorification. From here, the focus shifts to consider what Perkins believes about the resurrection and the eternal state. His eschatological hope is shaped in large part by his view of the realities of Christ's incarnation (i.e., what he became) and glorification (i.e., what he received) and how the believer shares in these two realities in glory. Concluding, the book then demonstrates how this eschatological hope directly influenced Perkins's personal spirituality and pastoral ministry.

There is only one treatise in which Perkins deals exclusively with eschatology: *A Fruitful Dialogue Concerning the End of the World*. While valuable, it is not the definitive work on his eschatology. His views and insights are scattered throughout his entire body of work. Many times, they arise in the context of his doctrinal "uses." While he does not provide a systematic analysis of eschatology, the frequency with which the subject arises in his sermon application confirms how central it is to the entirety of his thought.

By way of secondary resources, it is important to interact with Perkins's contemporaries who contribute in a significant way to discussions on eschatology. While the material is vast, particular attention is given to Robert Hill (d. 1623), George Gifford (1548–1620), and Thomas Brightman (1556–1607).[38] Assisting in this analysis of seventeenth-century eschato-

---

38. All three of these divines wrote treatises on eschatology and the apocalypse. They were contemporaries of Perkins and trained at Cambridge. Together, their works provide

logical paradigms are two modern scholars: Crawford Gribben and Peter Toon. In *The Puritan Millennium*, Gribben places English theologians in their proper historical context and demonstrates how that context shaped their understanding of eschatology. Gribben notes,

> Writers documenting the development of the puritan apocalyptic tradition have repeatedly set puritan ideologies in a vacuum, failing to recognize that eschatology was not something puritans studied so much as something in which they believed themselves to be involved, for the implications of their eschatology were not purely theoretical.[39]

Toon's *Puritans, the Millennium and the Future of Israel* is important as he demonstrates, in terms of eschatology, that most Puritans adhered to what he calls a "modified Augustinian historicist approach."[40] This paradigm provides a filter through which to interpret Puritan apocalyptic literature without becoming overwhelmed by the finer details.

## Thesis

J. I. Packer defined *spirituality* as "stockpiling resources for life in Christ."[41] William Perkins's spirituality (or "resources for life in Christ") is shaped in large part by his eschatological hope—what it means to be "crowned with immortal glory." In turn, his understanding of this hope is informed by his convictions concerning (1) the divine decrees, (2) the creation, (3) the incarnation, (4) the order of salvation, (5) the end times, and (6) the eternal state. For Perkins, what one believes about the future determines how one lives in the present.

While chiefly concerned with the field of biblical spirituality, this book makes secondary contributions. Historically, Perkins is a significant figure, as he ministered during a pivotal moment in the English Reformation. This study sheds further light on the role he played in securing the Reformation cause in England and beyond. Theologically, Perkins looms large because

---

a fuller understanding of eschatological thinking among Cambridge divines of the time period. Their views are found in appendices 1–4 of this book. Additionally, for views on Revelation that preceded Perkins, see Bullinger, *Hundred Sermons Upon the Apocalypse of Jesus Christ*. See also Fulke, *Praelections*; Junius, *Revelation of Saint Iohn*.

39. Gribben, *Puritan Millennium*, 13–14.

40. Toon, *Puritans*, 6.

41. Packer, *Concise Theology*, xii.

he shaped the development of Reformed theology. While John Calvin's work was a major influence during this time and his works were published "more times than any native theologian," Perkins was "his one serious rival"[42] as his influence extended to Continental Europe[43] and Colonial America.[44] When it comes to the particulars of his theology, little attention has been given to his eschatology. This work rectifies this oversight, while contributing to a better understanding of one of England's most influential theologians.

---

42. Hall, *Puritans*, 17–18.
43. Beeke and Thomas, "General Preface," 1:vii.
44. Morison, *Intellectual Life*, 11, 20, 134.

# 2

# A Perfect Vision of God

IN ORDER TO PROPERLY develop William Perkins's eschatological hope, things must be done decently and in order. Before considering the specifics of Perkins's concept of eschatological glory,[1] it is important to step back to establish the broad strokes of his eschatology,[2] then focus on key concepts which are prevalent throughout his writings. This will serve to demonstrate the intersect between Perkins's eschatology and spirituality.

## The Blessed Hope

Perkins was convinced that he was living in the last days.[3] He believed the Scriptures divide human history in two sections: "the old time" and "the latter days or last hour." For Perkins, "the old time" stretches from the beginning of creation to the incarnation of Christ, whereas the "last hour"

---

1. Perkins writes, "Blessedness is that whereby God Himself is all in all [to] His elect. . . . Blessedness has two parts: eternal life and perfect glory." Perkins, *Golden Chain*, 6:216. What is meant by "eschatological glory" is what Perkins calls "perfect glory." This is the understanding of the state/condition of the born-again man upon his death, resurrection, judgment, and entrance into the presence of the Triune God, that is, the consummation of "fellowship with God and life everlasting." Perkins, *Revelation*, 4:318. Again, a personal aspect of eschatological glory will be the main focus in this work.

2. For a fuller historical view of Puritan eschatology and how some Perkins's contemporaries interpreted John's Apocalypse, see appendices 1–4.

3. See Acts 2:15–17; 1 Tim 4:1; 2 Tim 3:1; Heb 1:2; Jas 5:3; 1 Pet 1:20; 2 Pet 3:3; 1 John 2:18. All Scripture citations are from the King James Version (KJV).

begins at Christ's first advent and extends to his second advent.[4] Although Christ will come "as thief in the night" (1 Thess 5:2), Perkins declares that the world may "continue on a hundred years or two hundred years longer."[5]

Perkins posits two reasons why the time between Christ's two advents is described as "the last hour." First, he appeals to the apostle Paul's declaration: "Now all these things happened unto them for ensamples: and they are written for our admonition, upon whom the ends of the world are come" (1 Cor 10:11). If the next age is "the end of the world," then the present age must be "the last hour." Second, Perkins argues that the incarnation of Christ marks the fullness of time (Gal 4:4). He explains,

> God altered the condition of His church and renewed His covenant from time to time. . . . But now Christ, being come, and that fullness of time wherein the former prophecies are fulfilled and accomplished, the shadows and ceremonies are abolished, and the new covenant of grace established. There remains no renewing thereof, neither any other alteration of it.[6]

Since Christ has come in the flesh, there is nothing more to be expected but his return in glory—what Paul calls "that blessed hope" (Titus 2:13).

## *The Millennium*

Perkins's conviction that the last hour encompasses the time between Christ's two advents is necessarily related to his view of the millennium. A survey of the apocalyptic literature between 1558 and 1616 reveals that the Puritans generally agreed that the millennium is a literal one-thousand-year period. From here, they fall into two distinct camps. Those who belong to the first believe that the millennium began with Christ and/or the apostles (AD 1/70) and ended in AD 1000/1070. Proponents include John Bale, Heinrich Bullinger, William Fulke, George Gifford, Arthur Dent, Thomas Pickering, and Hugh Broughton. This position was popularized in the 1599

---

4. Perkins, *Fruitful Dialogue*, 6:460–61. Perkins would divide these two main sections into four sub-divisions or "four ages": (1) from creation to the flood; (2) from the flood to the giving of the law; (3) from the giving of the law to the death of Christ; (4) from the death of Christ to the last judgment. Perkins, *Discourse of Conscience*, 8:19.

5. Perkins, *Fruitful Dialogue*, 6:461. Perkins was not implying that he believes the world would end in one or two hundred years. His point is that one cannot make the claim they know the year, month, day, or hour of Christ's return.

6. Perkins, *Jude*, 4:210.

Geneva Bible. Satan was bound so that the pure gospel and holy doctrine could spread to the nations. As the millennium ended, the influence of the papacy began to increase. At the time of Pope Sylvester II (AD 999) and/or Pope Gregory VII (AD 1073), Satan was loosed from the pit. This resulted in a full assault upon the church, and a great deception spread throughout the world. As Thomas Pickering notes,

> Corruption began to creep into the papacy.... [T]he bishops affected that sea, and aspired into it by diabolical arts.... [T]he canons, decrees, sentences, synodals, decretals, clementines, [and] extravagants, with other laws and constitutions, prevailed above the Scriptures, then Satan began again to erect his kingdom, and these works of iniquity to be set abroad.[7]

Those who belong to the second camp place the millennium a little later. They contend that it began around AD 300 and ended in AD 1300. Proponents include John Foxe, Laurence Deios, John Napier, John Foord, Robert Hill, Patrick Forbes, and Thomas Brightman. Satan was bound when Constantine became emperor (AD 306–337), and he was subsequently released at the time of Pope Boniface VIII (AD 1294–1303) in the west and the rise of the Ottoman Empire (AD 1299) in the east. The Papist and the Turk posed the greatest threats to the gospel of Christ. When the thousand years ended, says John Napier, "it pleased God to permit Satan, by his instruments, to raise up most terrible and universal wars for a season."[8]

Perkins stands in the second camp. He dates the binding of Satan in AD 295 and his release in AD 1295.[9] During this one-thousand-year period, the two prophets preached in sackcloth (chap. 11),[10] the first beast (the pagan

---

7. Pickering, "Epistle Dedicatory," 9:301.

8. Napier, *Plain Discovery*, 233.

9. Perkins, *Digest or Harmony*, 1:69. For Perkins, for the devil to be bound in chains means "that mighty power of God, which bridles and restrains the might and malice of the devils themselves, as the old dragon was bound for a thousand years (Rev 20:3). The power of God was the chain that curbed and overmastered him, and this is one part of his present punishment." Perkins, *Jude*, 4:124.

10. It is possible that Perkins saw these two witnesses as the saints and martyrs of the church. Perkins more than likely, staying in the same vein of his peers, saw the two prophets in the form of faithful ministers and teachers of God's Word who would preach in the midst of the slow and apostatizing church. It would be these faithful witnesses who would ultimately be killed by Rome (Rev 11:8, "Sodom and Egypt") at the hands of the Papacy in their attempt to suppress the true and pure Gospel and corrupt holy doctrine. See Perkins, *Jude*, 4:130; Perkins, *Treatise on God's Free Grace*, 6:442; Perkins, *Reformed Catholic*, 7:11.

Roman Empire) emerged from the sea (chap. 13),[11] and the second beast ("heretical apostatical Church of Rome") also emerged.[12] Perkins writes,

> "The man of sin" (which is that Antichrist)[13] "shall exalt himself above all that is called God, etc." (2 Thess 2:3–4). Now this whole chapter with all the circumstances thereof, most fitly agrees to the see of Rome and the head thereof. And the thing which then stayed the revealing of the man of sin [v. 6], is of the most expounded to be the Roman emperor . . . for the see of Rome never flourished until the Empire decayed, and the seat thereof was removed from the city of Rome. Again, [in] Revelation 13, mention is made of two beasts, one coming out of the sea, whom the papists confess to be the heathenish Roman Emperor; the second coming out of the earth, which does all that the first beast could do before him. And this fitly agrees to the popes of Rome, who do and have done all things that the emperor did or could do, and that in his very sight.[14]

For Perkins, the events of Revelation 20:1–8 followed directly upon the events of chapter 13. He writes, "Before the end there shall be a departure (2 Thess 2), and this departure is general in all nations (Rev 13:8, 16); and after a thousand years, there shall be the first resurrection (Rev 20:5); and this

---

11. Perkins points out that the Roman Empire (heathenism Rome) and the Roman church (ecclesiastical Rome) are essentially one and the same. Perkins writes, "Behold a vain and foolish distinction, for ecclesiastical Rome in respect of state, princely dominion, and cruelty in persecuting the saints of God, is all one with the heathenish empire, the see of the bishop being turned into the emperor's court as all histories do manifest." Perkins, *Reformed Catholic*, 7:10.

12. Perkins, *Revelation*, 4:307. Perkins writes elsewhere,

> Satan says, "all these will I give thee." This is the voice of the great red dragon; and the same is the voice of the pope of Rome, both registered in their canons and daily attempted in practice, to dispose of all the kingdoms of the earth; whereby he shows evidently, that he is that "beast coming out of the earth having two horns like the lamb, but he spake like the dragon" [Rev 13:11]. For the lamb's horns he shows in calling himself the servant of servants; and the voice of the dragon, that is, of the devil, in taking upon him to dispose of the sovereignties of these earthly kingdoms. (Perkins, *Combat between Christ and the Devil*, 1:145)

13. Perkins's views on the antichrist are clearly defined when he writes, "And so though antichrist is not one particular man but a state and company of men in the succession of popes, yet is that whole estate noted by the special name of one man—as that antichrist, man of sin, and son of perdition [2 Thess 2:3, 8]." Perkins, *Revelation*, 4:412–13. Perkins also believed that the antichrist was first revealed in AD 602 with Gregory I. Perkins, *Exposition of the Creed*, 5:289.

14. Perkins, *Reformed Catholic*, 7:132–33.

resurrection is the reviving and restoring of the gospel, after long ignorance and superstition."[15]

Additionally, Perkins sees the seals of chapters 6 and 7 as opened during this thousand-year period. The slaughter, famine, plague, etc., are the result of the rise of the Papacy and the Turks (chap. 9).[16] Yet, Christ remains faithful to his people and defends his church in "deed and word" (chap. 14), while bringing judgment upon his enemies (chap. 15). Perkins explains, "I gather that the true church of God is and has been in the present Roman Church as corn in the heap of chaff. Though popery reigned and overspread the face of the earth for many hundred years, yet in the midst thereof, God reserved a people unto Himself that truly worshipped Him."[17] Perkins identifies this as the fulfillment of the second half of Revelation 12:17 "And she still retains a remnant of her seed, which keep the commandment of God and have the testimony of Jesus Christ."[18]

In terms of what was yet to be fulfilled, Perkins expected the whore of Babylon (the Roman Church) and the beast (the Roman Bishop) to be overcome (chap. 17). This would be followed by the conquest of the dragon, the first resurrection,[19] the last judgment, and the glory of the saints (chap. 20).

15. Perkins, *Galatians*, 2:308.

16. In *Digest or Harmony*, Perkins only describes Rev 9 as "the horseman that destroy mankind" in AD 895. However, in his work *A Warning Against the Idolatry of the Last Times*, Perkins identifies "the horseman" of Rev 9 as "horseman from Euphrates, that is, Saracens or Turks, 'shall destroy them that worship idols of gold or silver' (Rev 9:20), that is, the idolaters of the Roman Church." Perkins saw the Turks as not only an enemy to the true church, but also an instrument in the hand of God to bring about judgment upon the Roman Church. Perkins, *Warning Against the Idolatry*, 7:467.

17. Perkins, *Reformed Catholic*, 7:149–50.

18. Perkins, *Reformed Catholic*, 7:150. Perkins's translation.

19. Regarding "the first resurrection," Perkins speaks of it in three different ways. (1) He believes it describes regeneration. "The first resurrection is spiritual," writes Perkins, "wrought in the soul by the Holy Ghost, causing him that is by nature dead in sin to rise to newness of life, whereof whosoever is a true partaker shall undoubtedly rise to glory." Perkins, *Cloud of Faithful Witnesses*, 3:377. (2) He believes it describes a great recovery and preaching ministry of the true gospel and holy doctrine after the time of the millennium in 1330. Perkins declares, "Before the end there shall be a departure (2 Thess 2), and this departure is general in all nations (Rev 13:8, 16); and after a thousand years, there shall be the first resurrection (Rev 20:5); and this resurrection is the reviving and restoring of the gospel, after long ignorance and superstition." Perkins, *Galatians*, 2:308. (3) He places "the first resurrection" after the defeat of all God's enemies and prior to final judgment and eschatological glory. This is a clear reference to the bodily resurrection of the living and the dead. Therefore, there are at least four possible ways to

## Signs of Christ's Coming

In accordance with Scripture, Perkins affirms that no one knows the day or hour when Christ will return.[20] That said, he seems to expect Christ to return in his day.[21] Regarding the "signs" of his coming, Perkins divides them into two groups. The first group consists of signs that occur *before* his coming. According to Perkins, there are seven. The first is the proclamation of the gospel throughout the whole world. This does not occur at one single moment, but "it shall be published distinctly and successively at several times."[22] The second sign is the revelation of the antichrist. For Perkins, this occurred in the days of Gregory I, "the first pope of Rome" (AD 607). Years later, Boniface III assumed the title "Universal Bishop, Pastor of the Catholic Church," and was, therefore, the first to be known as Antichrist.[23] The third sign is the great apostasy. Perkins believes this began with the Arian heresy in the fourth century, and continued with "the popish heresy," which spread itself over the whole earth.[24] The fourth sign is a general corruption in manners. Turning to 2 Timothy 3:1–5, Perkins writes, "This sign has been in former ages and is no doubt at this day in the world."[25] The fifth

---

interpret Perkins on this point: (1) Recognize that he is a fallible man and that there are inconsistencies in his writings. (2) Toward the end of his life, when *A Digest and Harmony* was written, his theological position regarding what this "first resurrection" is had changed. (3) Perkins had a three-tiered/three-layered understanding of what this "first resurrection" means. It is possible that Perkins saw this as speaking to all three positions: beginning with regeneration being applicable to all believers, next a historical understanding in seeing it as a great revival and renewal, and lastly, both of the former positions symbolizing and pointing to its ultimate and consummative end, the ultimate regeneration, the ultimate revival, the resurrection of the body of believers on the final day (cf. Matt 19:28). (4) The last possibility is that it is skewed regarding its placement, or a misprint of its title. It has been shown elsewhere that in *A Digest and Harmony* dates and numbers are clearly skewed and not aligned correctly. Thus, it is not out of the possibility that this is another example.

20. Perkins, *Fruitful Dialogue*, 6:456.
21. Bryan W. Ball, in his work on Protestant eschatology, goes as far to declare that "Perkins is clearly committed to the doctrine of an early advent." Ball, *Great Expectation*, 23.
22. Perkins, *Exposition of the Creed*, 5:289. Perkins explains elsewhere that "this sign is every day more and more accomplished." Perkins, *Fruitful Dialogue*, 6:462.
23. Perkins, *Exposition of the Creed*, 5:289.
24. Perkins, *Exposition of the Creed*, 5:289.
25. Perkins, *Exposition of the Creed*, 5:290. Second Tim 3:1–5 says,
> This know also, that in the last days perilous times shall come. For men shall be lovers of their own selves, covetous, boasters, proud, blasphemers,

sign is the coming of terrible and grievous calamities. This began with the early church and continued with the persecution of "the church of God" by "antichrist of Rome in the hundred years last past."[26] The sixth sign is the "exceeding deadness of heart." According to Perkins, people will grow so cold that neither God's judgments nor the preaching of the Word will have any effect upon them. "The small fruit that the Word of God brings forth in the lives of men," laments Perkins, "shows this to be most true."[27] The seventh sign is the conversion of the Jews.[28] It will be a great conversion, says Perkins, "to that religion which now they hate."[29] Because God promised Abraham that all the nations would be blessed in him (cf. Gen 12:3; Gal 3:8), "the nation of the Jews shall be called and converted to the participation of this blessing."[30] As far as Perkins is concerned, the first six signs had already taken place. The only sign that remained to be fulfilled was the conversion of the Jews. He announced that "the end cannot be far off."[31] Christ's return was as certain as it if were now present. Therefore, our duty is to consider the coming of Christ "as of a thing present."[32]

The second group is comprised of those signs that accompany Christ's coming. For Perkins, these are equivalent to "the sign of the Son of Man" (Matt 24:30).[33] They consist of heavenly disturbances: "And there shall be signs in the sun, and in the moon, and in the stars; and upon the earth distress of nations, with perplexity; the sea and the waves roaring" (Luke 21:25). "The heavens shall pass away with a great noise, and the elements

---

disobedient to parents, unthankful, unholy, Without natural affection, trucebreakers, false accusers, incontinent, fierce, despisers of those that are good, Traitors, heady, highminded, lovers of pleasures more than lovers of God; Having a form of godliness, but denying the power thereof: from such turn away.

26. Perkins, *Exposition of the Creed*, 5:290.

27. Perkins, *Exposition of the Creed*, 5:290.

28. This final sign would become "a staple component" of Puritan eschatology. According to Gribben, this "was firmly consolidated among English-speaking puritans, [and] Perkins' own influence in the University of Cambridge was reflected in the number of subsequent puritan leaders who studied there and themselves came to advocate the 'conversion of the Jews' motif." Gribben, *Puritan Millennium*, 38.

29. Perkins, *Fruitful Dialogue*, 6:462.

30. Perkins, *Galatians*, 2:166.

31. Perkins, *Exposition of the Creed*, 5:290.

32. Perkins, *Revelation*, 4:351.

33. While Perkins speaks of there being only "one" sign, it has several detailed elements, which will be discussed in the next section.

shall melt with fervent heat, the earth also and the works that are therein shall be burned up" (2 Pet 3:10). Perkins does not presume to expand on the particulars, writing, "Where God has no mouth to speak, there we must have no ear to hear."[34]

## The Day of Judgment

Immediately preceding Christ's second advent, there will be cosmic disturbances in the heavens. "The elect then living shall rejoice, but the reprobate shall shake every joint of them." At the same time, "the sound of the last trumpet shall be heard, sounded by the archangel" (1 Thess 4:16). Christ will come in the clouds with power, glory, and an angelic host (Matt 24:31).[35] "All men shall see Him with their own eyes," affirms Perkins, "all (I say) which were since the world began."[36] His appearance "in endless glory and majesty shall be more terrible and dreadful to the ungodly . . . and at the very sight thereof men shall desire the mountains to fall upon them and the hills to cover them."[37]

When the last trumpet blasts, the bodily resurrection will occur. "The elect which were dead shall rise with those very bodies which were turned to dust . . . and the souls of them shall descend from heaven and be brought again into those bodies."[38] The elect who are alive at Christ's return "shall be changed in the twinkling of an eye, and this mutation shall be instead of death. . . . [Their] bodies shall receive their full redemption; and all bodies of the elect shall be made like the glorious body of Christ Jesus and therefore shall be spiritual, immortal, glorious, and free form all infirmity."[39] As for the reprobate, "the living, being stricken with horror and fear, shall be changed in a moment," and the dead will rise to their condemnation.[40] All the reprobate, both living and dead, will receive immortal bodies yet without glory.

Following this bodily resurrection, all will appear before Christ's "majesty" to answer for themselves.[41] "All without exception must appear,

---

34. Perkins, *Exposition of the Creed*, 5:291.
35. Perkins, *Golden Chain*, 6:214.
36. Perkins, *Revelation*, 4:352.
37. Perkins, *Exposition of the Creed*, 5:294.
38. Perkins, *Golden Chain*, 6:215.
39. Perkins, *Golden Chain*, 6:215.
40. Perkins, *Golden Chain*, 6:259.
41. Perkins, *Exposition of the Creed*, 6:294.

as well high as low, rich as poor. None shall be able to withdraw themselves. ... [N]o excuse will serve the turn. Even the most rebellious of all creatures, whether man nor angel, shall be forced to appear."[42] When all are convened before the tribunal seat of Christ, the sheep will be separated from the goats (Matt 25:32). Perkins proclaims,

> For when all the kindreds of the earth and all unclean spirits shall stand before Christ, sitting in the throne of His glory, then as a good shepherd He shall separate them one form another the righteous from the wicked and the elect from the reprobate.... This full and final separation is reserved to Christ and shall not be accomplished till the last day.[43]

The books will be opened (Rev 20:12) and each one will be judged according to his works (2 Cor 5:10). This judgment is not "to make men just that are unjust," Perkins clarifies, "but only to manifest them to be just indeed which are just before and in this life truly justified."[44] Our works will be examined according to God's three books.[45] The first is the book of God's providence. His knowledge of all things—past, present, and future. The second is the book of God's judgment. It contains his knowledge of all people's affairs—their thoughts, words, and deeds. Man's conscience will bring to remembrance all that he has done and not done. The third is the book of life. It "is nothing else but the decree of God's election in which God has set down who be ordained to life eternal."[46]

Christ's sentence follows. "The secrets of all hearts must be disclosed," remarks Perkins, "and every man shall receive accordingly to that which he has done."[47] For the ungodly, the sentence is condemnation.[48] They will

---

42. Perkins, *Exposition of the Creed*, 5:294–95.

43. Perkins, *Exposition of the Creed*, 5:295.

44. Perkins, *Exposition of the Creed*, 5:296.

45. "Not properly," says Perkins, "but because all things are as certain and manifest to Him as if He had His registers in heaven to keep rolls and records of them." Perkins, *Exposition of the Creed*, 5:297.

46. Perkins, *Exposition of the Creed*, 5:297.

47. Perkins, *Jude*, 4:197.

48. Perkins defines and cautions about the ungodly when he writes, "The persons are set out by their property of ungodliness, which is a sin directly against God. And the ungodly man is he who denies God the honor due unto him." Perkins then gives them five notes or properties: (1) "he knows not or acknowledges not the true God according to His Word." (2) The ungodly "subjects not his body, soul, and conscience to the laws of God in all things, but takes liberty to live as he list." (3) "In heat and life [the ungodly] depends not

hear these words: "Depart from me, ye cursed, into everlasting fire, prepared for the devil and his angels" (Matt 25:41).[49] They will enter hell: "And these shall go away into everlasting punishment: but the righteous into life eternal" (Matt 25:46). "Neither the greatest rebel that ever was among men nor all the devils in hell shall be able to withstand . . . that fearful sentence of everlasting woe and condemnation which shall be pronounced upon the wicked."[50] "And whosoever was not found written in the book of life was cast into the lake of fire" (Rev 20:15). But for the godly, the sentence is absolution. The elect will hear these words: "Come, ye blessed of my Father, inherit the kingdom prepared for you from the foundation of the world" (Matt 25:34).

## The Beatific Vision

The nature of this blessing occupies a central place in Perkins's theology. As "the root of all the elect," Christ "conveys life both in body and soul to all who are united to Him."[51] This consists of spiritual life at regeneration and the full and final transformation of the body at the resurrection.[52] All those who are one with Christ share in his resurrection glory. Perkins highlights eight effects of Christ's resurrection. First, it shows that he is the true and perfect Savior of the world. Second, it shows that he is the true and natural Son of God. Third, it declares that he has made a full and perfect satisfaction for the sins of the world. Fourth, it secures our justification. When Christ arose from the dead "He acquitted and justified Himself from our

---

himself upon the will, power, providence, and good pleasure of God, but on something out of God Himself, or some other creature." (4) The ungodly worships not from his heart the true God. (5) The ungodly hates the church and the people of God; and when occasion shall serve, he will testify it by persecuting the same." Perkins, *Jude*, 4:198–99.

49. Perkins, *Exposition of the Creed*, 5:301. The estate of the wicked consists in three things according to Perkins: (1) a separation from all joy and comfort and the presence of God; (2) eternal fellowship with the devil and his angels, and (3) the feeling of the horrible wrath of God. Perkins writes, "Which shall seize upon body, soul, and conscience, and shall feed on them as fire does on pitch and brimstone, and torment them as a worm crawling in the body and gnawing on the heart. They shall always be dying and never dead, always in woe and never in ease. And this death is the more grievous because it is everlasting." Perkins, *Jude*, 4:156.

50. Perkins, *Exposition of the Creed*, 5:303.

51. Perkins, *Exposition of the Creed*, 5:401–2.

52. See Perkins, *Exposition of the Creed*, 5:401–2. See also Perkins, *Revelation*, 4:337; Perkins, *Estate of Damnation or in the Estate of Grace*, 8:483.

sins, and ceased to be any more a reputed sinner for us."[53] Fifth, it purchases all the gifts and graces that he bestows upon us. Sixth, it puts away the natural life that he received from Adam and takes to himself a spiritual life. This was done so as to "communicate the said life to all who believe in Him.... [He] renews us and makes us like to Himself in righteousness and life."[54] Seventh, it declares his victory over all his enemies and that he continues to conquer them in his people until all are put under his feet.[55] Eighth, it is the reason the body is raised "from the grave in the day of judgment to eternal glory."[56] Christ will "raise to eternal life all those who by the bond of the Spirit are mystically united to Him. For by means of this union, this raising power shall flow from the head to the dead bodies of them who are in Christ."[57]

According to Perkins, these eight effects have "endless efficacy" and, therefore, serve as the foundation for the believer's blessedness.[58] When the elect are raised in glory, the same divine power acted upon Christ's humanity is conveyed through the Holy Spirit to all his members. Christ's mystical body will be fully and finally conformed to their glorious, incorruptible, and immortal Head. While their bodies will be the same substance (i.e., physical bodies), they "shall be altered in quality, being made incorruptible and filled with glory."[59]

---

53. Perkins, *True Gain*, 9:68.

54. Perkins, *True Gain*, 9:69.

55. This effect is discussed in greater detail surrounding Christ's ascension. In his ascension, Christ did ascend up to heaven "to lead captivity captive" (Eph 4:8). Christ has triumphed over all the enemies of God on the cross and continues to triumph over them. He does this by his mighty power in his members by subduing and weakening the power of sin and Satan, "which He manifests every day by killing the corruption of their natures and the rebellion of their flesh." Perkins, *Exposition of the Creed*, 5:261. In the ascension, Perkins writes that Christ's led captivity, i.e., bondage to sin, misery, death, condemnation, and hell, captive. Christ vanquished "the devil and all his angels, under whom you lie bound," says Perkins, "and that not only in Himself, but in His members" (5:262). Christ truly sets free his elect from their captors. He not only freed those who were captive by their enemies, but captured these great enemies and "pinioned them fast, so as all the power they have is in Christ's hand" (5:262). Perkins concludes, "Surely, let him remember the end of Christ's ascension, which is to vanquish and subdue the rebellion of his nature, and labor too feel the benefit thereof." Perkins, *Exposition of the Creed*, 5:263

56. Perkins, *True Gain*, 9:69.

57. Perkins, *True Gain*, 9:69.

58. Perkins, *True Gain*, 9:69.

59. Perkins, *Exposition of the Creed*, 5:402.

The apostle Paul declares, "But we all, with open face beholding as in a glass the glory of the Lord, are changed into the same image from glory to glory, even as by the Spirit of the Lord" (2 Cor 3:18). For Perkins, the "glass" is the Word and sacraments. It is the means by which we are transformed into the image of Christ.[60] In this life, God's people see "as an old man through spectacles,"[61] but a day is coming when the earthly spectacles will be removed, and "we shall see God as He is to be seen, not as through a glass, but face to face."[62] For Perkins, this vision consists of two distinct (yet, inseparable) moments. The first is death when the soul enters God's presence. At this time, the believer sees God with the eye of the soul. The second moment is the resurrection, when the believer (with glorified eyes) beholds the glory of God in the face of Christ (2 Cor 4:6).[63] This moment is known as the Beatific Vision.[64]

---

60. It is significant to point out that the word for "change" (*mĕtamŏrphŏō*) in 2 Cor 3:18 is the same word used to describe Christ's transformation in his transfiguration. For an in-depth study of Christ's transfiguration and the believer's transformation within Puritan thought, see Jones, *Transfiguration and Transformation*.

61. Perkins, *Exposition of the Creed*, 5:409.

62. Perkins, *Exposition of the Creed*, 5:409.

63. Perkins defines God's glory or majesty as "the infinite excellency of His most simple and most holy divine nature." Perkins, *Golden Chain*, 6:19. Hans Boersma writes, "It is true that within the Calvinist tradition, the doctrine of the beatific vision flourished nowhere quite like it did among the Puritans . . . although the Puritans were by no means unique in recognizing that in the eschaton we will see God in Christ, it is perhaps true that the link between Christology and the beatific vision has nowhere been as sustained and profound as among the Puritans." Boersma, *Seeing God*, 315–16.

64. The beatific vision, or vision of God finds itself in essentially two groups historically, and both deal with the mediums whereby a person will see God. The two camps are: (1) those who believe that saints in heaven will see the unmediated divine essence, and (2) those who believe that the vision of God will be christologically mediated in some way. The former view is developed, defended, and held by medieval scholar and theologian Thomas Aquinas. See Aquinas, *Summa Theologica*, Suppl. Q. 92, a. 1–3. For example, Aquinas states: "Again, the vision whereby we shall see God in His essence is the same whereby God sees Himself, as regards that whereby He is seen, because as He sees Himself in His essence, so shall we also see Him. But as regards the knower there is the difference that is between the Divine intellect and ours. Now in the order of knowledge the object known follows the form by which we know, since by the form of a stone we see a stone: whereas the efficacy of knowledge follows the power of the knower: thus he who has stronger sight sees more clearly. Consequently in that vision we shall see the same thing that God sees, namely His essence, but not so effectively." Aquinas, *Summa Theologica*, Suppl. Q. 92, a. 1. Aquinas holds that a person can and will see the divine essence, but it will be seen apart from the mediation of the glorified Christ. Aquinas admits that while "a certain beatitude" is derived from seeing Christ's body, that

## The Sight of the Mind

Perkins equates the sight of the mind with "the knowledge or understanding of the mind."[65] It is imperfect in this life, yet perfect in the life to come. In this life, we see God by his "effects" in the Word and sacraments, and in his creatures. By these means, we perceive God as our Father, Christ as our Redeemer, and the Holy Spirit as our Sanctifier.[66]

Concerning the life to come, Perkins says that believers will possess "the perfect vision of God."[67] He defines this as "the perfect knowledge of God."[68] In describing this perfect vision, Perkins distinguishes between "literal" and "spiritual" knowledge, as well as "simple" and "comprehensive" sight. Spiritual knowledge "is when the mind is enlightened by the Spirit of God with the knowledge of God, by the Word and according to the Word, so as thereupon, men are transformed into the image of God."[69] Comprehensive sight is "when the creature sees God, so far forth as it is capable of His knowledge, and thus shall men see God in the world to come perfectly, and be filled therewith, though they know Him not wholly, as he is in

---

is not the vision of God. Aquinas, *Summa Theologica*, Suppl. Q. 92, a. 2. For Aquinas, the vision of God appears to be seen completely intellectually, and, therefore, in perfectly knowing God, man will perfectly see God. This is what Aquinas calls, "vision of face." Aquinas, *Summa Theologica*, Suppl. Q. 92, a. 1. Perkins's view, and what would become the dominant Reformed/Puritan view is of the latter. Perkins believed that the means and object of beholding the glory and majesty of the Triune God was through the ascended humanity of the glorified God-man, Jesus Christ both with the sight of the mind and the sight of the eye. Subsequent Puritans, such as Isaac Ambrose, John Owen, and Thomas Watson would hold and develop this same line of thought. See Ambrose, *Looking unto Jesus*; Owen, *Declaration of the Glorious Mystery*; Watson, *Beatitudes*. Recently, there has been debate/dialogue regarding these two views among Roman Catholics and Protestants alike. See Ortlund, "Will We See God's Essence?," 323–32; McDonald, "Beholding the Glory of God," 141–58; Gaine, "Thomas Aquinas and John Owen," 432–46; Strobel, "Jonathan Edwards' Reformed Doctrine," 171–88; Boersma, *Seeing God*; Mosser, "Recovering the Reformation's Ecumenical Vision," 3–24.

65. Perkins, *Sermon on the Mount*, 1:207.

66. Perkins, *Sermon on the Mount*, 1:207. Regarding Moses's sight of God's glory (Exod 33:17–23), Perkins remarks, "God would manifest His glory unto him by His effects, by which, as by a glimpse or imperfect representation, he might discern some part of His majesty, so far forth as he was able, in the infirmity of flesh and blood, to behold the same." Perkins, *Second Book*, 8:251.

67. Perkins, *Sermon on the Mount*, 1:207.

68. Perkins, *Exposition of the Creed*, 5:409.

69. Perkins, *Galatians*, 2:268. Perkins defines "literal" knowledge as "when the doctrine of God and His will is known without reformation of life." Perkins, *Galatians*, 2:268.

Himself."[70] In the life to come, every believer will attain to the spiritual and comprehensive knowledge of God. "The more apparent manifestation of God," writes Perkins, "is the contemplation of Him in heaven face to face."[71] He adds, "God indeed is infinite, and therefore the full knowledge of His majesty can no more be comprehended by the understanding of the creature, which is finite, than the sea by a spoon. Yet nevertheless God shall be known every way of man, so far forth as a creature may know the Creator."[72]

## *The Sight of the Eye*

At the resurrection, believers will receive glorified faculties, including perfect knowledge. They will also be fitted with gloried bodies, thereby acquiring perfect physical sight. Perkins insists that no one can see God. That which is corporeal (the eye) cannot behold that which is spiritual (and, therefore, invisible). The apostle Paul declares that God dwells "in the light which no man can approach unto" (1 Tim 6:16). In what sense, then, will glorified believers see God?

Christ provides the answer: "He that hath seen me hath seen the Father" (John 14:9). This is the case because Christ is "the image of the invisible God" (Col 1:15), and "the brightness of his glory, and the express image of his person" (Heb 1:3). Believers, therefore, will see the glory of God in the face of Christ, the incarnate Son of God, who came to make God known (John 1:18), and in whom are hidden are the treasures of wisdom and knowledge (Col 2:3).[73] As Perkins declares, "All men with their own eyes shall look on Him."[74] Christ will manifest and exhibit the fullness of his glory "immediately and visibly."[75] Christ in his glorified humanity is the foundation of all knowledge of God, as well as the only way in which the glory of God is seen. Christ, therefore, is the apex of

---

70. Perkins, *Sermon on the Mount*, 1:207. Perkins defines simple perfect sight as "when man sees a thing wholly as it is in itself, and thus God is not seen by the mind of men." Perkins, *Sermon on the Mount*, 1:207.

71. Perkins, *Golden Chain*, 6:19.

72. Perkins, *Exposition of the Creed*, 5:409.

73. According to Robert Louis Wilken, this notion of seeing God with the mind and also with the eye in the Person of Jesus Christ was the view and position of the early church. Therefore, Perkins can be seen in the historical footsteps of the Great Tradition. See Wilken, *Spirit of Early Christian Thought*, 1–24.

74. Perkins, *Revelation*, 4:353.

75. Perkins, *Lord's Prayer*, 5:436.

the believer's perfect vision of God, notional and visual. Perkins writes, "God in Himself and His own majesty is invisible, not only to the eyes of the body, but also to the very minds of men. And He is revealed to us only in Christ."[76] In this life, we see God as in a glass via the Word and sacraments. But in the life to come, we will see God face-to-face in the glorified humanity of Christ. "Now no man doubts," says Perkins, "but God in Christ may be seen," and upon entrance into the final state of eschatological glory, "we shall therewith behold our Lord Jesus Christ, who redeemed us by His blood, and made us kings and priests unto our God, to whom we shall sing praise, and honor, and glory forevermore."[77]

Perkins is committed to this Christ-centered understanding of the Beatific Vision.[78] The elect's communion with the triune God is first with Christ as he is a man.[79] In glory, there will be no temple because Christ is the temple. There will be no need for Word and sacrament in regard to fellowship with God, for Christ is their fellowship. There will be no need of celestial lights, for Christ is the light. Christ is the paradise of God.[80] Thus, for Perkins, all that is conveyed to the believer in glory comes through his union with Christ. In his "face the glory of God in His endless mercy is to be seen."[81] "Therefore," exhorts Perkins, "we must not know God and seek Him anywhere but in Christ. And whatsoever out of Christ comes unto us in the name of God is a flat idol of man's brain."[82]

---

76. Perkins, *True Manner of Knowing Christ Crucified*, 9:14.

77. Perkins, *Sermon on the Mount*, 1:207.

78. Boersma notes that three prominent and subsequent Puritans, Isaac Ambrose (1604–64), John Owen (1616–83), and Thomas Watson (1620–86) "argued that both in our contemplation today and in the future vision of God, we see him only in Christ." Boersma, *Seeing God*, 317.

79. Perkins, *Exposition of the Creed*, 5:407.

80. Perkins, *Exposition of the Creed*, 5:408.

81. Perkins, *True Manner of Knowing Christ Crucified*, 9:22. Boersma writes, "Since [the Puritans] meditated on Christ, his work, and his glory on a daily basis, it is hardly surprising that Christ was also central to their understanding of the ultimate vision of God. After all, daily meditation on Christ was simply preparation for heaven." Boersma, *Seeing God*, 316.

82. Perkins, *True Manner of Knowing Christ Crucified*, 9:15.

## Conclusion

Perkins is not overly concerned about interpreting the finer details of the book of Revelation, nor is he preoccupied with unlocking the signs associated with the end of world. He is far more concerned about how the truth of Christ's return applies to the present life. In short, it ought to have a sanctifying influence. John writes, "And every man that hath this hope in him purifieth himself, even as he is pure" (1 John 3:3). Perkins was convinced that believers must live in the light of Christ's coming. They must live as though every day were their last. "If this duty were practiced," exhorts Perkins, "we should find less corruption and more grace in our hearts and less sin and more obedience in our lives every day than another."[83] Seeing that earth will be purged with fire, how much more should believers be purged by "the heat of God's Spirit," which will "burn up sin and corruption in us and change us that we may be ready for Him against His coming."[84] Believers ought to pursue "moderation and sobriety . . . [for] whatsoever abuse shall come to God's creatures by our folly, the same shall then be abolished."[85] The need for God's purging of heaven and earth stems from man's sin, vanity, and corruption. God must "change the quality and abolish the corruption."[86] Therefore, believers should "acknowledge the greatness and wretchedness of [their] sins . . . [and] not be so slack in humbling [themselves]."[87]

Given the coming Day of Judgment, all people should "arraign, examine, cast, and condemn [themselves]."[88] They should "sue for pardon as for life and death," in order to "escape that fearful judgment."[89] Our actions should be to "approve our hearts unto God . . . [and] all our endeavors should be to please and obey Him."[90] Because God will not allow the guilty to go unpunished, we must "deny all ungodliness" and exercise ourselves unto godliness.[91] We must (1) learn and know God aright, his attributes and his affections toward his own; (2) subject our life, will, affections,

---

83. Perkins, *Revelation*, 4:352.
84. Perkins, *Exposition of the Creed*, 5:291.
85. Perkins, *Exposition of the Creed*, 5:291.
86. Perkins, *Exposition of the Creed*, 5:292.
87. Perkins, *Exposition of the Creed*, 5:291–92.
88. Perkins, *Jude*, 4:197.
89. Perkins, *Jude*, 4:197.
90. Perkins, *Jude*, 4:198.
91. Perkins, *Jude*, 4:199.

speech, and actions to all of God's law; (3) depend upon the good pleasure of God, living by faith, making him our rock, tower, fortress, and strong defense in all estates; (4) worship God not only outwardly, but serve him in spirit, giving him our whole heart; and (5) love all men, especially those of the household of faith.[92]

Lastly, for Perkins, the beatific vision implies that the joy of heaven is not rooted in a place, but in a person. As the psalmist declares, "In thy presence is fulness of joy; at thy right hand there are pleasures for evermore" (Ps 16:11). This is "the kingdom of glory," which is "the blessed estate of God's elect in heaven, whereby Christ becomes all things unto them immediately."[93] Drawing from Hebrews 11:10,[94] Perkins states the third heaven is "the seat of God's glory" where he reveals "His majesty in special manner to men and angels."[95] He believes he created heaven for two reasons. First, it is "His own glorious palace ... wherein He would make His glory most apparent, and wherein His glory should in a sort dwell."[96] Second, it reveals "His majesty and glory to His reasonable creatures, angels and men, and (by showing them His glory) to glorify them."[97] In heaven "God's glory shines more than any other place."[98]

But what makes heaven "the perfection of beauty and true happiness" is the presence of Christ.[99] He is our perfect peace, love, and fullness of joy. Because of him, heaven contains "all parts and perfection and all complements of happiness to make the state of God's children infinitely blessed."[100] We will see him face-to-face, and we will know as we are known (1 Cor 13:12). "Oh then," cries Perkins, "what glory it is to see Him as He is? Doubtless this sight of God is true happiness."[101]

> You are free denizens of the city of God; and therefore as free men in God's house let all your cares and duties, all your affairs and

---

92. Perkins, *Jude*, 4:199.
93. Perkins, *Sermon on the Mount*, 1:444.
94. "For he looked for a city which hath foundations, whose builder and maker is God" (Heb 11:10).
95. Perkins, *Cloud of Faithful Witnesses*, 3:159.
96. Perkins, *Cloud of Faithful Witnesses*, 3:163.
97. Perkins, *Cloud of Faithful Witnesses*, 3:164.
98. Perkins, *Cloud of Faithful Witnesses*, 3:165.
99. Perkins, *Cloud of Faithful Witnesses*, 3:161.
100. Perkins, *Cloud of Faithful Witnesses*, 1:160.
101. Perkins, *Sermon on the Mount*, 1:208.

doings be in heaven.... Christ Jesus has bought the kingdom of heaven for us (the most blessed purchase that ever was) and has paid the dearest price for it that ever was paid, even His own precious blood. And in this city He has prepared for us a dwelling place and made us free denizens of it. Therefore, all our joy and all our affairs ought to be there.[102]

---

102. Perkins, *Exposition of the Creed*, 5:266.

# 3

# God to Us: Eternal Union with Christ

IN HIS WORK, *A Golden Chain*, William Perkins writes, "God's decree, inasmuch as it concerns man, is called predestination, which is the decree of God by the which He has ordained all men to a certain everlasting estate—that is, either to salvation or condemnation, for His own glory."[1] The means whereby God accomplishes his work of predestination are the creation and the fall.[2] God directs his creation to a predetermined end. He manifests his

---

1. Perkins, *Golden Chain*, 6:26. Just prior to this statement, Perkins writes that God's work or action is "either His decree or the execution of His decree. The decree of God is that by which God in Himself has necessarily and yet freely from all eternity determined all things" (23).

2. Perkins writes, "Predestination is the counsel of God touching the last end or estate of man out of this temporal or natural life." Perkins, *Manner and Order of Predestination*, 6:305. Logically, therefore, predestination has two parts: election and reprobation. Perkins explains the decree of election as "that whereby God has ordained certain men to His glorious grace in the obtaining of their salvation and heavenly life by Christ." Perkins, *Manner and Order of Predestination*, 6:307. Perkins continues that in the decree of election there is a "double act" of (1) foreknowledge, "whereby [God] does acknowledge some men for His own before the rest"; and (2) predestination, "whereby He has determined from eternity to make them like to Christ" (6:307). See also Perkins's "Ocular Catechism" in appendix 5 of this book. Regarding "foreknowledge," a lengthy description is necessary. Perkins writes,

> This prescience or foreknowledge in God puts a difference between the true God and all creatures, *for the true God foresees all things that are to come*. So can no creature do. Indeed, some creatures foresee and foretell some things, yet herein they come short of the divine property. For God foresees all things by Himself without signs and outward means. But creatures only foresee some things not of themselves, but by means of signs and outward causes or by revelation from God, otherwise can no creature foresee things to come.

justice and mercy in (1) permitting the fall and (2) establishing the covenant of grace.³ Therefore, God's creation of man has an intended *telos*.⁴ It is eschatological. This means that humanity must be understood in terms of his four-fold estate: (1) as created; (2) as corrupted; (3) as renewed; and (4) as glorified.⁵ God's creation of man and God's covenant with man are, therefore, foundational to Perkins's concept of eschatological glory.

## God's Creation of Man

"In the beginning God created the heaven and the earth" (Gen 1:1). For Perkins, "creation" is "that by which God made all things very good of nothing—that is, of no matter which was before the creation . . . by His word alone without any instruments, means, assistance, or motion."⁶ The world which God made is "a most beautiful palace, framed out of a deformed substance and fit to be inhabited."⁷ God "began and finished the whole work in six distinct days," declares Perkins, and "in the end of the sixth day He made man."⁸ The sixth day culminates in these words: "And God said, Let us make man in our image, after our likeness . . . So God created man in his own image, in the image of God created he him; male and female created he them" (Gen 1:26–27).⁹ Perkins describes this

---

Now, as we said before, *this foresight in God includes His decree and ordination; for therefore did these things so come to pass because God ordained them. Whereby we see that God's prescience or foreknowledge is not idle but operative and joined with His will. . . . As all things in time come to pass, so God before all worlds willed—that is, decreed and appointed them.* And, under this large extent of God's will or decree, we must include the sinful actions of men. For God does not barely foresee them but decree the being of them and so will them after a sort, though not to be done by Himself yet by others. (Perkins, *Cloud of Faithful Witnesses*, 3:394, emphasis added)

3. Perkins, *Exposition of the Creed*, 5:82. The covenant of grace will be discussed at length in chap. 4.

4. Perkins writes, "Man was created that there might be a way prepared whereby God might show His grace and mercy in the salvation of some and His justice in the deserved damnation of others for their sins." Perkins, *Exposition of Creed*, 5:71.

5. Perkins, *Reformed Catholic*, 7:13.

6. Perkins, *Golden Chain*, 6:26.

7. Perkins, *Golden Chain*, 6:26.

8. Perkins, *Exposition of the Creed*, 5:50. For reasons why God created in six days, see pp. 5:50–51 of this same volume.

9. According to Perkins, the end of creation is the glory of God. God created in order that he might "communicate and make manifest His glory to His creatures and give them

estate according to seven realities: man's (1) place, (2) nature, (3) dignity, (4) subjection, (5) calling, (6) diet,[10] and (7) will.[11] Four of these are particularly relevant for our present discussion.

## *Man's Nature*

According to Perkins, the image of God in humanity consists of two principal parts. The first is knowledge. Because he was created in the image of God, Adam "knew God so far forth as it was convenient for a creature to know his Creator."[12] He also knew God's will "so far forth as it was convenient for him to show his obedience" unto him. Finally, he knew the "wisdom and will" of God regarding particular creatures.[13] In sum, Adam knew "the counsel of God in all His creatures."[14]

The second part of the image of God in man is holiness and righteousness. This entails "conformity of the will and affections and of the whole disposition of man both in body and soul to the will of God, his Creator."[15] Adam was created, formed, and fashioned in a perfect order. "And God saw everything that he had made, and behold it *was* very good" (Gen 1:31). For Perkins, "orderly comeliness is a part of the goodness of a thing."[16]

Because man was created in the image of God, he was endowed with a good conscience. Perkins defines the conscience as "that which rightly excuses and comforts, according to God's Word."[17] Adam's conscience was "good" and, therefore it could not accuse him but only excuse him. But Adam's will was mutable,[18] in that he was given the freedom to will either good or evil. Perkins demonstrates that Adam "was created with such liberty

---

occasion to magnify the same. For the reasonable creatures of God, beholding His glory in the creation, are moved to testify and declare the same among men." Perkins, *Exposition of the Creed*, 5:49.

10. Perkins notes that Adam's diet was "the herbs of the earth and fruit of every tree except the Tree of the Knowledge of Good and Evil." Perkins, *Golden Chain*, 6:31.

11. Perkins, *Golden Chain*, 6:30–31.

12. Perkins, *Exposition of the Creed*, 5:65.

13. Perkins, *Exposition of the Creed*, 5:65.

14. Perkins, *Golden Chain*, 6:30.

15. Perkins, *Exposition of the Creed*, 5:65.

16. Perkins, *Cloud of Faithful Witnesses*, 3:23.

17. Perkins, *Discourse of Conscience*, 8:56.

18. Pertaining to Perkins's understanding of Adam's liberty and mutability of will, see Perkins, *Treatise on God's Free Grace*, 6:405–7.

of will as that he could indifferently will either."[19] The freedom of Adam's will implied the (1) freedom to evil alone, (2) freedom to good alone, (3) freedom to do good in part, and (4) freedom to good or evil indifferently. This four-fold freedom, writes Perkins, "was in Adam before the fall, who, though he had no inclination to sin but only that which was acceptable to God, yet was he not bound by any necessity but had his liberty freely to choose or refuse either good or evil."[20] Perkins also makes a distinction in the freedom of the will through what he describes as a "double liberty of will." This distinction is made between the will in creation and the will in glory. Adam, by creation, received the freedom to will good or evil. The other is to will good alone, which is "reserved to the life to come."[21]

## *Man's Dignity*

Having been created in God's image, Adam is placed in the "most pleasant garden,"[22] and gifted with honor and dignity above all creation. This dignity includes blessed communion with the God. Adam and Eve are gifted with life by the Spirit,[23] and enjoy "blessed and immediate fellowship with God. . . . God revealed Himself in a special manner unto [Adam], so as his very body and soul was a temple and dwelling place of the Creator."[24] In this communion, "God rejoiced in His own image, so likewise man did fervently love God."[25] In addition, God established Adam as "lord and king" over all of creation. Their dignity also includes the "decency and dignity of the body. . . . Though naked, as nothing was unseemly, so was there in it imprinted a princely majesty."[26] As Perkins explains, man "had a wonderful beauty and majesty above all creatures in his body, whereupon David says the Lord has crowned him with 'glory and worship' [Ps 8:5]."[27] Finally, their dignity is evident in their calling to keep the garden (2:15). "If [Adam] had

---

19. Perkins, *Exposition of the Creed*, 5:65.
20. Perkins, *Exposition of the Creed*, 5:84.
21. Perkins, *Exposition of the Creed*, 5:85.
22. Perkins, *Golden Chain*, 6:30.
23. Perkins, *Golden Chain*, 6:36.
24. Perkins, *Exposition of the Creed*, 5:66.
25. Perkins, *Golden Chain*, 6:30.
26. Perkins, *Golden Chain*, 6:30.
27. Perkins, *Exposition of the Creed*, 5:66.

never fallen," expounds Perkins, "he should have labored in the garden, but so as he should never have been wearied therewith."[28]

## *Man's Calling*

Another component of Adam's state of innocence was his calling, which consisted of two expressions: particular and general. Adam's particular calling was to "dress" and "keep" the garden (Gen 2:15). "Adam in his innocency had all things at his will and wanted nothing," writes Perkins, "yet even then God employed him in a calling."[29] Adam's general calling was to worship God, "considering the moral law was written in his heart by nature."[30] In this state, Adam was not "clogged with sin," and therefore he was able to worship God according to his law.[31] Moreover, he worshiped God on the Sabbath, the seventh day from the beginning of creation. Perkins believes the two sacramental trees factored into Adam's worship in that they served to exercise Adam in obedience to God.[32]

As for the end for which God created man, Perkins points to the glory of God. To summarize, God created man to set forth and acknowledge his "wisdom, goodness, [and] mercy" in his creation and providence. Moreover, "having decreed to glorify His name," God created man to show his mercy in salvation and his justice in damnation. Therefore, says Perkins, God "has appointed the creation, especially of man to be a means of manifestation and beginning of the execution of His eternal counsel."[33]

## *Man's Subjection*

In his estate of innocence man was required to obey God's commands. First, Adam was bound by the *moral law*, as summed up in the *Decalogue*. These commands were written in "Adam's mind by the gift of creation,"[34] and they served as a "rule of life."[35] "Adam had fully before his fall written

---

28. Perkins, *Exposition of the Creed*, 5:67.
29. Perkins, *Exposition of the Creed*, 5:67.
30. Perkins, *Exposition of the Creed*, 5:67.
31. Perkins, *Exposition of the Creed*, 5:67.
32. Perkins, *Exposition of the Creed*, 5:68.
33. Perkins, *Exposition of the Creed*, 5:68.
34. Perkins, *Sermon on the Mount*, 1:243–44.
35. Perkins, *Galatians*, 2:253.

in his heart the moral law," reiterates Perkins.[36] In addition to the moral law, man was bound to obey two positive laws. The first focused on the tree of life (Gen 3:24) and the tree of the knowledge of good and evil (Gen 2:17), while the second focused on the Sabbath. Perkins calls these two trees "sacraments"[37] that were ordained "to be a proof and trial of man's obedience."[38] God gave the tree of life as a sign, so that "it might confirm to man his perpetual abode in the Garden of Eden, if he persisted in his obedience."[39] It also signified "assurance of life forever."[40] Perkins states, "It had in it virtue and power whereby it would have preserved [Adam] from death and old age."[41] By the "appointment and blessing of God," man was "immortal,"[42] "glorious,"[43] "righteous," and endowed with "power" to obey.[44] If Adam had continued in obedience, he would have lived "holily and happily,"[45] and there would "have been found no misery in men."[46] Given that Adam was told to "be fruitful, and multiply" (1:28),[47] he received all "for himself and his posterity."[48] "Had we continued in our innocence," writes Perkins, "all creatures had continued in their excellent order."[49]

The second sacramental tree was the tree of the knowledge of good and evil. Adam was commanded to abstain from eating its fruit. Attached to God's command was the threat of punishment—temporal and eternal death. Perkins adds, "This was a sign of death and had his name of the event because the observation thereof would have brought perpetual happiness, the violation gave experience of evil—that is, of all misery, namely punishment and guiltiness of sin."[50]

---

36. Perkins, *Golden Chain*, 6:179.
37. Perkins, *Exposition of the Creed*, 5:68.
38. Perkins, *Golden Chain*, 6:31.
39. Perkins, *Golden Chain*, 6:31.
40. Perkins, *Exposition of the Creed*, 5:68.
41. Perkins, *Revelation*, 4:453.
42. Perkins, *Exposition of the Creed*, 5:69.
43. Perkins, *Cloud of Faithful Witnesses*, 3:24.
44. Perkins, *Treatise on God's Free Grace and Man's Free Will*, 6:405.
45. Perkins, *Manner and Order of Predestination*, 6:321.
46. Perkins, *Exposition of the Creed*, 5:85.
47. Perkins, *Christian Oeconomie*, 10:124.
48. Perkins, *Jude*, 4:32.
49. Perkins, *Cloud of Faithful Witnesses*, 3:23.
50. Perkins, *Golden Chain*, 6:31.

## God's Covenant with Man

Much has been written on the history and development of what is called the covenant of works. It is granted creedal sanction in the Westminster Confession of Faith (1646), the Savoy Declaration (1658), and the Second London Baptist Confession (1677/1689).[51] One of the most exhaustive definitions of this covenant is found in James Ussher's *A Body of Divinity*. He defines the covenant of works as

> a Conditional Covenant between God and Man, whereby on the one side God commandeth the Perfection of Godliness and Righteousness, and promiseth that he will be our God, if we keep all his Commandments; and on the other side, Man bindeth himself to perform entire and perfect Obedience to God's Law, by that Strength where with God hath endued him by Nature of his first Creation.[52]

There is some debate concerning the place of the covenant of works in early Reformed theology.[53] According to Andrew Woolsey, the first use of the expression "covenant of works" (*foedus operum*) is found in Dudley Fenner's *Sacra Theologia*.[54] However, as J. V. Fesko notes, "the idea of an Adamic covenant . . . has roots in patristic theology as well as Roman Catholic theologians of the period."[55] Harrison Perkins agrees with Fesko, pointing out that the "covenant of works did not originate de novo in the sixteenth century and the notion of a covenant with Adam was an ancient idea." He adds, "Irenaeus of Lyons (c. 130–c. 200) and Augustine (354–450) both explicitly referred to a covenant made with Adam, even if they did not outline its content in an identical way to the early modern covenant of works."[56] Other scholars see something of the covenant of works in the early church father Tertullian (155–220) and the medieval theologian Thomas Aquinas

---

51. For statements on the covenant of works, see WCF: 7:2; 19:1, 6. SDF: 7:2; 19:1, 6. 2LBCF: 19:1, 6; 20:1.

52. Ussher, *Body of Divinity*, 111.

53. For a summary of this debate, see McGiffert, "Perkinsian Moment," 192.

54. Woolsey, *Unity and Continuity in Covenantal Thought*, 443. Dudly Fenner was an early English Puritan Divine (1558–87). He develops his "*De operum fœderc*" (The works of the Covenant) in his *Sacra Theologia*. Fenner, *Sacra theologia*, 88. Perkins, *Catholicity and the Covenant of Works*, 88.

55. Fesko, *Covenant of Works*, 6.

56. Perkins, *Catholicity and the Covenant of Works*, 88.

(1225–74).⁵⁷ However, there is little debate that it was not until the late sixteenth and early seventeenth centuries that the covenant of works was fully developed and ultimately embraced confessionally.⁵⁸

There are two main schools of thought concerning Perkins's position on the covenant of works. The first argues that Perkins "never provided a fully-fledged description of a covenant between God and Adam."⁵⁹ While he spoke of a covenant of works, he did not do so in reference to a "covenant with Adam," but to "the moral law."⁶⁰ Harrison Perkins explains, "Ussher taught that the moral law was embedded in the hearts of Adam and Eve at creation, but Perkins saw the moral law as essentially beginning at Sinai."⁶¹ He concludes, "Perkins taught many of the elements that became the covenant of works between God and man . . . [but], did not explicitly teach the doctrine even though he clearly taught pieces of it."⁶²

The second school of thought is summed up in Woolsey's exhaustive work, *Unity and Continuity in Covenantal Thought*. He maintains that Perkins holds to a pre-fall covenant of works. He rests his argument on the fact that Perkins (1) makes a substantive distinction between the covenant of works and the covenant of grace, (2) insists that the moral law (the Decalogue) was written upon Adam's heart, and (3) believes the promise of eternal life was contingent upon Adam's obedience.⁶³ For Woolsey, Perkins's view of the work of Christ

> revealed most conclusively the nature of Adam's relationship with God, and implied most strongly a pre-fall 'covenant of works' arrangement. . . . Christ as the second Adam came to undo what the first Adam had done and to restore what the first Adam had

---

57. Perkins, *Catholicity and the Covenant of Works*, 88.

58. Richard Muller, regarding the *foedus operum*, writes, "The specific language of a covenant of works rose to prominence in Reformed theology following 1590 in the works of Perkins, Rollock, Polanus, and others." Muller, *Dictionary of Latin and Greek Theological Terms*, 131. This is what McGiffert would call the "Perkinsian Moment," which "ran from about 1600 to about 1640. During those decades, federalism took form, caught on, gained strength—and grew problematic." McGiffert, "Perkinsian Moment," 124.

59. Perkins, *Catholicity and the Covenant of Works*, 94. Perkins footnotes, "There is one instance where Perkins made a passing reference to a covenant between God and Adam, but this does not constitute a rounded formulation of the doctrine." Perkins, *Catholicity and the Covenant of Works*, 94n50.

60. Perkins, *Catholicity and the Covenant of Works*, 95.

61. Perkins, *Catholicity and the Covenant of Works*, 96–97.

62. Perkins, *Catholicity and the Covenant of Works*, 98.

63. Woolsey, *Unity and Continuity*, 466–72.

lost.... [Perkins] interpreted Christ's redemptive work in terms of the second Adam providing salvation and justification through his obedience to, and satisfaction of, the righteousness of the law, in order to undo the devastation and death introduced by the disobedience of the first Adam.[64]

The most persuasive argument of those who deny that Perkins teaches a pre-fall covenant of works is that he never uses the expression in reference to the relationship between God and Adam.[65] "It is never mentioned," says Victor Lewis Priebe.[66] In sharp contrast, scholars, such as J. V. Fesko and T. F. Torrance argue that "the rise of the twofold covenantal architecture was largely due to the influence of William Perkins."[67] Woolsey presents a convincing case that a pre-fall covenant of works reflects the inner logic of Perkins's teaching. Even Harrison Perkins concedes that Woolsey demonstrates that Perkins taught "elements of the covenant of works and did not substantially diverge from those who wrote before or after him," adding that "he was in continuity with them in that he adopted theological structures from the previous generation and refined them, just as the generation after him did with his theological structures."[68]

## *The Covenant of Works*

Perkins defines God's covenant as "His contract with man concerning the obtaining of life eternal upon a certain condition."[69] He proceeds to explain that it consists of two parts: "God's promise to man; man's promise to God. God's promise to man is that whereby He binds Himself to man to be his God, if he performs the condition. Man's promise to God is that whereby he vows his allegiance to his Lord and to perform the condition between them."[70]

---

64. Woolsey, *Unity and Continuity*, 471–72.
65. Perkins, *Catholicity and the Covenant of Works*, 94n50, 98.
66. Priebe, "Covenant Theology of William Perkins," 42–43.
67. Fesko, *Covenant of Works*, 34. See Torrance, *Scottish Theology*, 61. The objection could be raised that no one is arguing Perkins does not teach a twofold covenant (works and grace). The issue is when the covenant of works was instituted. In that case, this would be a fair objection.
68. Perkins, *Catholicity and the Covenant of Works*, 99.
69. Perkins, *Golden Chain*, 6:65.
70. Perkins, *Golden Chain*, 6:65.

For Perkins, there are two kinds of covenants: legal (works) and evangelical (grace). The covenant of works (CW) is a "legal" covenant, and the covenant of grace (CG) is an "evangelical" covenant. In this legal covenant (CW), "life everlasting is promised to works—for that is the condition of the law: do these things and you shall live."[71] Ussher, likewise, sums up the nature of this covenant: "Do this, and thou shalt live: If thou dost it not, thou shalt die the death."[72] The condition of the covenant of works, according to Perkins, is "perfect obedience as expressed in the moral law."[73] He defines the moral law as "that part of God's Word which commands perfect obedience to man as well in his nature as in his actions, and forbids the contrary."[74] Specifically, this law contains "the edict commanding obedience and the condition binding to obedience. The condition is eternal life to such as fulfill the law, but to transgressors, everlasting death."[75]

According to Perkins, these two components of the law (edict and condition) were written upon Adam's heart in his state of innocence. Moreover, Adam received this law as the federal head of all humanity.[76] Perkins writes, "Adam must be considered not as a private man, but as a root or head bearing in it all mankind, or as a public person, representing all his posterity."[77] Turning to Romans 5, Perkins highlights the reality of the two humanities linked to two representative heads, Adam and Christ. All who are in Adam (all humanity) receive what Adam can give, life from his obedience or death from his disobedience. This reception can only be understood within a covenantal framework.[78] Perkins writes,

> Sentences of Scripture are either legal or evangelical: the law and the gospel being two several and distinct parts of God's Word. Now this former sentence (Gen 2:17) is legal and must be understood

---

71. Perkins, *Reformed Catholic*, 7:55. See also Perkins, *Sermon on the Mount*, 1:430.
72. Ussher, *Body of Divinity*, 111.
73. Perkins, *Golden Chain*, 6:65.
74. Perkins, *Golden Chain*, 6:65.
75. Perkins, *Golden Chain*, 6:66.
76. Perkins, *Golden Chain*, 6:36, 6:162.

77. Perkins, *Exposition of the Creed*, 5:88. That phrase, "not as a private man," is important for Adam, and will become an important descriptor in the next chapter when looking at the federal headship of Jesus Christ.

78. William Ames concurs, writing, "Adam was the first of mankind, from whom all men come, a law was given to him not only as a private person, as among the angels, but as a public person or the head of the family of man. His posterity were to derive all good and evil from him." Ames, *Marrow of Theology*, 113.

with an exception borrowed from the gospel or the covenant of grace made with Adam, and revealed to him after his fall. This exception is this: "You will certainly die whenever you eat the forbidden fruit, except I do further give you [the] means of deliverance from death, namely the seed of the woman to bruise the serpent's head."[79]

Several conclusions concerning Perkins's understanding of the covenants emerge. First, Perkins believes God gives the covenant of grace to Adam immediately after the fall. He also believes God gives an earlier covenant (with the "legal" stipulation) to Adam. The edict and condition are given prior to the fall (Gen 2:17) within a distinct covenantal context: "Do this, and thou shalt live; do not, and thou shalt die the death." This is the covenantal framework of blessing and cursing. Subsequently, the evangelical covenant (CG) was given to deliver from the consequence of breaking the legal covenant (CW). According to Perkins, for the covenant of grace to have any coherence, there must be a pre-fall covenant of works.

Perkins, therefore, shows how man inherits sin and death from Adam. God ordained that all of Adam's posterity would receive whatever Adam received. When Adam sinned, "he deprived first of all himself and then secondly all his posterity of the image of God, because all mankind was in his loins when he sinned."[80] Perkins adds, "The guilt of [Adam's] transgression goes all over mankind and continues still even to this hour and shall do so to the end of the world, in those which shall be born after."[81] Perkins sums up Adam's role and responsibility as covenantal head as follows:

> The reason hereof [that reason being all of mankind receiving the sin of Adam] is because we are his seed and posterity. We were then in his loins. He was the father of us all. And [he] was not a private man as we are now, but a public person, the pledge of all mankind, and [he] bore the person of us all at that time. Therefore, what he did then, he did it for himself and for us. What covenant God made with him was made for himself and us. What God promised him and he to God, he promised for himself and for us. What he received for himself and for us, and what he gained or lost by his fall, he gained and lost for us as for himself.[82]

79. Perkins, *Salve for a Sick Man*, 10:404.
80. Perkins, *Exposition of the Creed*, 5:90.
81. Perkins, *Exposition of the Creed*, 5:100.
82. Perkins, *Zephaniah* 2:1–2, 9:96–97. According to Priebe, Perkins did not hold to a pre-fall covenant of works. God did not make a covenant with Adam prior to the fall, nor

In Galatians 4:24–25,[83] Paul contrasts the bondage of law and the liberty of grace. He illustrates this dichotomy by appealing to the bondwoman (Hagar) and freewoman (Sarah), Sinai and Jerusalem, and Ishmael and Isaac. Each declares the basic dichotomy between works and grace, bondage and liberty.

In his exposition of these verses, Perkins states that Hagar represents the covenant of works, which is also allegorically interpreted as "Sinai." All those who place themselves under the law seek to justify themselves by the works of law (Gal 2:16; 3:20). Sinai is where God gave the law to Moses, thereby reiterating the stipulations of the covenant of works: "Do this and thou shall live."[84] Since they have Hagar as their mother, they are children

---

did God give the moral law until Sinai. Priebe, "Covenant Theology of William Perkins," 42–44. Further, Priebe claims that "Perkins's view of the two covenants is not understood in terms of successive stages of God's dealing with man, but rather, the two seem to be present and operative throughout history running simultaneously and concurrently." Priebe, "Covenant Theology of William Perkins," 44. Similarly, Harrison Perkins affirms that, for William Perkins, (1) the covenant of works is established after Adam's fall, (2) the moral law is given "essentially" at Sinai, and (3) the covenant of works and the covenant of grace are "parallel covenants of works and grace," which are instituted after the fall. Perkins, *Catholicity and the Covenant of Works*, 95–97.

83. "Which things are an allegory: for these are the two covenants; the one from the mount Sinai, which gendereth to bondage, which is Agar. For this Agar is mount Sinai in Arabia, and answereth to Jerusalem which now is, and is in bondage with her children."

84. Perkins believes that the Old Testament Scripture was an "unfolding" of that "old covenant of works," and the event at Mt. Sinai was the full "promulgation of the law." Perkins, *Art of Prophesying*, 10:292–93. Likewise, the Decalogue is an "abridgment" of the entire law and "the covenant of works." Perkins, *Golden Chain*, 6:66. Perkins holds that God had attached the promise of eternal life to the law (CoW), pre- and post-fall ("Do this and thou shall live." cf. Gen 2:17; Lev 18:5; Luke 10:28). At the same time, now living in a post-fall world, the legal sentence now shows "not what men can do, but what they should do." Perkins, *Golden Chain*, 6:235. Due to man's sinful nature, no man can merit eternal life because none can fulfill the law. In the attempt to attach and establish one's righteousness by keeping the law was to "come into bondage" and deprive oneself of the "inheritance of eternal life." Perkins, *Galatians*, 2:304. While the promise of eternal life was perpetually attached to the covenant of works, according to Perkins, that was never its ultimate purpose. He gives four reasons for the Sinaitic administration of the law: (1) It was to serve the Jews as a "guard of armed men" so that they should not "depart from their allegiance" to God. (2) As a "schoolmaster" (Gal 3:24), it "points out and shadows forth" the person and work of Christ. (3) It "urges and compels" men to go to Christ. Perkins, *Galatians*, 2:203–5. For Christ, by his obedience, fulfilled all that is contained in the law, that "we might have right to life everlasting, and according to the tenor of the law." Perkins, *Galatians*, 2:52. (4) With the ceremonial law now being abrogated (being fulfilled in Christ), the moral law and various judicial laws (laws linked to the moral law) were perpetual statues that are to serve the commonwealth in all times and places. See Perkins, *Galatians*, 206–9. See also Perkins, *Sermon on the Mount*, 1:243–45.

of "the bondwoman" and are born "according to the flesh."[85] For Perkins, Paul is not saying that the covenant of works was established at Sinai. If it were, then it would be necessary to say that it was established with Hagar since Paul is using Hagar and Sinai interchangeably. Woolsey provides a helpful explanation:

> It must be understood, however, that here Paul was referring to Judaizers who were troubling the Galatian church with their insistence on making obedience to the law a condition of salvation. In that context we can understand Paul emphasizing the place of the covenant of works in the Sinaitic administration. But doing so to demonstrate the difference between law and gospel in this way does not prove or imply that the covenant of law had no prior significance or existence.[86]

Perkins believes that Paul's goal is simply to demonstrate the contrast between law and gospel, bondage by works and freedom by grace. Following Paul's own words, Perkins interprets the illustrations allegorically.[87] One of the ways in which the law and gospel differ is that they are "two in substance or kind . . . the law was in nature by creation. The gospel is above nature and was revealed after the fall."[88] It is evident, therefore, that Perkins sees the covenant of works (and the moral law) as established before the fall.

## *The Covenant of Redemption*[89]

Perkins explains that Christ "was ordained in the eternal counsel of God to be our surety and pledge and to be a public person to represent all the

---

85. Perkins, *Galatians*, 2:297.

86. Woolsey, *Unity and Continuity*, 468.

87. By allegorical, Perkins means "one thing is said, and another thing is meant . . . expressed in borrowed or figurative speeches." Perkins, *Galatians*, 2:300–301.

88. Perkins, *Galatians*, 2:302–3.

89. Perkins never uses the term "covenant of redemption," "*pactum salutis*," or "*foedus redemptionis*." Richard Muller and J. V. Fesko locate the first usage of the term "covenant of redemption" or *foedus redemptionis* ca. 1638 in the work of David Dickson. Muller, "Toward the *Pactum Salutis*," 16. Also, see Fesko, *Trinity and the Covenant of Redemption*, 8. However, Muller notes that within Perkins, "whether in connection with [his] doctrines of predestination or in connection with [his] discussions of Christ, that there is an arrangement or agreement of some sort between the Father and the Son in the Godhead, according to which the Son is designated, appointed, or anointed to his office." Muller, "Toward the *Pactum Salutis*," 56. This section points out Perkins's terminology of

elect in His obedience and sufferings."[90] Christ was set apart, says Perkins, as the elect's Redeemer "in the eternal counsel of the Father, Son, and Holy Ghost."[91] Again, he writes, "The promises made to Abraham are first made to Christ, and then in Christ to all that believe in Him, be they Jews or Gentiles. . . . The promises of the gospel are first directed and made to Christ, and then by consequent to them that are by faith engrafted into Christ."[92] When were the promises of the gospel made to Christ? "In the eternal counsel of God," says Perkins. John von Rohr notes that Perkins's assertion is rooted in his understanding of the "intra-Trinitarian covenant of redemption," which is the "source for the covenant of grace."[93] According to Richard Muller,

> The pretemporal, intratrinitarian agreement of the Father and the Son concerning the covenant of grace and its ratification in and through the work of the Son incarnate. In the unity of the Godhead, the Son covenants with the Father to be the temporal sponsor of the Father's *testamentum* (q.v.) in and through the work of the Mediator. In that work, the Son fulfills his *sponsio* (q.v.) or *fideiussio* (q.v.), i.e., his guarantee of payment of the debt of sin in ratification of the Father's *testamentum*.[94]

In the covenant of redemption, God gives a people to his Son, and he makes promises to his Son, which are then fulfilled at the incarnation. These promises extend to all who are chosen in Christ before the foundation of the world and united to him by the Holy Spirit in time. This development takes us back to God's intended *telos* for man, specifically that he chooses a particular people in Christ for "the purpose of saving or conferring glory whereby He does ordain or set apart the very same men which were to fall

---

agreement within the eternal counsel of the Trinity regarding the role of Christ as Mediator and his relationship with the elect in history. Though in seed form, Perkins is one of several who helped lay a theological foundation for what would later be established as the covenant of redemption. For a more in-depth look at this development in Perkins, see Muller, "Toward the *Pactum Salutis*," 52–55.

90. Perkins, *Exposition of the Creed*, 5:94. See also Perkins, *Sermon on the Mount*, 1:334.

91. Perkins, *Galatians*, 2:180.

92. Perkins, *Galatians*, 2:189. Perkins elaborates later when he writes, "By His [the Father's] counsel and eternal decree whereby the Son was designed to the office of a mediator, and consequently to become man" (2:246).

93. Rohr, *Covenant of Grace*, 84.

94. Muller, *Dictionary of Latin and Greek*, 252. To see how these words find themselves being used in the context of the Covenant of Redemption, see Muller, *Dictionary of Latin and Greek*, 120, 342, 356.

in Adam to salvation and celestial glory."[95] Rohr concludes, "Thus the eternal covenant with Christ is also an eternal covenant with those who have been elected to receive his redemption. Ultimately the application of this redemption will be through the means which God has chosen to employ, that is, through the conditions of the covenant of grace."[96]

## The Covenant of Grace

For Perkins, the covenant of grace is "that whereby God, freely promising Christ and His benefits, exacts again of man that he would by faith receive Christ and repent of his sins."[97] This covenant was first revealed to Adam and Eve after the fall: "The seed of the woman shall bruise the serpents head" (Gen 3:15). It was then "continued and renewed with a part of Adam's posterity, as with Abraham, Isaac, Jacob, David, etc.; but it was most fully revealed and accomplished at the coming of Christ."[98] While one in substance, the covenant of grace is distinguished in the Old Testament by types and shadows which prefigured Christ. In the New Testament, Christ is declared to have come in the flesh and he is revealed in the gospel.[99] Rohr writes, "Despite the disobedience of the fall, despite the breaking of the first covenant by sin, despite the now corrupted character of the race, God has once again entered into the historical scene, not only to renew the broken relationship, but also to establish it in a radically different way."[100]

---

95. Perkins, *Manner and Order of Predestination*, 6:309. Perkins adds, "This act is in no wise to be severed from the former [electing certain men in Christ to everlasting love and favor], but to be distinguished in the mind (for orders' sake and for the better unfolding of it); for as by the former men were ordained to grace, so by this latter the means are subordained whereby grace may be conferred and manifested" (6:309).

96. Rohr, *Covenant of Grace*, 84.

97. Perkins, *Golden Chain*, 6:153.

98. Perkins, *Exposition of the Creed*, 5:94.

99. Perkins, *Golden Chain*, 6:153.

100. Rohr, *Covenant of Grace*, 45–46.

> It has been observed that, since the sixteenth century, the "concept" of the covenant of grace has been developed to establish the unity of redemptive history that began with the first promise, made to Adam . . . and culminated in the work of Jesus Christ as the Mediator of the covenant. . . . The covenant of grace represents God's gracious response to Adam's sinful failure to fulfill the condition of the covenant of works . . . [Therefore it] forms the heart and soul of Reformed soteriology and declares that salvation, whether in

Perkins compares the substantive differences between the old and new covenants. (1) The old propounds the justice of God without mercy, whereas the new reveals "the justice of God giving place to His mercy."[101] (2) The old requires perfect inward and outward righteousness, whereas the new "propounds unto us an imputed justice resident in the person of the mediator."[102] (3) The old promises life "upon condition of works," whereas the new promises "remission of sins and life everlasting upon condition that we rest ourselves on Christ by faith."[103] (4) The old was written in tables of stone, whereas the new is written on the "fleshly tables of our hearts."[104] (5) The old was in nature by creation, whereas the new is "above nature and was revealed after the fall."[105] (6) The old was mediated through Moses, whereas the new is mediated through Christ. (7) The old was "dedicated" by the blood of beasts, whereas the new was dedicated by the blood of Christ.[106] In summary, for Perkins, the covenant of works only "genders to bondage," while the gospel "genders to life." He adds, "For it [CG] is an instrument of the Spirit for the beginning and confirming of our regeneration and salvation."[107]

Perkins believes that the Old Testament saints ("believing Jews") ate the same spiritual meat and drank the same spiritual drink, thereby obtaining the same eternal life by faith (1 Cor 10:3), as the New Testament saints. However, he insisted that the administration of the covenant of grace does "far surpass the church of God in the old," and displays "the preeminence of the church" under the gospel.[108] This is true in five ways. (1) In the Old Testament, spiritual and heavenly things were propounded unto the church under temporal and earthly blessings. But now in the New Testament, "life

---

the Old or New Testament, is by grace alone, through faith alone in Jesus Christ. (Beeke and Jones, *Puritan Theology*, 259–60)

101. Perkins, *Galatians*, 2:302.

102. Perkins, *Galatians*, 2:302. Perkins previously notes, "The Son of God takes not Himself to the office of a mediator, but He is called and sent forth of His Father. Whereby two things are signified: one, that the office of a mediator was appointed by the Father; the other, that the Son was designed to this office in the eternal counsel of the blessed Trinity" (2:247). Again, this language points one back to an understanding of the eternal Covenant of Redemption.

103. Perkins, *Galatians*, 2:303.

104. Perkins, *Galatians*, 2:303.

105. Perkins, *Galatians*, 2:303.

106. Perkins, *Galatians*, 2:303.

107. Perkins, *Galatians*, 2:304.

108. Perkins, *Cloud of Faithful Witnesses*, 394–95.

everlasting is plainly promised to the believer without any such type or figure."[109] (2) In the Old Testament, Christ was shown and signified in ceremonies, rites, and types, which "were in number many and in significance some of them dark and obscure." But now in the New, "these types and ceremonies are abolished, the shadow is gone, and the substance come."[110] (3) In the Old Testament, "all the knowledge they had was in the law, and their understanding in the gospel was obscure and very slender. But in the New Testament not only the law is made manifest but also supernatural knowledge of the gospel."[111] (4) In the Old Testament, the law was only committed and published to the nation of Israel, but in the New, the gospel is spread and preached to all the world. (5) The church in the Old Testament looked forward to and believed in Christ who was to come. In the New, Christ has come manifested in the flesh, thus fulfilling all that had been promised concerning himself.[112] While the new covenant was given to our first parents in the garden, its full revelation and fulfillment came only in the time of Christ. Therefore, for Perkins, the foundation of the covenant of grace is the person of Christ.

### The Parties

The parties involved in both covenants are God and man. However, there is a difference. All people are included in the covenant of works because all are in Adam, but not all people are included in the covenant of grace because not all are in Christ. Entrance into the first comes by birth, whereas entrance into the second comes by a new birth. For Perkins, in the covenant of grace, God is the principal party, and "He promises righteousness and life eternal in Christ. Man again binds himself by God's grace to believe and rest upon the promise."[113] Therefore, not everyone is in the covenant of grace, "but only that little part of mankind which in all ages has been the church of God and has by faith embraced the covenant. . . . God makes no covenant of reconciliation without faith."[114]

---

109. Perkins, *Cloud of Faithful Witnesses*, 3:395.
110. Perkins, *Cloud of Faithful Witnesses*, 3:395.
111. Perkins, *Cloud of Faithful Witnesses*, 3:395.
112. Perkins, *Cloud of Faithful Witnesses*, 3:395.
113. Perkins, *Exposition of the Creed*, 5:94.
114. Perkins, *Exposition of the Creed*, 5:95.

Perkins shows that the covenant of works is universal, while the covenant of grace is particular. Prior to his fall, as the covenant head of humanity, Adam "did receive grace both for himself and for others also."[115] Likewise, in his fall, "[Adam] lost it both for himself and for all others."[116] After this, Adam received "the promise for himself alone and not for the whole world, otherwise the first Adam should not only have been a living creature but a quickening spirit, the which is proper to the second Adam."[117] Perkins draws on the language of Romans 5 and 1 Corinthians 15, to demonstrate that man receives from Adam only what Adam can give; namely, sin, corruption, misery, and death. And man receives from Christ only what Christ can give: forgiveness, holiness, joy, and life.[118] "The covenant of grace, and our being in Christ," Perkins exclaims, "is absolutely necessary, for no man, woman, or child, can be saved unless they have God for their God."[119] The covenantal relationship, therefore, is only found in Christ.

For Perkins, the sum of the covenant of grace is this: "Believe in the Lord Jesus Christ, and thou shalt be saved."[120] There is no knowledge of, or substance to, the covenant of grace apart from the person of Christ. Perkins writes, "The substance of the covenant is that righteousness and life everlasting is given to God's church and people by Christ."[121] Christ is the foundation upon which the covenant of grace is applied. Just as Adam was a public person who represented all humanity, Christ too is "a public person, representing all men that are to come to life eternal."[122] Christ's incarnation, therefore, is central to the covenant of grace and ultimately to eschatological

---

115. Perkins, *Golden Chain*, 6:257.

116. Perkins, *Golden Chain*, 6:257.

117. Perkins, *Golden Chain*, 6:257.

118. Perkins notes, "For Adam and Christ be two roots, as has been shown. Adam by creation first received God's image and after lost the same for himself and his posterity. Now Christ to remove the sin of man is made the second Adam and the root and very head of all the elect. His manhood was filled with holiness above measure, that from thence as from a storehouse it might be derived to all His members." Perkins, *Exposition of the Creed*, 5:127.

119. Perkins, *Case of Conscience*, 8:281.

120. Perkins, *Sermon on the Mount*, 1:430.

121. Perkins, *Reformed Catholic*, 7:43.

122. Perkins, *Exposition of the Creed*, 5:238. See also Perkins, *Sermon on the Mount*, 1:529. Perkins, *Galatians*, 2:132, 190, 255; Perkins, *Revelation*, 4:342; Perkins, *Exposition of the Creed*, 5:274, 334; Perkins, *True Gain*, 9:67.

glory. It is "in the gospel by the blood of Christ," declares Perkins, that the covenant of grace is "made and confirmed."[123]

According to Perkins, this means that the covenant of grace is rooted "in Christ," and that the heart of the covenant is "reconciliation to God in Christ."[124] Perkins reminds his reader that in the covenant of grace, the promises "are not made to any work or virtue in man, but to the worker—not for any merit of his own person or work, but for the person and merit of Christ."[125] Therefore, the sum and substance of the believer's life must be grounded upon "this covenant in Christ."[126] Salvation is by grace through faith in Christ, and man receives nothing outside of his covenantal head. Even the believer's works, and the rewards he is promised, are dependent upon this covenant. Perkins explains,

> The bond of all other promises of the gospel, in which God willingly binds Himself to reward our works, do not directly concern us, but have respect to the Person and obedience of Christ, for whose sake alone God binds Himself as debtor unto us and gives the recompense or reward, according to the measure of faith testified by our works... [our works and rewards are] but tokens, that the doer of the works is in Christ, for whose merit the promise [of the crown of life] shall be accomplished."[127]

Man brings nothing to God whereby he is accepted. "Bring faith in Christ," proclaims Perkins, "then is God your Father, and so you shall be welcome."[128]

According to Perkins, God's people have been living in the last days since the time of Christ's coming into the world.[129] Being the "fullness of time wherein the former prophecies are fulfilled and accomplished, the shadows and ceremonies are abolished," Perkins asserts, "the new covenant of grace" has now been established.[130] From the time that God first gave the covenant of grace in the garden to the coming of Christ, he had

---

123. Perkins, *Damned Art of Witchcraft*, 9:389.
124. Perkins, *Sermon on the Mount*, 1:430.
125. Perkins, *Reformed Catholic*, 7:55.
126. Perkins, *Sermon on the Mount*, 1:430.
127. Perkins, *Reformed Catholic*, 7:55.
128. Perkins, *Sermon on the Mount*, 1:430.
129. See also Perkins, *Exposition of the Creed*, 5:130–31.
130. Perkins, *Jude*, 4:210.

*GOD TO US: ETERNAL UNION WITH CHRIST*

"altered the condition of His church and renewed His covenant."[131] God promised (or pledged) it to Adam, renewed it with Noah, Abraham, David, and the returned Babylonian exiles. With the coming of Christ, however, "there remains no renewing thereof, neither any other alteration of it."[132] Having been fully and finally established in the incarnate Son of God, all that remains is the great expectation of Christ's "second coming in glory."[133] Christ, therefore, is the essential foundation to the covenant of grace, and he is the sum and substance pertaining to all our communion with God and the benefits we receive from our heavenly Father.

THE REQUIREMENTS

But how exactly does one become a beneficiary of the covenant of grace? Perkins identifies a twofold condition: faith and baptism."[134] "In the making of the covenant," writes Perkins, "there must be a mutual consent of the parties on both sides; and besides the promise on God's part, there must be also a restipulation on man's part. Otherwise, the covenant is not made."[135]

The first condition on man's part is faith. "For we are bound to believe in Christ if we would come to life everlasting," says Perkins, "or if we would be in the favor of God, or if we would be good disciples and members of Christ."[136] Elsewhere, he adds, "Again, be a man what he can be, unless he be within the covenant of grace, he cannot be saved. But he cannot be within the covenant but by faith. Therefore, no man can be saved by any means but by true faith, nor in any religion but that which teaches true faith."[137] When we believe in Christ, "we perform the condition of this covenant."[138]

Perkins adds an important qualifier to his assertion that faith is a condition of the covenant of grace: "The gospel has in it no moral condition of anything to be done of us. Indeed, faith is mentioned after the form and manner of a condition, but in truth it is the free gift of God, as well as life eternal. And it is to be considered not as a work done of us, but as an

---

131. Perkins, *Jude*, 4:210.
132. Perkins, *Jude*, 4:210.
133. Perkins, *Jude*, 4:210.
134. Perkins, *Discourse of Conscience*, 8:24.
135. Perkins, *Exposition of the Creed*, 5:96.
136. Perkins, *Discourse of Conscience*, 8:24.
137. Perkins, *Cloud of Faithful Witnesses*, 3:56.
138. Perkins, *Sermon on the Mount*, 1:430.

instrument to receive things promised."[139] Beeke and Yuille point out that, for Perkins, "faith is a gift of God's sovereign pleasure that moves us to respond to Christ through the preaching of the Word."[140] As to the nature of faith, Perkins believes there are three kinds: historical, temporary, and saving. As to saving faith specifically, he writes,

> In saving faith, there are four things: knowledge, assent, approbation, and apprehension—that is, an applying of the promises of God unto a man's self, whence proceeds joy.... Now the first two kinds of faith may be lost.... But hence it follows not that saving faith may be lost, for he that is endued therewith can never fall away.[141]

Historical and temporary faith may be lost because they are merely human actions, whereas saving faith is the fruit of divine activity. It is manifested in five degrees: (1) knowledge of the gospel; (2) hope of pardon for sin; (3) hungering and thirsting after the grace offered in Christ; (4) fleeing from the terror of the law and approaching the throne of grace to take hold of Christ; and (5) persuasion in the heart whereby the promises of the gospel are applied.[142] Each of these is the work of the Holy Spirit.

Consequently, entrance into the covenant through the condition of faith is in accordance with God's grace offered in Christ. "For by grace are ye saved through faith; and that not of yourselves: it is the gift of God: Not of works, lest any man should boast" (Eph 2:8–9). According to his own good pleasure, God places the elect in Christ by the Holy Spirit, thereby granting them faith to receive and apply Christ and all his benefits. While faith is a condition, it is a condition ultimately contingent upon God's grace.[143] "We may note that God's special love to a man, whereby He receives him into His covenant, is not grounded on man's behavior but on His own good will and pleasure."[144]

The second condition is baptism. Perkins states, "Now then, that we may attain to salvation by Christ, He must be given unto us really, as he propounded in the tenor of the foresaid covenant. And for the giving of Christ,

---

139. Perkins, *Galatians*, 2:193.

140. Beeke and Yuille, "Biographical Preface," 1:xiii.

141. Perkins, *Revelation*, 4:433.

142. Perkins, *Golden Chain*, 6:176–77. Additionally see "the necessity of faith" in Perkins, *Revelation*, 4:296–97.

143. Perkins, *Reformed Catholic*, 7:43.

144. Perkins, *Cloud of Faithful Witnesses*, 3:249.

God has appointed special ordinances, as the preaching of the Word and the administration of the sacraments."[145] Perkins understood that God uses means ("special ordinances") to accomplish his purposes.[146] One of these is baptism. For Perkins, the covenant of grace is "the foundation and substance of baptism,"[147] because it is "solemnified between God and the party baptized."[148] Baptism does not "make a Christian," but serves "to signify and declare a man to be a Christian by being within the covenant of grace."[149] God performs two actions in baptism. First, he makes the "promise of reconciliation, that is, remission of sins and life everlasting to them that are baptized and believe." Second, he makes "obsignation or sealing of this promise."[150] In these two actions, there is a double sealing: (1) inwardly by the Spirit, and (2) outwardly though the water and words of Matthew 28:19. Perkins, therefore, sees baptism as a means of conferring grace because it gives and exhibits "to the believing mind Christ with His benefits, and this it does by His signification. For it serves as a particular end and infallible certificate to assure the party baptized of the forgiveness of his sins and of his eternal salvation."[151]

---

145. Perkins, *Reformed Catholic*, 7:43.
146. Perkins, *Damned Art of Witchcraft*, 9:390.
147. Perkins, *Galatians*, 2:222.
148. Perkins, *Galatians*, 2:220.
149. Perkins, *Case of Conscience*, 8:284.
150. Perkins, *Commentary on Galatians*, 2:220.
151. Perkins, *Galatians*, 2:224–25. Perkins earlier says that "it is not the act of baptism to confer the first grace [regeneration] but only to confirm and seal it unto us [a second grace]. Adoption and life begins not in baptism, but before" (2:110). This carries major significance regarding infants being born in believing households. Perkins writes, "For the children of believers are born holy and Christian, and therefore dying in the want of baptism may for all that be saved. The seal of the covenant is not of like necessity with the covenant itself" (2:110). In the case of infant baptism (as well as adults), for Perkins, he distinguished between the covenant "made" and the covenant "accomplished." Perkins explains, "Men in their baptism enter covenant with God, but often start from it and will not stand to it, so as the covenant is only made. But when a man is effectually called, the covenant is not only made but truly accomplished, and that on man's part." Perkins, *Jude*, 4:30. Lastly, Perkins makes a distinction regarding the "kinds" of Christians when he writes, "There are three kinds of members: dead, decayed, and living. A dead member is that which is only in show a member, as a leg of wood or of brass in a man's body. A decayed member is a true member, though weak, as is a leg or arm that is taken with a palsy or sore wounded. But a lively member is that which does move and do all its functions perfectly." Perkins, *Revelation*, 4:434. See also Perkins, *Golden Chain*, 6:174.

Regarding the individual who is baptized, Perkins says that he "binds himself to give homage to the Father, Son, and Holy Ghost." This homage is believing all the promises of God in the covenant of grace and obeying all his commands.[152] "For as God (for His part) promises mercy in the covenant of grace, so we in baptism do make a vow and promise of obedience to Him in all His commands." Furthermore, God's promises to man and man's promises to God are then "renewed so often as we come to the Lord's Supper, and [it is] further continued in the daily spiritual exercise of invocation and repentance."[153]

## The Promises

Because the covenant is everlasting, it carries with it the promises of eternal reward. None of these promises are merited by man, but granted "by means of the covenant of grace." In the covenant, God promises his people "the pardon and remission of sin in and by Christ."[154] This is a sure promise because "the Lord contracts with His people" (1) to write his law in their hearts and (2) to become their God.[155] This relational aspect of the covenant is vitally important, in Perkins's estimation, because it means that it "is not for a day or an age or for a thousand years or ages, but is everlasting without end, so as God's people may say of God forever, 'God is our God.' And likewise, God will say of His church forevermore, 'This people is my people.'"[156]

When "God is our God," he (1) enters the church, (2) dwells among his people, (3) grants remission, (4) imparts salvation,[157] (5) gives assur-

---

152. Perkins, *Galatians*, 2:220.
153. Perkins, *Case of Conscience*, 8:284.
154. Perkins, *Jude*, 4:105.
155. Perkins, *Jude*, 4:105.
156. Perkins, *Exposition of the Creed*, 5:398.
157. Perkins, *Exposition of the Creed*, 5:97. Regarding the household, Perkins held that when a child is born into a Christian household, all of the posterity is made a "partaker" of the covenant of grace. Expounding on how this is the case, Perkins says, "The parent sustains a double person. First, he is to be considered as a child of Adam, and thus he brings forth a child having Adam's nature, Adam's corruption. Again, he is to be considered as a believer. And thus albeit he does not propagate his faith and holiness to the child; yet by means of his faith, his child is in the covenant and consequently is to be accounted holy in judgment of charity till God manifests the contrary." Perkins, *Galatians*, 2:110. Regarding children/infants, Perkins similarly says, "The children also sustain two persons. First, they are considered as children of the first Adam. And thus

ance of his favor, (6) bestows the comfortable presence of his Spirit, and (7) provides the presence and protection of his holy angels.[158] "Thus then," says Perkins, "the confession in which we acknowledge that we believe in Jesus Christ has a promise of fellowship with God and of life everlasting."[159]

The ultimate foundation to these sure promises is Christ. He is not only the substance of the covenant, but he is its Mediator; meaning he is both the bestower and the surety of these promises. By him we receive all the benefits of salvation, for in him "all the promises of God are yea and amen."[160] For Perkins, this is why Christ is called "the angel of the covenant" (Mal 3:1) and the "covenant of the people" (Isa 49:8) to be made with "all nations in the last age."[161] To be part of the covenant of grace is to be "made a partaker of Christ."[162] According to Perkins, as stipulated in the covenant of grace, (1) God promises to give Christ with all his merits and graces to all believers; (2) believers are united to Christ by the bond of the Spirit, whereby they are given to Christ and made one with him; and (3) by means of this union Christ communicates himself and all his benefits to believers.[163] This is done in two ways. The first is imputation, "which is an accounting and accepting of his obedience and sufferings as ours for the discharge of our sins and acquitting us from them." The second is propagation, "whereby grace is derived from his grace and infused into those that are set into Him."[164] Perkins illustrates,

> For as many candles receive light from one great torch or light, and as many streams flow from one foundation or headspring, and as from one root proceed many branches, even so all His members drink of His fountains, are enriched by His treasures of wisdom

---

they are conceived and born in sin and are children of wrath. Again, they are to be considered as children of believing parents. And thus by means of the covenant, they are children of God; and original sin which is in them is covered from their first beginning and not imputed to them." Perkins, *Galatians*, 2:110 (cf. n152).

158. Perkins, *Damned Art of Witchcraft*, 9:390.
159. Perkins, *Exposition of the Creed*, 5:97.
160. Perkins, *Exposition of the Creed*, 5:97.
161. Perkins, *Exposition of the Creed*, 5:97.
162. Perkins, *Damned Art of Witchcraft*, 9:391.
163. Perkins, *Jude*, 4:260.
164. Perkins, *Jude*, 4:260.

and knowledge, yea, indeed, and live by no other life than that which by His Spirit He inspires into the faces of their souls.[165]

In the covenant of grace, Christ is made of God to us wisdom, righteousness, sanctification, and redemption (1 Cor 1:30). Ultimately, he is made to us glorification—the resurrection of the body. "If God should leave His people in the grave under death forever," argues Perkins, "how could they be called the people of God. For He is the God of mercy and of life itself."[166] Believers possess the hope of the resurrection by "virtue of Christ's resurrection, whereof they are partakers by means of that blessed and indissoluble conjunction which they have in Christ."[167] By covenant, asserts Perkins, they "shall not remain [in the grave] so forever, but shall rise to glory at the last judgment."[168] Therefore, God's promised rewards in the covenant of grace are "not only the foundation of all our comfort in this life, but of our happiness after death itself, being the ground of those two main articles of our faith: the resurrection of the body and the immortality of the soul. For by virtue of this covenant alone shall we rise again after death to life, glory, and immortality."[169]

## Conclusion

The chapter set the foundation for Perkins's understanding of eschatological glory by considering his views on God's creation of man and God's covenant with man. For Perkins, these are the chief means by which man enters and enjoys the chief end for which he was created—eschatological glory. At the center of this eschatological glory, therefore, stands Jesus Christ—the One who has fulfilled the covenant of works on our behalf that we might (through union with him) enjoy the blessings of the covenant of grace.

---

165. Perkins, *Jude*, 4:260–61.
166. Perkins, *Exposition of the Creed*, 5:399.
167. Perkins, *Salve for a Sick Man*, 10:416.
168. Perkins, *Salve for a Sick Man*, 10:416.
169. Perkins, *Jude*, 4:106.

# God with Us: Historical Union with Christ

GIVEN THE CENTRALITY OF Christ in Perkins's covenant theology (Heb 8:6; 12:24), it is no surprise to discover that he views Christ's incarnation as "the foundation of all our comfort and all good things which we enjoy."[1] According to Perkins, "the whole Godhead indeed is incarnate, yet not as it is absolutely considered, but so far forth as it is restrained and limited to the person of the Son."[2] He adds, "To speak properly, the Godhead itself is not incarnate, but the very person of the Son, subsisting in the Godhead... [because] they really differ each from [the] other in regard of the peculiar manner of subsisting."[3] The only-begotten Son of God became man, meaning Jesus Christ possesses two distinct natures united in one person.[4]

## The Nature of the Incarnation

At the fall, human nature was corrupted by sin. Thus, all who come from Adam by natural generation receive a sinful (corrupt) human nature. Perkins explains that in the incarnation, God prevented the transmission of the sinful human nature by means of "the miraculous conception of the Holy

---

1. Perkins, *Galatians*, 2:251.
2. Perkins, *Exposition of the Creed*, 5:119.
3. Perkins, *Exposition of the Creed*, 5:119. Perkins illustrates his point by saying that just as "the soul of man is wholly in the head and wholly in the feet, yea, wholly in every part, and yet the soul cannot be said to use reason in the feet or in any other part, but only the head." Perkins, *Exposition of the Creed*, 5:119.
4. Perkins, *Jude*, 4:55–56.

Ghost, whereby He took the nature of man with the infirmities thereof, without the sin of man's nature or the guiltiness thereof... thus is Christ free from sin as He is man."[5] For Perkins, this means that "the manhood of Christ being but a creature [is] advanced to this dignity, that it should become a part of the Son of God."[6]

In his consideration of Christ's incarnation, Perkins focuses on three key actions, which are performed simultaneously. The first is the framing of Christ's manhood. He took to himself the whole and perfect nature of man in respect of "essence, namely the entire substance of a reasonable soul and human body."[7] The matter of Christ's body came from the virgin Mary, thereby making him the descendant of Adam, Abraham, and David, according to the flesh. He possessed "the powers of life, sense, motion, faculty of reason, will, and affection."[8] He knew thirst, hunger, weariness, sorrow, etc.[9] As for his soul, it was not derived from Mary, but came by "the very power of God and placed in the body, both of them [body and soul] from the first moment of their being having their subsistence in the person of the Son."[10]

The second action is the sanctifying of Christ's manhood. This entailed, first, the prevention of original sin and guilt. Perkins maintains that this was the case because Christ was not conceived by the normal manner of generation. Rather, the Holy Spirit overshadowed the virgin Mary whereby Christ assumed "the substance from the Virgin without the guilt and corruption of the substance."[11] This is what Perkins identifies as the "matter" and "manner" of the incarnation. The matter is the substance Mary, while the manner is the miraculous work the Holy Spirit. Second, the sanctifying of Christ's manhood involved "the infusion of all pureness and holiness into [it], so far forth as was meet for the nature of a Redeemer."[12] Christ's manhood "was filled with the gifts of the Holy Ghost above measure that He might in both natures be a perfect Savior."[13] This was essential, for "un-

---

5. Perkins, *Revelation*, 4:562.
6. Perkins, *Exposition of the Creed*, 5:124.
7. Perkins, *Galatians*, 2:248.
8. Perkins, *Galatians*, 2:248.
9. Perkins, *Golden Chain*, 6:49.
10. Perkins, *Exposition of the Creed*, 5:125.
11. Perkins, *Exposition of the Creed*, 5:126.
12. Perkins, *Exposition of the Creed*, 5:126.
13. Perkins, *Galatians*, 2:249.

less [Christ] had first been sanctified," declares Perkins, "[He] could not have been a fit Savior for us."[14]

The third action is the uniting of the Godhead and manhood in one person. The second person of the Trinity, the Son of God, "did unite unto Himself the human nature—that is, body and soul of man—so as the Godhead of the Son and the manhood, concurring together, made but one person."[15] In this union, the Son of God "makes the flesh or nature of man a part of Himself and communicates unto it His own subsistence,"[16] whereby the human nature, "having no proper subsistence, is as it were engrafted into the person of the Son and is wholly supported and sustained by it so as it should not be at all, if it were not sustained in that manner."[17] Perkins elaborates, "The manhood of the Son has no personality or personal subsistence, but is received into the unity of the second person and is sustained of it."[18] Again, "the Godhead of the Son is present and dwells with and in the manhood, giving unto it in some part His own subsistence. Whereby it comes to pass that this manhood assumed is proper to the Son."[19] It is Christ's soul that serves as the "mean or bond" that unites his Godhead and body together.[20] As for this union, Perkins makes the following observations. (1) The Godhead receives nothing from the manhood, yet the manhood is "perfected and enriched with unspeakable dignity."[21] (2) Together with the Godhead of the Son, the manhood is "adored and worshiped with divine honor, as in like case the honor done to the king himself redounds to the crown on his head."[22] (3) The Godhead of Christ "works all things in

---

14. Perkins, *Exposition of the Creed*, 5:127.
15. Perkins, *Exposition of the Creed*, 5:128.
16. Perkins, *Galatians*, 2:250.
17. Perkins, *Exposition of the Creed*, 5:128. See Perkins, *True Gain*, 9:49.
18. Perkins, *Galatians*, 2:250.
19. Perkins, *Exposition of the Creed*, 5:128. Perkins is sure to make clear that in this union (1) neither are the two natures turned into one another, (2) nor are they confused and mingled together, but (3) are now and remain without composition, conversion, or confusion really distinct in essence, properties, and operations. Perkins, *Exposition of the Creed*, 5:129.
20. Perkins, *Exposition of the Creed*, 5:228. Perkins continues to explain that in Christ's death, it was his Godhead that served as a "mean or middle bond" to unite his body and soul. Thus, sustaining and keeping the Hypostatic Union resolved, for both body and soul were never "severed from the Godhead of the Son" (5:228).
21. Perkins, *Exposition of the Creed*, 5:129.
22. Perkins, *Exposition of the Creed*, 5:129.

the matter of our redemption in and by the manhood."[23] By virtue of the Godhead, the manhood of Christ becomes "quickening flesh and the bread of life"[24] by way of the communication of personal subsistence.[25]

## The Purpose of the Incarnation

Turning to the purpose of the incarnation, Perkins begins by explaining why it was the Son who became man, and not the Father or the Spirit. He gives three main reasons. (1) The Father created man by the Son, therefore, man (now fallen) must be redeemed and recreated by the Son. (2) The Son is the "essential image" of the Father; therefore, he must assume man's nature to restore the image of God in man. (3) It is necessary that he who is the Son of God by nature should become a son of man so that we who are the sons of man "should be made the sons of God."[26] Each of these reasons is eschatological. In other words, the chief reason the Son became flesh was to ensure eschatological realities for his people; namely, their final redemption, their complete and perfect renewal in the image of God, and their attainment of sonship.[27]

As for the incarnation, it begins in humiliation. Christ made himself of "no small reputation in respect of His deity" by taking the form of a servant in the likeness of sinful flesh (Rom 8:3; Phil 2:7–8). Furthermore, he became "execrable, which is, by the law accursed for us."[28] Christ veiled his power and majesty, lived in a fallen world, and bore the curse of the law

---

23. Perkins, *Exposition of the Creed*, 5:129.

24. Perkins, *Exposition of the Creed*, 5:130.

25. Perkins, *Galatians*, 2:250. For a fuller understanding and development of the *communicatio idiomatum*, or the communication of properties within early Reformed thought, see Mosser, "Gospel's End and Our Highest Good," 83–108.

26. Perkins, *Exposition of the Creed*, 5:118.

27. This incorporates all the elect including Old Testament saints. Perkins shows how this can be before Christ became incarnate. He says, "The body and blood of Christ, though then it was not subsisting in the world, yet was it then present to all believers [in] two ways. First, by divine acceptation, because God did accept the incarnation and passion of Christ to come, as if it had been accomplished. Secondly, it was present to them by means of their faith, which is a subsistence of things that are not seen, and consequently it makes them present to the believing heart." Perkins, *Galatians*, 2:31.

28. Perkins, *Golden Chain*, 6:58.

upon the cross, thereby satisfying divine justice.[29] The result is eternal life and holiness for God's elect.[30]

As J. Stephen Yuille notes, Perkins "was convinced that Christ's chief purpose in the incarnation was to fulfill His role as Mediator on behalf of His people."[31] God's "majesty was infinitely offended," by man's sin. Consequently, man is under the wrath of God, the tyranny of the devil, and the power of death.[32] In other words, he stands in need of a Savior. Commenting on Perkins's understanding of Christ's mediation, Joel Beeke and Greg Salazar remark,

> Predestination does not affect anyone apart from the work of Jesus Christ. Without Christ, man is totally hopeless. Christ is the foundation of election, as the center of Perkins's chart [*A Golden Chain*] shows. He is predestined to be Mediator. He is promised to the elect. He is offered by grace to the elect. And, finally, He is personally applied to their souls in all His benefits, natures, offices, and state.[33]

For there to be reconciliation between God and man, there "must be such a one as may make request or speak both to God and man."[34] For a mediator serves as a middle person, "making intercession between two other persons—the one offended, the other offending."[35] Christ is the only person who can speak to the Father on behalf of his people, bringing their prayers to the Father. God speaks to us by Christ alone, and we speak to God by Christ alone.[36] Perkins understands Christ's role of Mediator in terms of his threefold office of Priest, Prophet, and King.[37]

---

29. Perkins, *Exposition of the Creed*, 5:121.
30. Perkins, *Golden Chain*, 6:48.
31. Yuille, preface to *The Works of William Perkins*, 1:xxxv.
32. Perkins, *Golden Chain*, 6:48.
33. Beeke and Salazar, preface to *The Works of William Perkins*, 6:xxxiii-xxxiv.
34. Perkins, *Exposition of the Creed*, 5:121.
35. Perkins, *Exposition of the Creed*, 5:121.
36. Perkins, *Exposition of the Creed*, 5:121.
37. "*Munus triplex*"—threefold office. Richard Muller points out that this Christological term that refers to the threefold work/office of Christ was developed and taught by Calvin and "became standard" among Reformed theologians in the sixteenth century. Muller, *Dictionary of Latin and Greek*, 225. See also Muller, *Christ and the Decree*, 31–33.

## Priest

Regarding the first, Christ "performed all those things to God whereby is obtained eternal life."[38] This consists chiefly in his works of satisfaction and intercession. Perkins defines satisfaction as "that whereby Christ is a full propitiation of His Father for the elect."[39] The first part of Christ's satisfaction is his passion, consisted of the following. (1) His agony, whereby he endured "a vehement anguish" arising from his desire to obey the Father and yet avoid death. (2) His sacrifice, whereby he offered himself to "God the Father as a ransom for the sins of the elect."[40] (3) The Father's acceptance of his sacrifice. (4) The imputation of man's sin to Christ, "whereby His Father accounted Him as a transgressor, having translated the burden of man's sins to His shoulders."[41] (5) Christ's humiliation, which is the entirety of his earthly life, culminating in his becoming a curse for his people.[42] In his passion, Christ was "captivated of death" that he might abolish its sting (sin in the human heart),[43] overcome the first and second death, and satisfy God's justice.[44] Having ratified his last will and testament, he has changed the nature of death "from a curse into a blessing," whereby it has become "a middle way and entrance to convey men out of this world into the kingdom of glory in heaven."[45] Perkins declares that we must "by faith apprehend it [Christ's passion] as it is a satisfaction or a means of reconciliation for our offences," for in this is "all our joy and rejoicing."[46]

The second work of Christ's priestly office is his intercession. Perkins describes Christ as "an advocate and entreater of God the Father for all the faithful."[47] Christ intercedes according to both of his natures. In his humanity

---

38. Perkins, *Golden Chain*, 6:55.
39. Perkins, *Golden Chain*, 6:56. See Perkins, *Exposition of the Creed*, 5:138–39, 176–97.
40. Perkins, *Golden Chain*, 6:57.
41. Perkins, *Golden Chain*, 6:58.
42. Perkins, *Golden Chain*, 6:57–58. For Perkins, this curse included an inward accursedness in the sense of God's fearful anger upon the cross, and an outward accursedness in Christ's death on a cross, his burial to ratify the certainty of his death, and descending into hell, i.e., "the time of His abode in the grave" when he was under the "ignominious dominion of death." Perkins, *Golden Chain*, 6:59.
43. Perkins, *Exposition of the Creed*, 5:198.
44. Perkins, *Golden Chain*, 6:59.
45. Perkins, *Exposition of the Creed*, 5:197.
46. Perkins, *Exposition of the Creed*, 5:139.
47. Perkins, *Golden Chain*, 6:59.

beginning of the new spiritual world.... And as in the first day of the first world light was commanded to shine out of darkness upon the deeps, so in the first day of this new world the Sun of Righteousness rises and gives light to them that sit in darkness and dispels the darkness that was under the Old Testament."[58] Christ's resurrection, therefore, marked the beginning of the "world to come"; namely, "a new heaven and a new earth" in which the people of God, "zealous of good works," keep "an eternal Sabbath unto God."[59]

As for the nature of Christ's resurrection, Perkins believes that Christ raised himself (his manhood) from the dead by virtue of his Godhead. This was the beginning of Christ's exaltation, which Perkins defines as "that glorious or happy estate into which Christ entered after He had wrought the work of our redemption upon the cross. And He was exalted according to both natures, in regard of His Godhead and also of His manhood."[60] By the power of his Godhead, Christ reunited his body and soul, thereby quickening his manhood.[61] He did so for all who are united to him. As Christ stood as a public person, representing all the elect, in his obedience, suffering, and death, so too Christ arose from the dead "not as a private man" but a public man for "all men that are to come to life eternal."[62] When Christ rose from the dead, "all of the elect rose with Him and in Him."[63] Thus, Christ's resurrection becomes the elect's resurrection, as the apostle writes, "For if we have been planted together in the likeness of his death, we shall be also in the likeness of his resurrection" (Rom 6:5).

Perkins recognized the essential nature of Christ's resurrection for the salvation of his people (1 Cor 15:13–17). First, it demonstrates that his people have conquered death. When Christ was raised from the dead, he conquered death. As a result, the believer's conscience is fully persuaded that Christ has made full and perfect satisfaction for his people. Second, it confirms that his people inherit eternal life. As God, Christ is the Author

---

Breward, *Work of William Perkins*, 79. For a helpful overview of English Sabbatarianism, see Lee, "Origins of English Puritan Sabbatarianism," 103–19; Sprunger, "English and Dutch Sabbatarianism," 24–38.

58. Perkins, *Exposition of the Creed*, 5:241–42.
59. Perkins, *True Gain*, 9:69.
60. Perkins, *Exposition of the Creed*, 5:236.
61. Perkins, *Revelation*, 4:337; Perkins, *Exposition of the Creed*, 5:238.
62. Perkins, *Exposition of the Creed*, 5:238.
63. Perkins, *True Gain*, 9:67.

of life. It was, therefore, "neither meet nor possible for Him to be beholden of death, but he must needs rise from death to life."[64] Third, it declares that Christ has made atonement for the sins of his people. As high priest, he offered himself to make satisfaction for sin. He was raised to "perform the second part" of his priesthood, that is, to apply the virtue of his crucifixion resurrection to his people and make intercession for them.[65] Fourth, it declares that Christ has defeated his people's enemies. By his resurrection, he made a "full victory and conquest" over death, the world, and the devil.[66] Fifth, it confirms that Christ has secured his people's future resurrection. He conveys life to all his members in their resurrection from death to life. Perkins states, "Christ's resurrection did make acceptable unto God the resurrection of all His members."[67]

When Christ rose from the dead, there was a significant change. Christ lives a "heavenly and spiritual life," unbeholden to the infirmities and dependencies of the natural world.[68] He is no longer hungry, thirsty, or weary. He no longer possesses a body that is subject to change and weakness. Having been raised by virtue of his Godhead, his manhood is now clothed with glory and power. He was raised imperishable and immortal (1 Cor 15:42–54). According to Perkins, Christ "put off" all servile conditions and infirmities, and "put on" such gifts that "have so great and so marvelous perfection as possibly can befall any creature."[69] When he was raised from the dead, he "began by degrees to make manifest the power of His Godhead in His manhood."[70] Perkins notes that Christ's body and soul "were beautified and adorned with all qualities of glory. . . . [His mind] was enriched with as much knowledge and understanding as can possible befall any creature and more in measure than all men and angels have."[71] Moreover, his body was "endued with agility to move as well upward and downward, as may appear by the ascension of His body into heaven."[72] Perkins affirms

---

64. Perkins, *Exposition of the Creed*, 5:238.
65. Perkins, *Exposition of the Creed*, 5:238.
66. Perkins, *True Gain*, 9:67.
67. Perkins, *Revelation*, 4:337.
68. Perkins, *True Gain*, 9:67.
69. Perkins, *Golden Chain*, 6:61.
70. Perkins, *Exposition of the Creed*, 5:236.
71. Perkins, *Exposition of the Creed*, 5:237.
72. Perkins, *Exposition of the Creed*, 5:237.

that Christ did not assume this exalted life for himself alone, but that he might communicate it to all who believe in him.[73]

Christ's glorified body now shines in resemblance to what was seen at His transfiguration (Matt 17:1–13; Mark 9:1–13; Luke 9:28–36). Commenting on this, John Calvin declares that Christ

> in the brightness of an unusual form of His Godhead might become visible . . . [and] gave them a taste of his boundless glory, such as they were able to comprehend . . . for this was not a complete exhibition of the heavenly glory of Christ, but, under symbols which were adapted to the capacity of the flesh, he enabled them to taste in part what could not be fully comprehended.[74]

Similarly, for Perkins, the transfiguration was but "a shadow of the eternal glory"[75] which Christ would come to possess. It was a foretaste of beatific delight. First, it pointed to the immediate and eternal fellowship that exists between the triune God and his people. Perkins quotes Augustine as follows:

> There shall be exceeding peace in us, and among us, and with God Himself. Because we shall see Him, and enjoy Him always and everywhere. Therefore, blessed shall that life be for the thing which we shall enjoy, for we shall enjoy God Himself, all other means ceasing. For the measure of enjoying Him, for we shall fully enjoy Him. For the time, for we shall eternally enjoy Him. For the certainty, whereby we shall know that it shall be so. For the place, for we shall enjoy Him in heaven. Lastly, for the companions joined with us, for they shall be the elect.[76]

Second, the transfiguration pointed to the eternal joy that awaits believers in glory. Third, it pointed to the transformation of the believer into the likeness of Christ's glorified body.[77] Fourth, it pointed to man's dominion over

---

73. Perkins, *True Gain*, 9:68–69.

74. Calvin, *Harmony of the Evangelists*, 310.

75. Perkins, *True Gain*, 9:76.

76. Perkins, *True Gain*, 9:76. Perkins cites Augustine's "Sermon de. Temp. 148" in his margin. I have been unsuccessful in locating this exact quote in Augustine's works.

77. Perkins writes, "For then our bodies shall be spiritual, that is, immediately and eternally preserved by the operation of the Spirit of God, *as now the body of Christ is in heaven.*" Perkins, *True Gain*, 9:75, emphasis added. This spiritual body comes from the "spiritual life" that flows from union with Christ. Perkins defines spiritual life as "that most happy and blessed estate in which all the elect shall reign with Christ, their Head, in the heavens after this life and after the day of judgment forever and ever." Perkins, *Exposition of the Creed*, 5:407.

all creation in Christ. Referring to the eternal estate of the elect, Perkins writes, "They that be wise, shall shine as the brightness of the firmament, and they that turn many to righteousness, shall shine as the stars for evermore [Dan 12:3]."[78]

## Christ's Ascension

Following his resurrection from the dead, Christ says to Mary, "Touch me not; for I am not yet ascended to my Father: but go to my brethren, and say unto them, I ascend unto my Father, and your Father; and to my God, and your God" (John 20:17). When Christ ascended into heaven before the eyes of his disciples, he sat down at the right hand of his Father, crowned with all glory and splendor. Perkins describes Christ's ascension as his "passage ... to glory."[79] Christ's body was lifted up "really," "actually," and "visibly" by "the mighty power of His Godhead" and by "the supernatural property of a glorified body" into heaven.[80]

After his ascension, Christ sat down at the right hand of God the Father. Perkins clarifies that God, being spirit, does not have a body. The language of "right hand," is borrowed "from earthly kings and potentates, whose manner and custom has been to place such persons at their right hands whom they purpose to advance to any special office or dignity."[81] At his ascension, therefore, Christ (as God-man) was advanced to a position of authority, honor, dignity, and glory. In addition, it marked his "full and

---

78. Perkins, *Exposition of the Creed*, 5:412. The theme of transformation seen in the Transfiguration can be traced beyond Perkins to other Puritans, such as Thomas Manton. For example, Manton writes that Christ was transfigured to show what we shall be; for Christ is the pattern: (1) Christ will communicate his glory and "adorn and beautify our earthly and obscure bodies." Manton, *Transfiguration of Christ*, 1:356. (2) Christ reveals that glorification is the "instance and pattern to us. For if the head be glorious, so will the members also" (1:357). And, (3) Christ's transfiguration displays that in glory "the substance and natural properties" of the body are not taken away," but "freeth us from natural infirmities.... Christ hath showed in his own body what he can or will perform in ours—these same bodies, but otherwise adorned" (1:357). Manton then declares, "Be transformed that you may be transfigured.... The change must begin in the soul, and then it is conveyed to the body. The lustre of grace maketh way for the splendour of glory" (1:357).

79. Perkins, *Exposition of the Creed*, 5:258.

80. Perkins, *Exposition of the Creed*, 5:260.

81. Perkins, *Exposition of the Creed*, 5:270.

manifest exaltation into the authority and government of His kingdom, which spreads itself over heaven and earth."[82]

Prior to his ascension, he "lifted up his hands, and blessed" his disciples (Luke 24:50). In this act, says Perkins, Christ "did not only pronounce or foretell a blessing that should come to His disciples, but did confer and give the same unto them."[83] The apostle Paul declares that believers possess every spiritual blessing in the heavenly places in Christ (Eph 1:3). All that they receive comes by means of their union with Christ. This is true of the ascension. As Perkins makes clear, Christ's ascension was not "personal or private." Rather, "Christ ascended in the room and stead of all the elect, and they ascended together in and with Him, and now after a sort are together in and with Him in glory."[84]

Seated at the right hand of the Father, Christ now fulfills his mediatorial office as King. His regal office is "that whereby He distributes His gifts and disposes all things for the benefit of the elect."[85] After his humiliation, Christ "was by little and little exalted to glory, and that in sundry respects according to both His natures."[86] Perkins's understanding of Christ's mediatorial office as King focuses on his anointing, majesty, and dominion.

## Anointing

As priests, prophets, and kings were anointed with oil in the Old Testament, the incarnate Christ was "the anointed Savior and Redeemer" and, therefore, the ultimate King, Priest, and Prophet.[87] Perkins acknowledges that the Old Testament anointing with oil served as a type. Christ was not anointed "with bodily oil" but "by the Spirit."[88] This occurred at his baptism.[89] While Christ possessed the Holy Spirit before this event, he received

---

82. Perkins, *Exposition of the Creed*, 5:271.

83. Perkins, *Exposition of the Creed*, 5:259.

84. Perkins, *True Gain*, 9:50.

85. Perkins, *Golden Chain*, 6:61.

86. Perkins, *Golden Chain*, 6:61. The phrase "by little and little exalted to glory" is spoken of pertaining to Christ's resurrection, ascension into heaven, and sitting at the right hand of God the Father, which has already above been discussed.

87. Perkins, *Exposition of the Creed*, 5:103. See Perkins, *Jude*, 4:56; Perkins, *Sermon on the Mount*, 1:615.

88. Perkins, *Exposition of the Creed*, 5:103.

89. Just as David was *anointed* as king first (1 Sam 16), and then *appointed* as king later (2 Sam 5), Perkins would take the same view with Christ who was anointed as King

at his baptism "a greater measure of the Spirit than He had before."[90] Perkins elaborates, "And at His baptism, being inaugurated into His mediatorship, He received such fullness of the Spirit as was behoveful for so high an office, which because it was far greater than before He needed."[91]

For Perkins, this anointing was a significant event because it demonstrated that (1) Christ is publicly and solemnly "invested into the office of His mediatorship," (2) Christ is the "knot and bond of both covenants," having been both circumcised and baptized, and (3) Christ is "sufficiently furnished with both gifts and authority."[92] God's people "reap great benefit and comfort" from Christ's anointing because they too are "to be partakers thereof."[93] First, they are set apart as spiritual kings, priests, and prophets. Second, they receive the "same oil," that is, the same Spirit of God. Perkins celebrates, "the unspeakable goodness of God that has advanced us to the dignity of kings, priests, prophets before Him and has given His unto us to enable us to be so indeed."[94]

## *Majesty*

The prophet Isaiah describes Christ in his humiliation as one who "hath no form nor comeliness; and when we shall see him, there is no beauty that we should desire him. He is despised and rejected of men" (Isa 53:2–3). By means of his exaltation, Christ now possesses "glory and majesty, dominion and power, both now and forever. Amen" (Jude 25). Perkins defines this majesty as "that highness and greatness of God and Christ whereby He is in Himself, in His works, and every way wonderful."[95] Christ is now exalted above all earthly and creaturely kingdoms, thrones, dominions, and

---

at his baptism, and then appointed as King later upon his resurrection and ascension. See Perkins, *Cloud of Faithful Witnesses*, 3:89.

90. Perkins, *Sermon on the Mount*, 1:94.

91. Perkins, *Sermon on the Mount*, 1:94.

92. Perkins, *Golden Chain*, 6:54. Perkins writes elsewhere that "Christ's anointing is according to both His natures; for in what nature He is a mediator, in the same He is anointed. But according to both His natures jointly He is a mediator. The Godhead is no mediator without the manhood, nor the manhood without the Godhead. And therefore His anointing extends itself both to His Godhead and to His manhood." Perkins, *Exposition of the Creed*, 5:103.

93. Perkins, *Exposition of the Creed*, 5:104.

94. Perkins, *Exposition of the Creed*, 5:105.

95. Perkins, *Jude*, 4:263.

powers. He reigns over His kingdom with all power and authority, "directing the hearts and consciences of men."[96] First, he does so by making laws, ordaining ministers as his instruments, and giving grace to quicken his people. He governs them by his holy scepter of Word and Spirit.[97] Second, he does so by destroying the kingdom of darkness, which Perkins defines as "the whole company of Christ's enemies."[98] Unlike earthly kings who can only destroy the body, Christ destroys both body and soul.[99] In sum, Christ displays his majesty in governing all, friend and foe. Because he is "a prince of the greatest monarchs of the world and is far above them, we must then with all fear and trembling reverence His high majesty.... We cannot conceive what honor we owe unto Him, which is advanced in the throne of all majesty."[100]

## Dominion

Christ's sovereign rule extends to all things. He has received all authority in heaven and on earth (Matt 28:18). Perkins declares that Christ has "absolute power to command and forbid, to condemn and absolve, and therefore has the keys of heaven and hell to open and shut."[101] In Psalm 2, the nations and their rulers are commanded to "kiss the Son" (v. 12). This homage is due to Christ because God has set him upon his holy hill to reign over all. Because this psalm was fulfilled in Christ, Perkins announces that (1) "all princes must do Him service, for they are all inferior and subject to Him," (2) "all earthly princes are bound to plant and establish in their kingdoms the religion of Christ," and (3) "Christ alone is Prince of the kings of the earth" and, therefore, all governing authorities are subject to him at all times and in all places.[102] In addition, Perkins teaches that,

---

96. Perkins, *Revelation*, 4:338.

97. Perkins, *Exposition of the Creed*, 5:372; Perkins, *Golden Chain*, 6:63.

98. Perkins, *Golden Chain*, 6:63. Perkins identifies Christ's enemies as the devil, Satan's angels, unbelievers (atheists, magicians, idolaters, Turks, Jews, heretics, apostates, false christs), and that antichrist (the pope of Rome). These are all members of the kingdom of darkness (6:63).

99. Perkins, *Jude*, 4:56.

100. Perkins, *Revelation*, 4:338.

101. Perkins, *Exposition of the Creed*, 5:279. Elsewhere Perkins writes that Christ has the sovereign power to prescribe, judge, save, and destroy. Perkins, *Revelation*, 4:566.

102. Perkins, *Revelation*, 4:339.

as King, Christ conveys to his people the means of salvation.[103] This is accomplished by (1) gathering them unto himself, (2) guiding them in the way of everlasting life, (3) disciplining them unto obedience, (4) defending his church, and (5) confounding His enemies.[104] After Christ has gathered his elect, subdued his enemies, and judged the living and dead two things will occur:

> (1) the surrendering over of His kingdom to God the Father, as concerning the manner of regiment and spiritual policy, consisting in word and Spirit together; (2) the subjection of Christ only in regard of His humanity. The which then is when the Son of God shall most fully manifest His majesty, which before was obscured by the flesh as a veil, so that the same flesh remaining both glorious and united to the Son of God may by infinite degrees appear inferior. We may not therefore imagine that the subjection of Christ consists in diminishing the glory of the humanity, but in manifesting most fully the majesty of the Word.[105]

## Conclusion

For Perkins, the incarnation is the means whereby "we have access to God."[106] This "access" begins with union with Christ. By virtue of the incarnation (Christ's humiliation and exaltation), all believers are united to Christ, and therefore united to the very Son of God. This is the result of the "communication of grace,"[107] by which believers are authentically united to Christ.

> God becomes a man that we men might be partakers of the divine nature. Christ is made bone of our bone and flesh of our flesh by His incarnation that we might be made bone of His bone and flesh of His flesh by regeneration. The Son of God was made the Son of man that we which are the sons of men might be made the sons of God. . . . The Godhead is the fountain of all good things, and the flesh or manhood [of Christ] is a pipe or conduit to convey

---

103. Perkins, *Foundation of Christian Religion*, 5:499.

104. Perkins, *Exposition of the Creed*, 5:279–84.

105. Perkins, *Golden Chain*, 6:64. Perkins states, "For though the efficacy of His offices are everlasting, yet the execution of them shall then cease." Perkins, *Estate of Damnation or in the Estate of Grace*, 8:505.

106. Perkins, *Galatians*, 2:251.

107. Perkins, *Galatians*, 2:250.

the same unto us. If we would then receive true comfort, we must hunger and thirst in our hearts after Christ, and by our faith eat His flesh and drink His blood.[108]

---

108. Perkins, *Galatians*, 2:250–51.

# 5

# God in Us: The Mystical Union with Christ

HAVING LAID THE GROUNDWORK for William Perkins's development of eschatological glory within its covenantal and incarnational context, this chapter turns attention to the believer's mystical union with Christ.[1] J. V. Fesko writes that while Perkins "is known for his *Golden Chain*, he is also a theologian of union with Christ."[2] Victor Priebe supports this claim, noting, "Mystical union occurs under the broader heading of the covenant and soteriology. Thus, mystical union is a relationship not between some Supreme being or Creator and created beings, but between the Redeemer and man as sinner."[3] In this mystical union, the crown of immortal glory comes into greater focus.

For Perkins, eschatological glory does not come to the elect apart from Christ (in his manhood) entering glory. He writes,

> And though the manhood of Christ be not Lord of angels, yet being received into the unity of His Godhead, it is thereby exalted above all angels by many degrees. Wherein we may behold the endless goodness of God, in advancing our nature . . . far above the angels in degree, by reason of this conjunction which it has with the nature of God in the person of Christ.[4]

---

1. Mark Shaw points out this next logical step toward eschatological glory when he writes, "Entrance into the covenant of grace was equivalent to mystical union between the believer and Christ which occurs when God offers the gift of grace to us and we receive it by faith." Shaw, "Drama in the Meeting House," 48.
2. Fesko, "William Perkins on Union with Christ and Justification," 24.
3. Priebe, "Covenant Theology of William Perkins," 106.
4. Perkins, *Combat between Christ and the Devil Displayed*, 1:162. Perkins prefaces

According to Perkins, Christ (by his exaltation) advances human nature far above angelic nature, and we are the beneficiaries of this advancement. This relationship rests on three realities. (1) At the incarnation, Christ's manhood (body and soul) was united to the second person of the Trinity. (2) Because of his Godhead, Christ's manhood possesses all fullness of grace and all the gifts of the Holy Spirit in the highest degree of perfection. (3) Christ's manhood receives this excellency of gifts and graces "that it may be (as it were) a pipe or conduit to convey the same graces to all the elect."[5] In short, therefore, the advancement of Christ's exalted humanity is conveyed to all who are one with him. "Our salvation and life," exclaims Perkins, "depends on the fullness of the Godhead which is in Christ."[6]

The purpose of this chapter is to consider Perkins's understanding of this union in greater detail, focusing on its (1) necessity, (2) nature, (3) means, (4) order, (5) fruit, and (6) benefits.

## Its Necessity

Union with Christ is essential for spiritual life.[7] Perkins demonstrates that apart from "the root of life," man cannot possess spiritual life. As the root, Christ has life in himself "that He may convey it to all that believe in Him."[8] Therefore, Perkins says, "He is our root, in whom are hid the treasures of graces (Col 2:3) and of whose fullness we all receive grace for grace (John 1:16)."[9]

Thomas Tuke aids in explaining the need for union with Christ by way of a biblical metaphor. As members of a physical body have neither "sense nor motion" unless they are united to the head of the body, so too believers have no "spiritual life or motion" unless they are united to Christ. When we are "united and knit to Him, we receive sense and sap, life and motion."[10] Simply put, therefore, there is no life outside of Christ.

---

this statement by saying Christ, "the man-God, is Lord of all angels, and they do Him homage and service" (1:162).

5. Perkins, *True Gain*, 9:46.

6. Perkins, *True Gain*, 9:46.

7. For Perkins, spiritual life "is the beginning of eternal life," and stands in four things: (1) reconciliation with God, (2) peace of conscience, (3) joy of the Holy Spirit, and (4) newness of life. Perkins, *How to Live*, 10:10–15.

8. Perkins, *Galatians*, 2:135.

9. Perkins, *Jude*, 4:185.

10. Tuke, "Dedication Epistle," 6:285.

To benefit from the root, we must be grafted into it. "There must be a union with Christ before we can receive life from Him, and He live in us."[11] Trees of righteousness do not grow by nature but must be planted. Men are but "wild olives" who need to be transplanted from the first Adam into the second Adam. "We must be engrafted with [Christ]," says Perkins, "before we can be conformable to His death and resurrection."[12] The way in which God executes this engrafting is by (1) giving Christ in and by the Word and sacraments, and (2) giving "power to the believer to apprehend [Christ] and receive Him with His merits unto salvation, and that by the only hand of faith."[13] By the bond of the Holy Spirit and the virtue of the covenant of grace, a real and substantial union is made between believers and Christ, whereby he "communicates Himself unto us."[14]

This union not only concerns believers and Christ, but by extension believers and the church (the body of Christ). Perkins defines the church as "a peculiar company of men predestinated to life everlasting and made one in Christ."[15] He sees that the cause of the church is God's predestination to life everlasting a particular company of men, that is, the elect chosen in Christ before the foundation of the world. As the first and principal cause, God (out of the good pleasure of his will) "purposed to advance His elect to eternal life . . . [and be] made one with Christ." "They must be mystical members of Christ," declares Perkins, "and visible members of His church. And out of Christ and His church, [there is] no possibility of salvation."[16] This union between the elect and Christ means that there is "one mystical body." Christ is the head, and every believer is a member of the one body.[17] Perkins declares, "So if man be out of Christ and out of His church, no gold nor silver, no honor nor glory, no wit nor policy, no estimation nor authority, no friends nor favor, no wisdom nor learning, no hills of happiness, nor mountains of gold can save his soul. But he must perish in the flood of God's eternal wrath."[18]

---

11. Perkins, *Galatians*, 2:135–36.
12. Perkins, *Galatians*, 2:136.
13. Perkins, *Jude*, 4:185.
14. Perkins, *Galatians*, 2:136.
15. Perkins, *Exposition of the Creed*, 5:324.
16. Perkins, *Cloud of Faithful Witnesses*, 3:101.
17. Perkins, *Cloud of Faithful Witnesses*, 3:115.
18. Perkins, *Cloud of Faithful Witnesses*, 3:102.

## Its Nature

In its most basic form, Perkins defines *union with Christ* as "a work of God whereby all believers are made one with Christ."[19] This is not to be understood metaphorically, for it is not a union "in conceit or imagination," but is "a real conjunction."[20] This means that "every believer is spiritually and yet truly and really conjoined to Christ."[21] First, they are not one "by consent of heart and affection," as if they merely agree in sentiment and affection toward one another. In that sense, "all familiars and friends are one."[22] Second, they "are not one in substance." The substance of the Godhead is incommunicable, and the body of Christ is in heaven and, therefore "it cannot be mixed or compounded with our substance."[23] Just as the two natures of Christ are not mixed or compounded, Christ and believers are not compounded. Third, they are not one "by transfusion of the properties and qualities of the Godhead or manhood unto us."[24]

For Perkins, the starting point for understanding the nature of this union is regeneration. Turning to John 3:5,[25] he affirms that when the "natural man" is born again, he is made new, not in regard of his body or soul, but in regard of "God's image restored and renewed by Christ."[26] In this restoration a "new quality of righteousness and holiness" is implanted. By the work of the Holy Spirit, there is an "infusing" of new graces into the heart. The root, from which this change arises, is Christ who was crucified, buried,

---

19. Perkins, *Galatians*, 2:234.
20. Perkins, *Galatians*, 2:234.
21. Perkins, *Cloud of Faithful Witnesses*, 3:114–15.
22. Perkins, *Galatians*, 2:234.
23. Perkins, *Galatians*, 2:234. Thomas Tuke clarifies, "The Lord has united all His elect and dear children to Christ by His Spirit and by a true and lively faith. And by reason of this union, they are after asort united to the whole Trinity: Father, Son, and Holy Ghost. Yea, hence it is that we are partakers of Christ's benefits." Tuke, "Dedication Epistle," 6:285.
24. Perkins, *Galatians*, 2:234. The key word in this negative assertion is "transfusion." Perkins makes a distinction between "transfusion" and the synonymous terms of "communication," "infusion," and "diffusion." The language is specific to deny and guard against the claim that one somehow loses their individual personhood and becomes a part of Christ's Person, or is absorbed into the Godhead. Perkins speaks in similar language when dealing with the two natures of Christ in the Incarnation.
25. "Jesus answered, 'Verily, verily, I say unto thee, Except a man be born of water and of the Spirit, he cannot enter into the kingdom of God.'"
26. Perkins, *Jude*, 4:64–65.

raised, and exalted. Believers are members of his body, "of His flesh and of His bones."[27] Perkins sees a parallel in God's creation of Eve. Just as "Eve was made of the side of Adam, so is every believer of the body of Christ."[28] Just as every sinful man "springs from the first Adam, so does every man, so far as he is renewed, spring from the second Adam."[29] From this renewal, man is taken out of the "wild olive," Adam, and engrafted into "new stock," Christ. The believer receives from Christ "holiness" regarding his soul, and "incorruption" regarding his body, seeing that "the whole man is united unto Christ, and so both soul and body receive immortality and glory."[30]

In this union, the believer is united to the whole Christ, God and man. Since no man can "receive saving virtue from Christ unless first of all he receives Christ Himself," he must receive all of Christ. This "donation of Christ," explains Perkins, is an "action or work of God the Father by the Holy Spirit whereby Christ as Redeemer in the appointed time is really communicated to all ordained to salvation."[31] Consequently, believers can say that "Christ Himself with all His benefits is theirs, both in respect of right thereto and in respect of all fruits redounding thence."[32] The whole Christ, and all that belongs to him, is shared with every believer whereby it becomes theirs. Perkins states, "For by reason of this mystical union between Him and us, all blessings of salvation in Him . . . are diffused into us as His members or branches, and yet are as properly still in Him."[33]

## Its Means

R. Tudor Jones observes that the doctrine of union with Christ was "woven into the fabric of Protestant thinking," and that "faith, union with Christ, and regeneration are contemporaneous. And all this is the work of the Holy Spirit."[34] Perkins says that one must look to the means whereby God gives his Spirit to his people, chiefly the Word and sacraments.[35] This is the happy

- 27. Perkins, *Jude*, 4:65.
- 28. Perkins, *Jude*, 4:65.
- 29. Perkins, *Jude*, 4:65.
- 30. Perkins, *Jude*, 4:65.
- 31. Perkins, *Exposition of the Creed*, 5:365.
- 32. Perkins, *Exposition of the Creed*, 5:366.
- 33. Perkins, *Cloud of Faithful Witnesses*, 3:115.
- 34. Jones, *Union with Christ*, 187, 191.
- 35. Perkins, *Sermon on the Mount*, 1:639.

state of every child of God, says he, "for they are united to Christ by the Spirit of grace, by which they are regenerate, and in Christ they are adopted for sons and daughters, and so enjoy God's special grace and favor."[36] The Holy Spirit, proceeding from the Father and the Son, is sent by the Father and the Son to dwell in believers, making them "the temples of the Holy Ghost, who is said 'to dwell in men.' [Rom 8:9; 1 Cor 3:16]."[37] By this gracious indwelling, the Spirit "testifies His presence by His special operation and gifts of grace."[38] These include the (1) imputation of Christ's righteousness; (2) impartation of life; (3) resurrection of the body; (4) knowledge of reconciliation with God; (5) direction of the mind, will, and affections; (6) impartation of comfort in times of distress; and (7) strengthening the heart in the performance of their callings.[39]

As for the mechanics of this union, Perkins explains that it is "by one and the same Spirit dwelling in Christ and in all the members of Christ... all the saints in heaven and all believers upon earth, having one and the same Spirit of Christ dwelling in them, are all one in Christ."[40] There is no mixing or compounding of Christ with believers.[41] It is by way of the communion and operation of the indwelling Spirit. He dwells "both in Christ and us,"[42] and "conjoins those things which are of themselves far distant from each other."[43] This union is "celestial and spiritual... [and] the very same Spirit of God that dwells in the manhood of Christ and fills it with all graces above measure is derived thence and dwells in all the true members of the church and fills them with the like graces in measure."[44] Perkins urges his readers to lay hold of this union through faith, and labor to feel it by experience in the heart rather than merely conceive of it in the mind:

> God the Father has made an evangelical covenant with His church in which of His mercy He has made a grant of His own Son unto

---

36. Perkins, *Sermon on the Mount*, 1:214.
37. Perkins, *Exposition of the Creed*, 5:311.
38. Perkins, *Galatians*, 2:151.
39. Perkins, *Galatians*, 2:136; Perkins, *Exposition of the Creed*, 5:312–15.
40. Perkins, *Galatians*, 2:234–35.
41. Perkins, *Exposition of the Creed*, 5:368.
42. Perkins, *True Gain*, 9:55.
43. Perkins, *Golden Chain*, 6:173. Elsewhere Perkins notes, "Distance of place does not hinder this conjunction, because the Holy Ghost which links all the parts together is infinite." Perkins, *Exposition of the Creed*, 5:369.
44. Perkins, *Exposition of the Creed*, 5:368.

us with righteousness and life everlasting in Him; and we again by His grace accept of this grant and receive the same by faith. And thus by mutual consent according to the tenor of the covenant any repentant sinner may truly say, "Though I now have my abode upon earth, and Christ in respect of His manhood be locally in heaven, yet is He truly mine to have and to enjoy. His body is mine; His blood is mine."[45]

According to Perkins, we become one with Christ in his death and resurrection by means of faith and baptism:

> First, we must believe that we are crucified with Christ; that is, as we conceive ourselves to be in Christ by faith, whereby we have communion with Him, so we must conceive that this communion with Christ, is in His death and burial, so as our sinful nature, with all our corrupt affections, were nailed to His cross and buried in His grave.[46]

"By the power of His Godhead" Christ, "did overcome the grave and power of death in His own person."[47] By this same power, all his members experience "a spiritual death and burial of sin and natural corruption."[48] Therefore, sin no longer reigns in our mortal body, nor does it produce fruits that leads to death (Rom 6:12; Gal 5:16–24). "So let a man that is dead in sin be cast into the grave of Christ," says Perkins, "that is, let him by faith but touch Christ dead and buried—it will come to pass by the virtue of Christ's death and burial that he shall be raised from death and bondage of sin to become a new man."[49]

All this is explained in Romans 6:3–4, where the apostle Paul writes, "Knew ye not that so many of us as were baptized into Jesus Christ were baptized into his death? Therefore we are buried with him by baptism into death: that like as Christ was raised up from the dead by the glory of the Father, even so we also should walk in newness of life." The apostle Peter says something similar: "The like figure whereunto *even* baptism doth also now save us (not the putting away of the filth of the flesh, but the answer of a good conscience toward God,) by the resurrection of Jesus Christ" (1 Pet 3:21). Referencing these texts, Perkins remarks,

---

45. Perkins, *Exposition of the Creed*, 5:367.
46. Perkins, *Sermon on the Mount*, 1:298.
47. Perkins, *Exposition of the Creed*, 5:229.
48. Perkins, *Exposition of the Creed*, 5:229.
49. Perkins, *Exposition of the Creed*, 5:229.

> In the right and lawful use of baptism, God according to His own promise engrafts them into Christ that believe. And the inward washing is conferred with the outward washing. For these causes, they that are washed with water in baptism are said "to put on Christ." In the same manner must other phrases be understood; as when it is said that baptism "saveth" (1 Pet 3:21); that men must be baptized for the remission of sins (Acts 22:16); that "we are buried by baptism into the death of Christ" (Rom 6:3).[50]

Perkins is quick to note that the key element in baptism is the inward washing by the Holy Spirit. "The outward baptism," he says, "without the inward is not the mark of God's child, but the mark of the fool that makes a vow and afterward breaks it (Eccl 5:4)."[51] That said, Perkins sees a "sacramental union" in baptism. First, the outward washing points to Christ's blood, which washes away the stain of sin. Second, the outward washing "seals and confirms" God's "engrafting or incorporating of the party baptized into Christ." It also seals and confirms his "spiritual regeneration." Third, the outward washing confirms three realities. (1) "The shedding of the blood of Christ for the remission of all our sins and the imputation of His righteousness." (2) The "mortification of sin by the power of Christ's death . . . and a continual increase of mortification by the power of both Christ's death and burial." (3) "Our spiritual vivification to newness of life in all holiness and justice, the which we attain by the power of Christ's resurrection."[52] So, if a man would be "saved by his baptism," he "must look that baptism work this effect in him to make him die and be buried with Christ, that afterward he may rise and reign with Christ. And then shall baptism save us."[53]

## Its Order

Perkins believes that the whole believer is united to the whole Christ, but there is a definite order to this union. It entails donation and reception. Eternal life "depends on that fullness of the Godhead which is in Christ," and we are united to that Godhead by means of our union with Christ's humanity. The Godhead, therefore, is given and communicated to every

---

50. Perkins, *Galatians*, 2:217.
51. Perkins, *Galatians*, 2:216.
52. Perkins, *Golden Chain*, 6:164.
53. Perkins, *Cloud of Faithful Witnesses*, 3:103.

believer "in the flesh and by the flesh of Christ."[54] In this way, therefore, the whole Christ (Godhead and manhood), is given to the believer. One is first joined to Christ's manhood, and then his Godhead. This means that it is by Christ's humanity that one has fellowship with God. "It serves as a pipe or conduit to derive the efficacy and operation of the Godhead to us," says Perkins.[55] The reason for this particular order is because "[Christ's] humanity without His Godhead, or the Godhead without the humanity, does not reconcile us to God."[56]

The logic in Perkins's thinking is as follows. (1) Christ's manhood profits nothing by itself. But, united to the Godhead and subsisting in the Son of God, it becomes the vehicle of eternal life and blessing. (2) Christ's manhood, by virtue of the Godhead, receives "quickening virtue to revive and renew all those to whom it shall be given."[57] (3) Every believer receives "eternal life from the Godhead, and by it God is joined to man and man to God."[58] (4) By means of his humiliation and exaltation, Christ stores up blessings and rewards in his manhood.[59] (5) Some of these blessings are given by imputation. Christ gives his "merit and satisfaction"[60] when "we are justified by [His] righteousness"[61] and our "sins are covered."[62] (6) Some of these blessings are given by infusion. Christ gives "the efficacy of His Spirit"[63] to make his people conformable to himself in holiness, which is in "the manhood of Christ and derived from it, as the light of one candle from another."[64] (7) The Word and sacraments "are (as it were) the hand of God, whereby He exhibits Christ unto us with all His benefits."[65]

---

54. Perkins, *Golden Chain*, 6:173. Regarding how the Godhead is "communicated," Perkins says it is not the substance of the Godhead, for that is incommunicable, but is "merely energetical," being as it operates in and through the manhood of Christ. Perkins, *Exposition of the Creed*, 6:366. See also Perkins, *Galatians*, 2:235.

55. Perkins, *True Gain*, 9:55.
56. Perkins, *Exposition of the Creed*, 5:366.
57. Perkins, *Exposition of the Creed*, 5:366.
58. Perkins, *Galatians*, 2:235.
59. Perkins, *Exposition of the Creed*, 5:366.
60. Perkins, *Galatians*, 2:235.
61. Perkins, *Exposition of the Creed*, 5:366.
62. Perkins, *Galatians*, 2:235.
63. Perkins, *Galatians*, 2:235.
64. Perkins, *Exposition of the Creed*, 5:366.
65. Perkins, *Galatians*, 2:235.

This is how God offers Christ. For our part, we receive. Since the Word and sacraments are "the hand of God," whereby he gives Christ to his people, our faith is the hand by which we take hold of Christ and are therefore united to him, thereby receiving him and all his benefits.[66] "This receiving," says Perkins, "is done by a supernatural act of the mind whereby we believe Christ with His benefits to be ours."[67]

Regarding the quality or quantity of faith required, it does not need to be perfect but true. "Though it is so little as a grain of mustard seed, and feeble like a young born babe, and that sore diseased too," it is enough to grasp and apply the Savior.[68] This is the case because even the "smallest measure of renewing grace have the promises of this life, and the life to come."[69] The rationale behind this, as Joel Beeke points out, is that "the object of faith is not the sinner or his experiences or faith itself; it is Jesus Christ alone."[70] For Perkins, faith is the "passive instrument or hand" that God grants in order that the elect may embrace all of Christ, and "when Christ is received, faith responds to the gift of grace. Thus, the response is most active when it has completely yielded to and is centered in the person it has received."[71] While exhorting his readers to strive for an increase of faith, Perkins assures them that "one little sparkle of true faith is sufficient to engraft us into Christ."[72] Once we are united to Christ through faith, we gain communion with Christ and, therefore, we enjoy him and his benefits forever, partly in this life and fully in the life to come.[73]

---

66. For Perkins, "faith gives [the believer] his life and sense." Perkins not only likens faith to (1) the hand of the soul "whereby we lay hold on Christ and receive Him with all benefits," but faith also as (2) the eye of the mind "whereby we behold Christ in the Word and sacraments," (3) the mouth of heart "whereby we feed on Christ, eating His body and drinking His blood to eternal life," (4) the feet of the soul "that makes us walk with God," (5) an ear "whereby we hear God speak to us in His Word," and (6) the tongue of the soul "whereby we speak to God by invocation of His holy name." Perkins, *How to Live*, 10:14.

67. Perkins, *Galatians*, 2:235.

68. Perkins, *Case of Conscience*, 8:626.

69. Perkins, *Grain of Mustard Seed*, 8:645.

70. Beeke, "William Perkins and His Greatest Case of Conscience," 266.

71. Beeke, "William Perkins and His Greatest Case of Conscience," 267.

72. Perkins, *Case of Conscience*, 8:626.

73. See Perkins, *Combat of the Flesh and the Spirit*, 9:170. John Flavel (1628–91) makes this same distinction: "The believer knows, how sweet soever his communion with Christ is in this world, yet that communion he shall have with Christ in heaven, will far excel it: there it will be *more intimate and immediate . . . more full and perfect . . . more constant and continued . . . more pure and unmixed . . . more durable and perpetual.*"

## Its Fruit

The apostle Paul writes, "I am crucified with Christ: nevertheless I live; yet not I, but Christ liveth in me" (Gal 2:20). Commenting on this verse, Perkins says that the apostle sets down the true preparation to spiritual life: "For God first kills, and then He makes alive."[74] This is important to his understanding of the believer's future glory. As Paul says in Romans 6:5, "For if we have been planted together in the likeness of his death, we shall be also in the likeness of his resurrection."

All have sinned and fall short of the glory of God (Rom 3:23; 6:23). Man has fallen from life and glory to death and misery, but Christ has come to reverse the curse. He has come to bring many sons to glory (Heb 2:10). To live, we must die and be made alive in Christ: "For your soul cannot live while your sins, the old man—that is, your corruptions—do live," writes Perkins, "but they must die and be buried, and then your soul lives."[75] On the cross, Christ "stood not as a private person, but as a public person in the room, place, and stead of all the elect."[76] When Christ was crucified, writes Perkins, "all believers were crucified in Him."[77] He adds, "And he that thus dies not, never lives. And he that thus is not buried never rises to true life."[78]

## Its Benefits

Being united in Christ's death, "the cross and passion of Christ is as verily made ours as if we had been crucified in our own persons."[79] This means that we now share in his life. Christ has "taken away the sting of death, and has changed the condition of [death] by making it of the gate of hell to be the way to eternal life."[80] Those who have been engrafted into Christ have full confidence that this union will continue forever. "So firm and certain

---

Flavel, *Tenth Meditation*, 6:450. The distinction Flavel makes between the believer's joys in Christ on earth now and their joys of the future in heaven is not of kind, but of degree. For they will be of greater quantity, constancy, purity, efficacy, society, and durability. Flavel, *Sermon X*, 4:228–29.

74. Perkins, *Galatians*, 2:132.
75. Perkins, *Cloud of Faithful Witnesses*, 3:102.
76. Perkins, *Galatians*, 2:132.
77. Perkins, *Galatians*, 2:132.
78. Perkins, *Cloud of Faithful Witnesses*, 3:102.
79. Perkins, *Galatians*, 2:132.
80. Perkins, *True Gain*, 9:45.

is this engrafting," assures Perkins, "that it once being made can never be dissolved but is everlasting—for the root living and abiding forever, so also do the branches, being set into the same, and that by the hand of the 'good husbandman,' God Himself [John 15:1]."[81]

God declares his love to his Son, and then his love to the elect in Christ. The apostle Paul declares his desire "be found in [Christ], not having [his] own righteousness, which is of the law, but that which is through the faith of Christ, the righteousness which is of God by faith" (Phil 3:9). Perkins notes that Paul expresses his desire that "God would respect him as a member of Christ and accept him into His favor eternally for Christ."[82] The elect are not first loved by God because something in them is worthy of love. They are not the originators of God's love to them. Rather, God "begins His love in Christ, whom He loves simply for Himself." Then, he "descends to them who are united to Christ."[83] Perkins says that God now considers "them even as parts of Christ, whom also He loves, yet not simply but respectively in and for Christ."[84] And, therefore, God's love "is that whereby God does freely love all such as are chosen in Christ Jesus, though in themselves altogether corrupt."[85] God looks upon "things of divers kinds through a green glass, yet beholds them all to be green. Even so, they whom God respects in and for Christ are loved by God as he is loved, and righteous as He is righteous."[86] This love is everlasting and according to God's free and good pleasure. Perkins writes,

> In the decree of election, the first act is a purpose or rather a part and beginning of the divine purpose whereby God does take certain men which are to be created to His everlasting love and favor, passing by the rest, and by taking makes them vessels of mercy and honor. And this act is of the sole will of God without any respect either of good or evil in the creature. And God does wrong none, although He choose not all, because He is tied to none, and because He has absolute sovereignty and authority over all creatures.... The second act is the purpose of saving or conferring

---

81. Perkins, *Jude*, 4:186.
82. Perkins, *True Gain*, 9:55.
83. Perkins, *True Gain*, 9:55. See Eph 1:3–4.
84. Perkins, *True Gain*, 9:55.
85. Perkins, *Golden Chain*, 6:170.
86. Perkins, *True Gain*, 9:55.

of glory whereby He does ordain or set apart the very same men which were to fall in Adam to salvation and celestial glory.[87]

The benefits of union with Christ are manifold. (1) We are made a new creature in Christ. (2) We are united to the triune God and enjoy eternal fellowship with him. (3) We receive the righteousness of Christ, and therefore stand justified before God. (4) We die to sin and are renewed in righteousness and holiness. (5) We have the protection of God's angels. (6) We recover our title to the creatures of God and enjoy their holy and lawful use.[88] Regarding this last benefit, Paul declares, "Therefore let no man glory in men. For all things are yours" (cf. 1 Cor 3:21). For Perkins, this means that "in Adam, you are poor and blind and miserable; in Christ, you are rich and glorious, you are a king of heaven and earth, fellow heir with Him, and shall as surely be partaker of it as He is even now."[89] These are but a sampling of the benefits of union with Christ, and each is a direct result of God's declaration of love.

In *A Golden Chain*, Perkins explains the four-fold declaration of God's love to those united to Christ: (1) calling, (2) justification, (3) sanctification, and (4) glorification. This four-fold declaration is essential to understanding the full benefits that accrue to believers in Christ. All who are one in Christ receive this four-fold declaration of God's love along with the myriad of benefits which accompany each.

## *Calling*

Perkins defines effectual calling as that "whereby a sinner being severed from the world is entertained into God's family."[90] It consists of two parts. First, the sinner is severed "from the cursed estate of all mankind." As Christ

---

87. Perkins, *Manner and Order of Predestination*, 6:309.

88. Perkins, *Exposition of the Creed*, 5:369–70. For Perkins, this final benefit is eschatological and will be enjoyed in the future and final state of glory. He writes,

> But some will say, if this be so, then a Christian man may have and enjoy all creatures at his pleasure and therefore the goods of other men. *Answer.* The reason is not good, for in this life we have no more but right unto the creature and right in it—that is, actual possession—is reserved for the life to come. Therefore, we must content ourselves with our allowed portions given unto us by God, by His grace using them in holy manner, expecting by hope the full fruition of all things till after this life. (5:370)

89. Perkins, *Estate of Damnation or in the Estate of Grace*, 8:568.

90. Perkins, *Golden Chain*, 6:172.

declares, "I have chosen you out of the world" (John 15:19). Second, there is a "reciprocal donation." This is the "free gift of God the Father whereby He bestows the sinful man to be saved upon Christ, and Christ again actually and most effectually upon that sinful man.... That admirable union or conjunction" wherein a man is engrafted and saved into Christ.[91]

God executes of the effectual call by certain means. The first is the preaching and hearing of God's Word. The Holy Spirit first applies law, thereby "showing a man his sin and the punishment thereof, which is eternal death." He then applies the gospel, "showing salvation by Christ Jesus to such as believe"[92] Here the Spirit "inspires him with some spiritual motions, and begins to regenerate and renew the inward powers of his soul."[93] It is termed "effectual call" because it is a work of the Holy Spirit who actually and truly brings about a change. This, says Perkins, is that "which is the beginning of grace in us, He Himself laying the first foundation of it by giving power to receive the word, to mingle it with faith, and bring forth the fruits of new obedience."[94]

The second means is the mollifying (or softening) of the heart. "Is not my word ... like a hammer that breaketh the rock in pieces?" (Jer 23:29). Perkins insists that the heart "must be bruised in pieces that it may be fit to receive God's saving grace offered to it."[95] This bruising takes place by four principal blows: (1) the knowledge of God's law; (2) the knowledge of sin, original and actual, and what punishment is due to them; (3) the compunction (or pricking) of the heart—namely, a sense and feeling of the wrath of God for sin; and (4) a holy desperation of a man's own power in obtaining eternal life.[96] As a result of these blows, the individual possesses "a willing mind steadfastly to believe in the Lord Jesus" and endeavors to "please the

---

91. Perkins, *Golden Chain*, 6:172.

92. Perkins, *Golden Chain*, 6:174. Perkins shows that to rightly preach Christ and his salvation contains "four ministerial actions": (1) to teach the doctrine of the Incarnation and the three offices of Christ (kingly, prophetical, and priesthood); (2) to teach faith as that which apprehends and applies Christ and his benefits; (3) to certify and reveal that it is the will of God to save him by Christ in particular; and (4) to certify and reveal to every hearer that they are to apply Christ and his benefits to himself particularly. Perkins, *Galatians*, 2:58.

93. Perkins, *Grain of Mustard Seed*, 8:644.

94. Perkins, *Jude*, 4:27.

95. Perkins, *Golden Chain*, 6:175.

96. Perkins, *Golden Chain*, 6:175.

Lord in all things."[97] His heart is "made tractable and pliable." Such a heart, says Perkins, "can relish the sure promises of the gospel."[98]

The third means is faith, which "is a miraculous and supernatural faculty of the heart apprehending Christ Jesus being applied by the operation of the Holy Ghost and receiving Him to itself."[99] Christ is given by grace and received by faith. This faith is but an "instrument to apprehend and receive that which Christ for His part offers and gives."[100] Christ is received when the individual "does particularly apply to himself Christ with His merits by an inward persuasion of the heart." And this comes about "but by the effectual certificate of the Holy Ghost concerning the mercy of God in Christ Jesus."[101]

## *Justification*

The second declaration of God's love is justification. Those who "believe are accounted just before God through the obedience of Christ Jesus."[102] For Perkins, Christ fulfills the law in three ways. First, in his doctrine, Christ fulfills the law by restoring "its proper meaning and true use," and "by revealing the right way, whereby the law may be fulfilled."[103] Second, in his person, Christ fulfills the law "by becoming accursed to the law, in suffering death upon the cross for us," and "by performing perfect obedience unto the law, doing all that the law required, for the love of God, or of His neighbor."[104] Third, in his people, Christ fulfills the law "by creating faith in their hearts, whereby they lay hold on [Him]," and "by giving them His own Spirit, which makes them endeavor to fulfill the law."[105] As for the reprobate, Christ fulfills the law "when He executes the curse of the law upon them, for that is part of the law, and the execution and enduring of the curse, is a fulfilling of the law."[106]

---

97. Perkins, *Jude*, 4:29.
98. Perkins, *Jude*, 4:29.
99. Perkins, *Golden Chain*, 6:175.
100. Perkins, *Grain of Mustard Seed*, 8:652.
101. Perkins, *Golden Chain*, 6:176.
102. Perkins, *Golden Chain*, 6:181.
103. Perkins, *Sermon on the Mount*, 1:245–46.
104. Perkins, *Sermon on the Mount*, 1:246.
105. Perkins, *Sermon on the Mount*, 1:246.
106. Perkins, *Sermon on the Mount*, 1:246.

There is a double act in Christ's obedience. The first is his passive obedience: "His passion or suffering of whatsoever the justice of God had inflicted on man for sin, whether for soul or body."[107] The second is his active obedience: "His perfect fulfilling of the moral law in all duties to God or man in thought, word, or deed—and all this for us, in our stead and on our behalf."[108] Therefore, for Perkins, Christ is the "meritorious cause of our justification.... Seeing therefore we cannot perform the things contained therein by ourselves, we must perform them in the person of our mediator, who has satisfied for the threatening of the law by His passion, and has fulfilled the precepts of the law by His obedience in all duties of love to God and man."[109]

As for the act of justification, Perkins identifies two components: the remission of sin and imputation of Christ's righteousness.[110] The believer "is freed from the guilt and punishment of sin by the passion of Christ,"[111] and receives "the imputation of Christ's own righteousness."[112] Therefore, justification is "an action of God, whereby He absolves a sinner and accepts him to life everlasting for the righteousness and merit of Christ."[113] By this imputation of Christ's righteousness, God "accounts and esteems that righteousness which is in Christ, as the righteousness of that sinner which believes in Him."[114]

In the act of justification, therefore, there is a double imputation, "a kind of translation of the believer's sins to Christ and again Christ's righteousness to the believer by a reciprocal or mutual imputation."[115] Perkins teaches that when an individual believes in Christ, God accepts the

---

107. Perkins, *Cloud of Faithful Witnesses*, 3:113.

108. Perkins, *Cloud of Faithful* Witnesses, 3:113.

109. Perkins, *Galatians*, 2:113.

110. Perkins speaks of two types of righteousness regarding justification: (1) the *righteousness of faith*, "whereby a sinner is justified through grace in Christ, and so stands righteous before God, having the pardon of all his sins"; and (2) *inward righteousness*, "whereby a man is sanctified and made holy, having God's image renewed in him by the Spirit of grace, which was lost by the fall of our first parents.... We must understand righteousness, which is that spiritual grace of God the fountain of all blessings, whereby sinners are justified and sanctified." Perkins, *Sermon on the Mount*, 1:193–94.

111. Perkins, *Golden Chain*, 6:182.

112. Perkins, *Reformed Catholic*, 7:34.

113. Perkins, *Reformed Catholic*, 7:34.

114. Perkins, *Reformed Catholic*, 7:34.

115. Perkins, *Golden Chain*, 6:182.

obedience of Christ for him, as if he had perfectly satisfied God's justice and obeyed God's will in his own person. "Therefore," Perkins proclaims, "nothing can procure unto us an absolution and acceptance to life everlasting but Christ's imputed righteousness."[116]

Closely related to justification is adoption. "All such as are predestinate to be adopted receive power to be actually accounted the sons of God by Christ."[117] Perkins declares that "the Son of God was made the Son of man that we which are the sons of men might be made the sons of God."[118] By the grace of adoption, "God accepts men for His children," and "men are born of God when the image of God is restored in them in righteousness and holiness."[119] By the means of adoption God bestows many "notable privileges" upon His children. (1) They are "the Lord's heirs."[120] (2) They are "fellow heirs with Christ, yea kings." (3) "All their afflictions, yea even their wants and offences are turned to trials or fatherly chastisements, inflicted upon them for their good." (4) They have "dominion over all creatures, yet so as that in this life they have only right to the thing, but after this life they shall have right in the same. (5) They have "angels as ministering spirits attending upon them for their good."[121] Perkins notes the eschatological reality that flows from justification:

> Christ as mediator is first of all elected, and we in Him. Christ is first justified, that is, acquit of our sins, and we justified in Him. He is heir of the world, and we heirs in Him. He died upon the cross, not as a private person, but as a public person representing all the elect; and all the elect died in Him and with Him. In the same manner they rise with Him to life and sit at the right hand of God with Him in glory.[122]

## Sanctification

Sanctification is never severed from justification, but bears "the fruits thereof, whereby the old man being mortified, and the new man in Christ

---

116. Perkins, *Reformed Catholic*, 7:37.
117. Perkins, *Golden Chain*, 6:184.
118. Perkins, *Galatians*, 2:250.
119. Perkins, *Galatians*, 2:211.
120. Perkins, *Golden Chain*, 6:184.
121. Perkins, *Golden Chain*, 6:185.
122. Perkins, *Galatians*, 2:189–90.

renewed, according to His image, in knowledge, righteousness, and true holiness, the whole person is turned unto God, and made careful to please Him, both in thought, word, and deed."[123] Sanctification, therefore, is the third declaration of God's love. For Perkins, "such as believe, being delivered from the tyranny of sin, are little and little renewed in holiness and righteousness."[124]

This deliverance from sin and Satan, and progressive renewal in holiness, takes place in all believers. Because they are "mystically bone of His bone and flesh of His flesh,"[125] Christ performs three works in them by means of the Holy Spirit. First, his death works effectually the death of sin, thereby breaking the power of the flesh. "For it is a corrosive," writes Perkins, "which being applied to the part affected, eats out any venom and corruption. And so the death of Christ, by faith applied, frets out and consumes the concupiscence and the corruption of the whole man."[126] Second, Christ's burial causes the burial of sin, as it were in a grave. Third, Christ's resurrection sends a "quickening power into them, and serves to make them rise out of their sin, in which they were dead and buried, to work righteousness and to live in holiness of life."[127] Perkins describes this reality on the basis of John 11:

> Lazarus's body lay four days and stank in the grave, yet Christ raised it and gave him life again, and made him do the same works that living men do. So also Christ deals with the souls of the faithful. They rot and stink in their sins, and would perish in them if they were left alone; but Christ puts a heavenly life into them, and makes them active and lively to do the will of God in the works of Christianity, and in the works of their callings.[128]

According to Perkins, sanctification has two parts: mortification and vivification. Mortification is "when the power of sin is continually weakened, consumed, and diminished," or "whereby the power of sin is abated

---

123. Perkins, *Sermon on the Mount*, 1:262.
124. Perkins, *Golden Chain*, 6:186.
125. Perkins, *Estate of Damnation or in the Estate of Grace*, 8:483.
126. Perkins, *Estate of Damnation or in the Estate of Grace*, 8:483.
127. Perkins, *Estate of Damnation or in the Estate of Grace*, 8:483.
128. Perkins, *Estate of Damnation or in the Estate of Grace*, 8:483. To read Perkins expound upon how sanctification is applied to the mind, memory, will, affections, and body see Perkins, *Estate of Damnation or in the Estate of Grace*, 8:484–88.

and crucified in the faithful."[129] From Christ's death and burial, writes Perkins, "proceeds such virtue as the first giving sin its deadly wound does bereave it of power to rage and reign in man and causes it to die and consume as it were in a grave."[130] By the power of his deity, Christ in his humanity vanquished all sin and guilt that was imputed to him. By this same power, he will "abolish the corruption of sin" in all his members.[131] As a result, believers seek to obey God's commands.[132]

Perkins affirms that mortification "is the way to heaven; and death, the way of life eternal. And, he that is not thus mortified in his corruption, let him never look to be quickened to grace or glory."[133] We must, therefore, "exercise and inure ourselves in dying by little and little so long as we live here upon earth, before we come to die indeed. And as men, who are appointed to run a race, exercise themselves in running so that they may get the victory, so we should begin to die now while we are living so that we might die well in the end."[134]

The second part of sanctification is vivification. This is when Christ dwells in the believer's heart by his Spirit, and inherent righteousness is augmented, enlarged, and increased.[135] The foundation for vivification is the virtue of Christ's resurrection, "which is nothing else but the power of His Godhead raising His manhood and freeing Him from the punishment and tyranny of our sins."[136] This power is conveyed from him to all his members who are "mystically conjoined with Him" whereby they are raised from spiritual death and given the power to walk in newness of life.[137] Perkins teaches that when Christ conquered death and sin, and was exalted to glory, he transferred this efficacious power by the Holy Spirit to all his members, creating holiness and righteousness in them. This causes them to endeavor to live according to the will of God. They are renewed and made

---

129. Perkins, *Estate of Damnation or in the Estate of Grace*, 8:483.
130. Perkins, *Golden Chain*, 6:186.
131. Perkins, *Golden Chain*, 6:186. See also Perkins, *Jude*, 4:33–34.
132. Perkins, *Zephaniah 2:1–2*, 9:136–37. See also Perkins, *Jude*, 4:33–34.
133. Perkins, *Cloud of Faithful Witnesses*, 3:102–3.
134. Perkins, *Salve for a Sick Man*, 10:426.
135. This definition has been harmonized by three different definitions given by Perkins. See Perkins, *Jude*, 4:34; Perkins, *Estate of Damnation or in the Estate of Grace*, 8:483; Perkins, *Golden Chain*, 6:186.
136. Perkins, *Jude*, 4:34.
137. Perkins, *Jude*, 4:34.

like Christ in righteousness and life. "The head quickened with spiritual life will not suffer the members to remain in the death of sin."[138]

Perkins ties justification and sanctification together in an eschatological expectation: "Righteousness indeed is imputed to them that believe, and that in this life, yet the fruition and the full revelation thereof is reserved to the life to come when Christ our righteousness shall appear and when the effect of righteousness, namely sanctification, shall be accomplished in us."[139]

## *Glorification*

The fourth declaration of God's love is glorification, which Perkins defines as "the perfect transforming of the saints into the image of the Son of God."[140] This is the end for which the elect were predestined: (1) "their eternal life and glory in heaven," and (2) "that the glory of [God's] grace may be known, and eternally made manifest."[141] The elect must be brought into everlasting glory. Perkins explains, "That election, vocation, faith, adoption, justification, sanctification, and eternal glorification, are never separated in the salvation of any man, but as inseparable companions go hand in hand."[142]

Perkins sees glorification as the climax (or fulfillment) of the grace found in union with Christ. He tracks the logical progression from effectual calling to celestial glory. First, he speaks of election, whereby we are predestined to glory. Second, he marks the promises of God given in the covenant of grace. Third, he applies the offices of Christ (Prophet, Priest, and King) whereby he imparts spiritual life and guards the elect. Lastly, he shows that the graces of faith, justification, sanctification, etc., "endure to life everlasting."[143] All this reaches a culmination when God's people are presented before him, holy and blameless, partly in the day of death and partly in the day of judgment. Perkins exhorts, "Believers need not fear the

---

138. Perkins, *True Gain*, 9:69.
139. Perkins, *Galatians*, 9:329.
140. Perkins, *Golden Chain*, 2:212.
141. Perkins, *Case of Conscience*, 8:628.
142. Perkins, *Case of Conscience*, 8:153.
143. Perkins, *Jude*, 4:37.

day of death or judgment. Nay, rather they may rejoice in it as the day of their redemption, yea, and of triumph."[144]

Glorification, therefore, begins at death, but "it is not accomplished and made perfect before the last day of judgment."[145] Death is a type of sleep "whereby the body and soul are severed: the body, that after corruption it may rise to greater glory; the soul, that it being fully sanctified may immediately after departure from the body be transported into the kingdom of heaven."[146] When the believer's soul is transported into the presence of God, he remains there until the day of judgment. In this intermediate state, he will "magnify the name of God" and (2) "wait and pray for the consummation of the kingdom of glory and full felicity in body and soul."[147]

Perkins writes, "We must mark the end to which we are predestined, and to which we say that one day we shall be brought."[148] In *A Case for Conscience*, Perkins he gives thirteen benefits believers receive from predestination unto eschatological glory in union with Christ.

1. The Lord Jesus, with His obedience, merits, death, resurrection, [and] glory; namely, in that respect He is made Mediator between God the Father and His people, as the Head of all the elect.... Therefore, seeing Christ is the first effect of predestination, He is also the cause of all other effects, by whom we are made partakers of them.

2. The effectual calling to Christ and to His gospel, in which the elect only are called, because it is by the purpose and grace of God which is given us in Christ.

3. After effectual calling follows faith, which is said to be peculiar unto the elect. And without which it is not possible to please God. For by it they are engrafted into Christ, and are made the members of Christ, and without faith no man can be saved.

4. Next, is justification; that is, a free pardoning of all their sins, and the imputation of the righteousness of Christ ... by the pardoning of all their faults and by the imputation of His perfect obedience.

---

144. Perkins, *Iude*, 4:37–39.
145. Perkins, *Golden Chain*, 6:212.
146. Perkins, *Golden Chain*, 6:212.
147. Perkins, *Golden Chain*, 6:213.
148. Perkins, *Case of Conscience*, 8:628.

5. With justification is joined regeneration and sanctification by the Holy Spirit: namely, the elect are made new creatures by Him, and the sons of God too, not only by adoption, but also by regeneration.... He takes from them their stony heart, and gives them a fleshly heart of His own ... strips them of the old man, and puts on His new man ... [and] takes away the corruption of their nature, and makes them partakers of His divine nature.

6. What then follows is a love of righteousness and detestation of sin. For in regeneration, the affections are principally changed, namely the affections of the corrupt nature and flesh into the affections of the divine nature and Spirit.

7. From these two affections, arises a care and endeavor to do good works, that is, to flee [from] sin and to fulfill the law of God.

8. This results in one's calling upon God, that in this fight the Lord would give us aid against the devil, the world, and the flesh. For this is the property of the Spirit, which the elect have to stir them up to prayer.

9. From these proceed a perpetual repentance for one's daily slips, and a continual desire to be bettered in godliness. Here one has a heartily desire to be dissolved out of this world and to be with Christ, for this end, that he might sin no more.

10. There is a desire that Christ may come and make an end of all their misery and sins, and perfectly restore His own kingdom.

11. Then appears true patience, that is, not only true comfort but also a rejoicing in adversity.... And, therefore, a certain taking up of courage and recovery of strength against his enemies; whereby it comes to pass that all things turn to the salvation of the elect.

12. Ensuing, they fight so long, till they are made conquerors and are assured of the victory and of the crown.

13. Lastly, the gift of perseverance unto the end in faith and a true confession of Christ, joined with a manifest care to live a godly life and a desire to glorify Him.[149]

These gifts and promises become the believer's supreme comfort in life and death. Perkins writes,

---

149. Perkins, *Case of Conscience*, 8:629–35.

> And when they shall come to the end of their lives, they shall be received into the heavenly glory, until such time as their bodies also being raised up, they may take full possession of eternal life.... Thus, we see that it is very certain that those who are elected to eternal life are also predestined to use those means by which, as by certain steps and stairs, they climb into that heavenly dwelling place... because we were elected to eternal life, according to the purpose and grace of God.[150]

All these benefits and promised rewards are the glorious declaration of God's love for his children, who have been graciously chosen in his beloved Son, Jesus Christ. "Blessed be the God and Father of our Lord Jesus Christ, who hath blessed us with all spiritual blessings in heavenly places in Christ" (Eph 1:3).

## Conclusion

By way of summary, every believer who is united to Christ by the Holy Spirit receives life from Christ and is transformed by Christ. In the incarnation, the manhood of Christ is united to his Godhead, which is the eternal spring of life. Christ's manhood, exalted in glory, is the fountainhead of life for all who are united to him by the Spirit. They become partakers of Christ because they are made real members of his body, thus partakers of the divine nature (2 Pet 1:4). In short, all that Christ's humanity receives and becomes in glory is given to all who are one with him. This is the reason Perkins believes that union with Christ is "the ground of the conveyance of all grace."[151] The gifts and benefits are myriad, and the transformation promised is magnificent—eschatological glory.

---

150. Perkins, *Case of Conscience*, 8:635.
151. Perkins, *Exposition of the Creed*, 5:369.

# 6

# The Hope of Glory

WILLIAM PERKINS RECOGNIZED THAT a cognitive understanding of biblical truth and doctrine was no guarantee that a believer would endure to the end. Something more was required; namely, a change in the affections. To that end, he sought to preach as one who spoke "the oracles of God" (1 Pet 4:11). He longed for his hearers to love God with all their heart, soul, mind, and strength, to be renewed in the full knowledge of God, and to be conformed to the image of Christ in righteousness and holiness (Mark 12:29–30; Rom 8:29; Eph 4:24; Col 3:10).[1] Perkins's emphasis on the affections mirrored the spirit of John Calvin who declared that doctrine "is not apprehended by the understanding and memory alone, as other disciplines are, but it is received only when it possesses the whole soul, and finds a seat and resting place in the inmost affection of the heart."[2]

Perkins's affective theology is particularly evident in his musings on eternal life. He believed it consisted of three degrees. The first begins in this life when a person repents of sin and believes in Christ, and can truly say, "he lives not but Christ lives in him."[3] Perkins provides his own testimony of this reality: "I find, partly by the testimony of my sanctified conscience and partly by experience, that Christ my Redeemer by His Spirit guides me and governs my thoughts, will, affections, and all the powers of body

---

1. For a more in-depth look at affective theology in Puritan spirituality, see Yuille, *Puritan Spirituality*, 33–39, 72–75.
2. Calvin, *Institutes*, 3.6.4.
3. Perkins, *Salve for a Sick Man*, 10:413. See also Perkins, *First Book of the Cases of Conscience*, 8:191.

and soul, according to the blessed direction of His holy will."[4] The second degree of eternal life occurs when a person dies. His body is buried in the ground, but his "soul is carried by the angels into heaven."[5] His body is prepared "so that it may be fit to enter into eternal happiness together with the soul" already in heaven.[6] The third degree takes place on the day of judgment, when the believer's body is raised from the dead and reunited with his soul. They "go both together into eternal [happiness] and everlasting glory."[7]

For those who have received eternal life in Christ, death is to be viewed as "gain" (Phil 1:21). This is the case because Christ "has taken away the sting of death and has changed the condition of it by making it of the gate of hell to be the way to eternal life."[8] This hope compels believers to live at present in light of what they will receive in glory. "For he who would live forever in eternal happiness," writes Perkins, "must begin in this world to rise out of the grave of his own sins (in which by nature he lies buried) and live in newness of life (Rev 20:6)."[9]

It is this promise of eschatological reward in Christ that invariably shaped Perkins's spirituality—his vision of the Christian life, particularly his (1) practice of biblical meditation, (2) method of pastoral ministry, (3) pursuit of personal holiness, (4) approach to personal suffering, and (5) engagement in polemical theology.

## Living the Promises

In *A Treatise Tending unto a Declaration whether a Man is in the Estate of Damnation or in the Estate of Grace*, Perkins provides seven persuasive reasons for embracing Christianity. The sixth is the promise of "eternal life." This, says Perkins, "is a thing desired of all men, yet none shall be made partakers of it but the true Christian, and the glorious estate of this life

---

4. Perkins, *Salve for a Sick Man*, 10:425.

5. Perkins, *Salve for a Sick Man*, 10:413. See also Perkins, *First Book of the Cases of Conscience*, 8:191.

6. Perkins, *First Book of the Cases of Conscience*, 8:191.

7. Perkins, *First Book of the Cases of Conscience*, 8:191. See also Perkins, *Salve for a Sick Man*, 10:413.

8. Perkins, *True Gain*, 9:45.

9. Perkins, *Salve for a Sick Man*, 10:424.

would move any to be a Christian."[10] This is the case because of the great blessings attached to the "glorious estate." (1) Christians will be freed from "all pains, sicknesses, infirmities, hunger, thirst, cold, weariness; from sin, as anger, forgetfulness, ignorance; from hell, death, damnation, Satan, and from everything that causes misery."[11] (2) They will enter the "presence of God's majesty in heaven, there to 'behold his face,' that is, His glory."[12] (3) They will experience "such an excellent communion with God, that He shall be unto them 'all in all.'"[13] (4) They will be filled with "an unspeakable joy and gladness."[14] (5) They will "love God with all their hearts, with all their souls, and strength," and this love will show itself "in that they are eternally occupied in worshipping God by singing of songs of praise and thanksgiving unto Him."[15]

As recorded in Revelation 2–3, Christ sends seven letters to the seven churches in Asia Minor. According to Perkins, while the letters speak directly to the first-century churches, they are a "prophetic history" and, therefore, they also speak to "the state of the church to the end."[16] Perkins believes the book of Revelation has a message for the church between Christ's two advents. While penned during the reign of Domitian (AD 81–96),[17] the book "concerns the present and future state of the church."[18] It makes known "things to come" for "the great good and comfort of [God's] children to the end of the world."[19] Perkins explains all this in *A Godly and Learned Exposition, or, Commentary Upon the First Three Chapters of Revelation*. In this work he divides each of the seven letters into three main sections: *Preface*, *Proposition*, and *Conclusion*. As he expounds the *Conclusion* of each letter, Perkins gives special attention to the *Recipient* and the *Reward*.

---

10. Perkins, *Estate of Damnation or in the Estate of Grace*, 8:505.

11. Perkins, *Estate of Damnation or in the Estate of Grace*, 8:505. Perkins elsewhere adds, "No ignorance, no unbelief, no distrust in God, no ambition, no envy, no anger, nor carnal lusts, nor terror in conscience, or corrupt affection." Perkins, *Exposition of the Creed*, 5:408.

12. Perkins, *Estate of Damnation or in the Estate of Grace*, 8:505.

13. Perkins, *Estate of Damnation or in the Estate of Grace*, 8:505.

14. Perkins, *Estate of Damnation or in the Estate of Grace*, 8:506.

15. Perkins, *Estate of Damnation or in the Estate of Grace*, 8:506.

16. Perkins, *Revelation*, 4:324.

17. Perkins, *Revelation*, 4:361–62.

18. Perkins, *Revelation*, 4:318.

19. Perkins, *Revelation*, 4:308.

## The Recipients

In the concluding remarks spoken to each of the seven churches, Christ grants a promise to those who "overcome" (Rev 2:7, 11, 17, 26; 3:5, 12, 21). Perkins expounds these promises by asking two questions. (1) "Who are these who overcome?" (2) "What do they receive?"

Perkins defines the one who overcomes as "him that in fighting prevails against all the spiritual enemies of his salvation: sin, Satan, hell, and condemnation."[20] Starting with the church at Ephesus, Perkins shows three foundational truths concerning the one who overcomes: (1) he is born anew in Christ, (2) he has true faith, and (3) he keeps faith.[21] Therefore, in order to overcome, one must be regenerate and have faith in Christ.[22] For Perkins, the work of Christ and union with Christ are the foundation for assurance that we will overcome the world and receive eschatological glory.

Again, they are those who are born again, possess true faith, and persevere to the end.[23] In other words, they are those who are one with Christ. Perkins begins his discussion of this reality by speaking of Christ's divine nature: "In respect of His Godhead, He is coeternal with the Father and with the Holy Spirit, living of Himself that uncreated and eternal life, which is all one with the Godhead, being eternal, without beginning or ending."[24] Yet the eternal Son of God became man, fulfilled all righteousness, died upon the cross, rose again, and then "ascended up to heaven, where in full

---

20. Perkins, *Revelation*, 4:452.

21. Perkins, *Revelation*, 4:452. Perkins expounds upon these three declaring: "So by regeneration he is freed from the bondage of hell, death, sin, and Satan.... For when a man is in Christ, by faith he is made partaker of Christ victory upon the cross and by it receives power to subdue his own corruptions, the world, and the devil ... [one] must keep faith—that is, true religion and a good conscience—standing out in life and death against all adversarial Power whatsoever." Perkins, *Revelation*, 4:452.

22. Regarding "faith," Perkins writes, "The gospel has in it no moral condition of anything to be done of us. Indeed faith is mentioned after the form and manner of a condition, but in truth it is the free gift of God, as well as life eternal. And it is to be considered not as a work done of us, but as an instrument to receive things promised." Perkins, *Galatians*, 2:193.

23. Perkins, *Revelation*, 4:452. Perkins explains these three as follows: "So by regeneration he is freed from the bondage of hell, death, sin, and Satan.... For when a man is in Christ, by faith he is made partaker of Christ victory upon the cross and by it receives power to subdue his own corruptions, the world, and the devil ... [one] must keep faith—that is, true religion and a good conscience—standing out in life and death against all adversarial Power whatsoever." Perkins, *Revelation*, 4:452.

24. Perkins, *Revelation*, 4:405.

glory He enjoys immediate fellowship with the Godhead... His manhood being wholly and immediately sustained by His Godhead."[25] As the God-man, Christ now gives eternal life to every member of his body.

Perkins explains that Christ's "manhood has quickening virtue in it, yet not of itself or by itself, but as it is the manhood of the Son of God; for from the Godhead it receives this quickening power to give eternal life unto the church."[26] He illustrates this reality as follows: "For as the root of a tree lives not for itself but for the body and for all the branches, even so Christ Jesus has eternal life in Him—not for Himself alone, but that He may convey the same to all His members."[27] Christ is life and he conveys life to his people by "virtue of that mystical union which is between Him and every member of His church."[28] This means that his people inherit eternal life—that is, "glory and bliss in body and soul in heaven forever and ever."[29] When Christ is given to his people, his manhood "is given both for the *substance* and in regard of all the *benefits* that are conveyed to man by it."[30] Perkins explains,

> When God gives Christ to any, He does with all give unto the same party the Spirit of Christ... and this Spirit creates in his heart the instrument of faith by which Christ given of the Father is received and apprehended, both His body and blood and the efficacy and the benefits thereof.... And the same Spirit that works this faith does knit the believer unto Christ, really, though mystically, making him one with Christ, so as Christ is the Head and the believer a member. And thus is this mystical conjunction wrought, from whence proceeds this eternal life.[31]

---

25. Perkins, *Revelation*, 4:405.

26. Perkins, *Revelation*, 4:406.

27. Perkins, *Revelation*, 4:406. John Calvin, commenting on Rom 6:5, writes, "[The] apostle does not exhort, but rather teach us what benefit we derive from Christ... for between the grafting of trees, and this which is spiritual, a disparity will soon meet us: in the former the graft draws its aliment from the root, but retains its own nature in the fruit; but in the latter not only we derive the vigour and nourishment of life from Christ, but we also pass from our own to his nature." Calvin, *Romans*, 223.

28. Perkins, *Revelation*, 4:406.

29. Perkins, *Revelation*, 4:406–7.

30. Perkins, *Revelation*, 4:406, emphasis added.

31. Perkins, *Revelation*, 4:406. Concerning "eternal life," Perkins distinguishes between "uncreated life" and "created life." Uncreated life is "the very Godhead itself whereby God lives absolutely in Himself, from Himself, and by Himself, giving life and being to all things that live and have being... [and] is not communicable to any

In sum, by virtue of his divinity, Christ's humanity is exalted and glorified, and by virtue of his union with his people, he becomes to them the well-spring of life. Moreover, all that Christ's humanity receives in glory becomes theirs.[32] Perkins's understanding of Christ's nature and exaltation, and of the believer's union with Christ, is foundational to his view of eschatological glory.

## *The Rewards*

While "the power of grace does change [the elect's] carnal nature,"[33] Perkins insists that a future perfection awaits God's people. This is the "reward"[34] (or prize) that they will receive in eschatological glory, and it is the chief cause of their hope (see Phil 3:11–14). Commenting on Hebrews 11:40, Perkins writes, "Indeed, all true believers before Christ were justified and sanctified and in soul received to glory before us; yet perfected in soul and body both they must not be before us, but we must all be perfected together."[35] This perfection will be realized at Christ's second coming. For

---

creature." "Created" life is a quality in the creature that is "natural and spiritual." Natural life is the understanding that men in this world "live by meat and drink and all such means by God's providence." Spiritual is "that most happy and blessed estate in which all the elect shall reign with Christ, their Head, in the heavens after this life and after the day of judgment forever and ever . . . and it consists in an immediate conjunction and communion or fellowship with God Himself." Perkins, *Exposition of the Creed*, 5:406–7.

32. John Calvin writes,

> As this secret power to bestow life, of which he has spoken, might be referred to his Divine essence, he now comes down to the second step, and shows that this *life* is placed *in his flesh*, that it may be drawn out of it. . . . But an objection is brought, that the flesh of Christ cannot give life, because it was liable to death, and because even now it is not immortal in itself; and next, that it does not at all belong to the nature of flesh to quicken souls. I reply, though this power comes from another source than from the flesh, still this is no reason why the designation may not accurately apply to it; for as the eternal Word of God is the fountain of *life* (John 1:4), so his flesh, as a channel, conveys to us that *life* which dwells intrinsically, as we say, in his Divinity. And in this sense it is called life-giving, because it conveys to us that life which it borrows for us from another quarter. (Calvin, *John*, 262)

33. Perkins, *Sermon on the Mount*, 1:200.

34. "For as a reward is given to a workman after his work is done, so everlasting life is given unto men after the travels and miseries of this life are ended." Perkins, *Exposition of the Creed*, 5:411.

35. Perkins, *Cloud of Faithful Witnesses*, 3:396.

Perkins, the eschatological rewards promised to the seven churches delineate exactly what this blessing will entail.[36]

## Entering Paradise

"To him that overcometh will I give to eat of the tree of life, which is in the midst of the paradise of God" (Rev 2:7). In this promise to the church at Ephesus, Christ says that they may "eat of the tree of life." For Perkins, the act of eating signifies "immediate fellowship with Christ."[37] At present, Christ conveys "quickening spiritual life to all that believe in Him."[38] In eternity, his people will enjoy an "immediate partaking with Christ in all His blessings. So that when Christ is all in all unto us immediately, then we do eat of the tree of life and thereby shall live eternally."[39]

Christ also says in the promise that his people will enter "the paradise of God." According to Perkins, this is the third heaven:

> The Lord does manifest Himself in His glorious majesty, and which He has prepared for the glory of all His elect . . . which is therefore called paradise, because it is a place of endless joy and pleasure . . . a great and most excellent place. . . . There, God communicates Himself to all the elect and becomes all things unto them immediately, so that this must needs be a place of all joy and comfort. . . . But the joys and glory of this paradise of God are endless and unspeakable.[40]

At the consummation, Christ's members will hear these words: "Well done, thou good and faithful servant: thou hast been faithful over a few things, I will make thee ruler over many things: enter thou into the joy of thy lord. . . . Come, ye blessed of my Father, inherit the kingdom prepared for you from the foundation of the world" (Matt 25:21, 34).

---

36. For Perkins's views on the signs before Christ's coming, the signs at Christ's coming, the resurrection, and the final judgment, see Perkins, *Exposition of the Creed*, 5:286–303, 398–406; Perkins, *Fruitful Dialogue*, 6:460–62; Perkins, *Golden Chain*, 6:214–15.
37. Perkins, *Revelation*, 4:453.
38. Perkins, *Revelation*, 4:453.
39. Perkins, *Revelation*, 4:454.
40. Perkins, *Revelation*, 4:454.

## Escaping the Second Death

"He that overcometh shall not be hurt of the second death" (Rev 2:11).[41] For Perkins, the second death is "the condemnation of the soul and body forever and ever.... When soul and body are both severed forever from God's comfortable presence."[42] The glory of this reward is that, although the regenerate will experience physical death (the separation of body and soul), they will never experience eternal death (or damnation). They will never be "severed from God to go into that lake that burns with fire and brimstone. Which is a most gracious and happy promise."[43] Instead, they will enjoy the fullness of joy found in the triune God.

## Eating Hidden Manna

"To him that overcometh will I give to eat of the hidden manna, and will give him a white stone, and in the stone a new name written, which no man knoweth saving he that receiveth it" (Rev 2:17). These three gifts, says Perkins, signify "the election, vocation, justification, and glorification of God's people."[44] Specifically, "the hidden manna" is Christ—"the true food of life eternal."[45] "Our life," says Perkins, "comes out of Christ's death."[46] All that has been given to Christ's exalted and glorified humanity, by virtue of his Godhead, become ours by virtue of our union with him. Elsewhere, Perkins states, "The exaltation of His humanity is the putting off from Him His servile condition and all infirmities and the putting on of such habitual gifts, which, albeit they are created and finite, yet they have so great and so marvelous perfection as possible can befall any creature." He adds, "The gifts of His mind are wisdom, knowledge, joy, and other unspeakable virtues; of His body, immortality, strength, agility, brightness."[47] Christ

---

41. In Rev 2:10, Christ promises "the crown of life." It is given to those who are martyred for the faith. Perkins says they receive this crown "not for his sufferings, but because he is a member of Christ and by suffering death has shown his faith in Christ, for whose merit alone he is so rewarded. And so must this and all other promises of like sort be understood." Perkins, *Revelation*, 4:470.

42. Perkins, *Revelation*, 4:472.

43. Perkins, *Revelation*, 4:472.

44. Perkins, *Revelation*, 4:500.

45. Perkins, *Revelation*, 4:501.

46. Perkins, *Revelation*, 4:501.

47. Perkins, *Golden Chain*, 6:61.

then bestows these same gifts upon his people in glory. "We shall then be," asserts Perkins, "partakers of the divine, not essence (for then we should be deified), but nature, that is divine virtues and qualities."[48]

Perkins defines "perfect glory" as "that wonderful excellency of the elect whereby they shall be in a far better estate than any heart can wish."[49] The reasons are as follows. (1) They will behold the face of God—His glory and majesty. (2) They will be conformed to Christ—"just, holy, incorruptible, glorious, honorable, excellent, beautiful, strong, mighty, and nimble." (3) They will "inherit the kingdom of heaven; yea, the new heavens and the new earth shall be their inheritance."[50] (4) They will have "dominion and lordship over heaven and earth."[51]

Turning to Philippians 3:21 and 1 Corinthians 15:44, Perkins notes the similarity between the glorified body of Christ and the glorified bodies of the elect. (1) As Christ's body is *incorruptible*, "so shall our bodies be void of all corruption."[52] (2) As Christ's body is *immortal*, "so ours in the kingdom of heaven shall never die." (3) As Christ's body is *spiritual*, "so shall ours be made spiritual." This means that we will have no need for food, drink, sleep, medicine, etc., because our body will be preserved "by the immediate power of God's Spirit forever and ever." (4) As Christ's body is now a "shining body," so "the bodies of the elect shall be shining and bright, always remaining the same for substance." (5) As Christ's body has a "property of agility" such as "swiftness to pass from earth to the third heaven," so the bodies of the saints "shall be able as well to ascend upward as to go downward and to move without violence, and that very swiftly."[53]

The second gift, promised to those who overcome, is "a white stone." According to Perkins, it is a "token of absolution."[54] He explains, "First, the judge in giving a sentence used white stones and black stones. The giving of a white stone was a token of absolution; the giving of a black stone, a sign of condemnation. Here then the giving of a white stone may signify absolution from Christ of all a man's sins and trespasses."[55] Because of the

---

48. Perkins, *True Gain*, 9:76.
49. Perkins, *Golden Chain*, 6:217.
50. Perkins, *Golden Chain*, 6:217.
51. Perkins, *True Gain*, 9:76.
52. Perkins, *Exposition of the Creed*, 5:410.
53. Perkins, *Exposition of the Creed*, 5:410.
54. Perkins, *Revelation*, 4:504.
55. Perkins, *Revelation*, 4:503–4.

finished work of Christ, the overcomers receive a token of the reality that all their sins are forgiven. They live in true and eternal blessedness, knowing that there is no guilt, punishment, or condemnation.

The third gift is "a new name," written on the stone.[56] To explain this, Perkins turns to 1 John 3:1, and declares that it is an honor and privilege "to be called sons of God." "Beloved, now are we the sons of God, and it doth not yet appear what we shall be: but we know that, when he shall appear, we shall be like him; for we shall see him as he is" (1 John 3:2). God's people will enjoy "the perfect vision," whereby they will behold the fullness of God with the eye of the mind and "be filled therewith . . . even as a vessel cast into the sea may be perfectly full of water, though it receives not all the water in the sea."[57]

## Ruling the Nations

"And he that overcometh, and keepeth my works unto the end, to him will I give power over the nations: And he shall rule them with a rod of iron; as the vessels of a potter shall they be broken to shivers: even as I received of my Father. And I will give him the morning star" (Rev 2:26–28). Perkins identifies two gifts in this promise.

The first is "power over the nations." As Christ received power and authority to rule over the nations, so too those who are in Christ participate in "the fruit and benefit of this power in his salvation."[58] Perkins describes this power in two ways. (1) Christ makes all his servants "partakers of His glory in heaven." They sit with him and "there approve of the just condemnation of all the wicked." (2) Christ enables all his servants "to overcome all the enemies of their salvation." This means that all who are united to Christ and partake of his exaltation, by virtue of his power, will receive power "in themselves over their sins, over death, hell, the world, and all the enemies of their salvation."[59]

---

56. Perkins, *Revelation*, 4:504. Perkins adds, "We must not think this an idle name or a bare title only; but withal God gives him a new condition whereof this name is a token and title." Perkins, *Revelation*, 4:504.

57. Perkins, *Sermon on the Mount*, 1:207.

58. Perkins, *Revelation*, 4:539.

59. Perkins, *Revelation*, 4:539.

The second gift is "the morning star." This, for Perkins, is the full reception of Christ.[60] It consists of two principle "benefits." (1) Perfect illumination whereby "ignorance shall be whole taken away after this life, when man shall know God fully, so far forth as a creature can know the Creator. (2) Perfect glory whereby "we shall be made to shine as stars. Yea, we shall become saints in light."[61] Those who are in Christ will receive perfect knowledge and perfect holiness, so far forth as any creature may know and reflect the Creator.[62]

## Receiving White Raiment

"He that overcometh, the same shall be clothed in white raiment; and I will not blot out his name out of the book of life, but I will confess his name before my Father, and before his angels" (Rev 3:5). Just as the saints are arrayed with the glory of Christ, they will walk with Christ in white garments. This is the promise of living with Christ in glory. These garments, according to Perkins, "have always been used to signify joy, happiness, life, and glory."[63] Sin is that which separates man from God. The removal of sin, therefore, is the restoration of fellowship with God. This removal is secured by Christ and enjoyed in Christ. Perkins states,

> For when God will save any man, He gives Christ unto that man truly and really, so as he may say, "Christ is mine." And with Christ God gives His Spirit which works in his heart true saving faith, whereby he does receive Christ. And so Christ and His righteousness belong unto that man really, and by virtue thereof he is worthy [of] life everlasting.[64]

---

60. According to Perkins, the "morning star" is Christ for three reasons. (1) Christ illumines people with the "light of understanding and his church with the knowledge of the will of his father." (2) Christ is the fulfillment of Numbers 24:17; He is the "star of Jacob." (3) As the physical morning star rises at the end of night, before the sun dawns, likewise, "Christ came not in the beginning or middle of the dark time under the law, but in the last age of the world." Perkins, *Revelation*, 4:541.

61. Perkins, *Revelation*, 4:541.

62. Perkins, *Exposition of the Creed*, 5:409–10.

63. Perkins, *Revelation*, 4:558.

64. Perkins, *Revelation*, 4:558–59. Perkins adds elsewhere, "Now if Christ is ours, then His obedience is not only His but ours also, [It is] His because it is in Him. [It is] ours because with Him it is given us by God." Perkins, *True Gain*, 9:61.

In addition to "white raiment," God's people receive two blessings. First, their names are included in the Book of Life.[65] Second, their names are confessed before the Father. Elsewhere, Christ declares, "Whosoever therefore shall confess me before men, him will I confess also before my Father which is in heaven" (Matt 10:32). Perkins explains that, on that day, Christ will separate his people from the wicked, set them on his right hand, and advance them to glory. There Christ will pronounce before the angelic host and his Father that they are his. "He will confess [them] to be His and receive [them] to His own glory."[66]

## Becoming a Pillar

"Him that overcometh will I make a pillar in the temple of my God, and he shall go no more out: and I will write upon him the name of my God, and the name of the city of my God, which is new Jerusalem, which cometh down out of heaven from my God: and I will write upon him my new name" (Rev 3:12). It is here, says Perkins, that "Christ does most notably express the state and condition of eternal life."[67] When we want to remember a loved one or honor a heroic figure, we erect a monument (or pillar) in his name. In this way we "immortalize" them. Perkins makes the point that Christ does not merely erect a pillar to honor his people; rather, he "makes" them "a pillar durable and everlasting, whose memory shall always continue."[68] In sum, he is given immortality.

The location of these pillars is extremely significant—God's temple. For Perkins, this is a description of "the church triumphant."[69] In the Old Testament, the temple was the place where God's people gathered to worship him. It was also the place where God manifested his glory in a special manner. Likewise, in eschatological glory, God's people will dwell with him in the "most glorious and comfortable manner." This dwelling has no duration, for they "shall go no more out," meaning they "shall remain forever

---

65. For Perkins, the Book of Life is "nothing else but God's predestination or eternal decree of election whereby He has chosen some unto salvation upon His good pleasure." Perkins, *Revelation*, 4:559.

66. Perkins, *Revelation*, 4:561.

67. Perkins, *Revelation*, 4:590.

68. Perkins, *Revelation*, 4:590.

69. Perkins, *Revelation*, 4:590.

and ever, and no time shall ever come wherein [they] shall cease to be a pillar in the same."⁷⁰

Engraved on these pillars are three names: (1) the name of God; (2) the name of the city of God; and (3) Christ's new name. Regarding the first, Perkins explains that Christ will "manifest that this man is indeed the son of God, and that God is all in all unto him." The second name discloses the location of these pillars—the highest heaven. The third name reveals that they will share in Christ's exaltation—dignity, power, and glory.⁷¹ Perkins concludes:

> And thus we have eternal life set out unto us by the author of life Himself. The sum whereof is this: that he which overcomes shall be made a true member of the triumphant church and there continue forever and shall have three names written on him, the name of God, having this made evident that he is the child of God; the name of God's city, being made partaker of the privileges of God's kingdom of heaven; and the new name of Christ, *communicating with Christ in His glory and majesty*.⁷²

## Sitting upon Christ's Throne

"To him that overcometh will I grant to sit with me in my throne, even as I also overcame, and am set down with my Father in his throne" (Rev 3:21). Contained in this final eschatological promise is the reaffirmation of Christ's "gracious promise of fellowship" to all who are one with him.⁷³ "For the saints of God," writes Perkins, "shall have an actual fruition of God Himself and be as it were swallowed up with a sea of His love and wholly

---

70. Perkins, *Revelation*, 4:590.

71. Perkins, *Revelation*, 4:591–92.

72. Perkins, *Revelation*, 4:592, emphasis added. "By this," says Perkins, "it is plain that no man can have fellowship with God but by Christ. We must not look to have immediate fellowship with God of ourselves or by any other, but by Christ. God hears not, God helps, not, God saves not, but by Christ. Nay, God is no God unto us out of Christ. For first He is a God unto Christ, and then in Him and by Him unto us." Perkins, *Revelation*, 4:593–94. Perkins goes on to expound that Christ will make the believer a partaker of that glory and dignity wherewith Christ himself is glorified since His death and resurrection. "Mark this," proclaims Perkins, "all that after this life must have Christ's new name must in this life become new creatures.... Would we then partake with Christ in His glory? We must here be partakers of His grace." Perkins, *Revelation*, 4:594.

73. Perkins, *Revelation*, 4:622.

ravished therewith."[74] When Christ promises, "I will grant to sit with me in my throne" (Rev 3:21), he is guaranteeing them "fellowship with [Him] in glory."[75] They will participate in Christ's glory, "so much as shall suffice for [their] happiness," and will "advance" them into "the participation of His glory."[76]

## Summary

For Perkins, this eschatological glory is central to the Christian life. Believers are to make this future hope a present reality. This is clearly evident in Perkins's spirituality, particularly his (1) practice of biblical meditation, (2) method of pastoral ministry, (3) pursuit of personal holiness, and (4) approach to personal suffering.

## The Focus of Meditation

The apostle Paul writes in Philippians 4:8, "Finally, brethren, whatsoever things are true, whatsoever things are honest, whatsoever things are just, whatsoever things are lovely, whatsoever things are of good report; if there be any virtue, and if there be any praise, think on these things." Thinking (or meditating) on biblical truth was a vital exercise within Puritan spirituality.[77] Joel Beeke notes, "Meditation was a daily duty that enhanced

---

74. Perkins, *Exposition of the Creed*, 5:409.

75. Perkins, *Revelation*, 4:626.

76. Perkins, *Revelation*, 4:626.

77. U. Milo Kaufmann identifies two "sharply divergent" lines of thought within Puritan meditation: (1) the Joseph Hall Line and (2) Heavenly meditation. Kaufmann, *Pilgrim's Progress*, 120, 133. Regarding the former, Kaufmann notes that Puritan's such as Joseph Hall (1574-1656), Thomas Hooker (1586-1647), Edmund Calamy (1600-1666), and Isaac Ambrose (1604-64) saw that the use of imagination "had no proper place in the process in which man confronted the revealed Word" (126). This was a rejection of the Roman Catholic method of meditation, which emphasizes the use of the imagination on particular events in the life of Christ as the center of meditation rather than scriptural and doctrinal truths. According to the Roman Catholic view, the Scriptures merely serve as an outline "to be expanded upon by the imagination so that the person in meditation might enter fully into the scriptural scene" (126-27). This method of meditation finds roots in twelfth and thirteenth century practices where an emphasis was placed "on emotional engagement . . . with the person inserting himself or herself into a visualized reenactment of a biblical event." Hancock, "Meditation," in *Dictionary of Christian Spirituality*, 607. The Scriptures in Roman Catholic meditation are, therefore, subservient to the imagination and are to only serve as a means to something beyond the meaning of the text itself. Hancock gives

delight as "savoring the things of the Spirit."[86] For Perkins, meditation is the means whereby we retain and preserve the grace of the Spirit given through God's Word. Meditation, therefore, is a chain reaction: as our thoughts are consumed with God's Word, our affections are engaged thereby producing delight and satisfaction within the soul.[87] "We must do what we can to stir up in our hearts a desire to believe," says Perkins, "and to strive against doubting and distrust."[88] To neglect meditation, according to Perkins, is to neglect God's "good means" for obtaining his grace.[89]

## The Subject of Meditation

When it comes to the subject of meditation, Perkins focuses on those things that are best suited to work upon the heart: the nature of God, the truth of the gospel, the mystery of providence, and the hope of glory. Regarding the last, Perkins breaks it down into three main foci.

### THE PERSON AND WORK OF CHRIST

"We must in mind and meditation come to the cross of Christ," says Perkins.[90] In particular, God's people are to meditate upon the magnitude of Christ's suffering and the extent of his love. The "consideration of this love will move us to love Him again, and the Father in Him."[91] Referencing Colossians 2:3, Perkins declares that believers are to seek out those treasures that are hidden in Christ by meditating on him who is "the spirit of wisdom and revelation" (Eph 1:17). In so doing, Christ reveals to his church those things which can only be known by the children of God; namely, "our election, vocation, justification, and sanctification in this life and our eternal glorification after this life."[92]

---

86. Perkins, *Galatians*, 2:186.
87. Perkins, *Galatians*, 2:186.
88. Perkins, *Sermon on the Mount*, 1:570.
89. Perkins, *Sermon on the Mount*, 1:638. Other subjects of meditation for Perkins are God's works, Word, creation, and providence. See Perkins, *Sermon on the Mount*, 1:96, 292, 336, 340.
90. Perkins, *Galatians*, 2:25.
91. Perkins, *Galatians*, 2:25.
92. Perkins, *Exposition of the Creed*, 5:203.

CROWNED WITH IMMORTAL GLORY

## The Prospect of Death and Judgment

The writer of Hebrews states, "And as it is appointed unto men once to die, but after this the judgment" (9:27). Commenting on this, Perkins writes, "All people are warned by this to meditate of the future judgments of God."[93] By meditating upon the future judgement, believers are instructed "above all things to seek God's kingdom [in heaven] and to establish it in [their] hearts."[94] They are deterred from returning to the works of the flesh thereby losing the kingdom of God.[95] Such meditation moves us daily to the "practice of true repentance" and to "employ the good gifts and blessing we receive from God, like good servants, unto the best advantage of His glory."[96] Perkins adds this warning:

> For when we shall stand before the judgment seat of Christ, He then, knowing all things in His eternal counsel, shall reveal unto every man His own particular sins, whether they were in thought, word, or deed. And then also by His mighty power, He shall so touch men's consciences that they shall afresh remember what they have done. Now indeed, the wicked man's conscience is shut up as a closed book. But then it shall be so touched and as it were opened, that he shall plainly see and remember all the particular offences which at any time he has committed, and his very conscience shall be as good as a thousand witnesses, whereupon he shall accuse and utterly condemn himself. The consideration of this ought to terrify all those that live in their sins; for howsoever they may hide and cover them from the world, yet at the last day God will be sure to reveal them all.[97]

Many people do not believe in the reality of the last judgment because they are not "smitten with fear and reverence" for it.[98] This is primarily due to the fact, says Perkins, that they do not meditate on it.

---

93. Perkins, *Galatians*, 2:381.

94. Perkins, *Galatians*, 2:381. The brackets were added to this quote because Perkins defines "God's kingdom" here as "a state or condition in heaven whereby God and Christ is all things to the elect," and, therefore, "not to enjoy the kingdom of God is to be in torment in hell." Perkins, *Galatians*, 1:301.

95. Perkins, *Galatians*, 2:382.

96. Perkins, *Treatise of Man's Imaginations*, 9:251.

97. Perkins, *Exposition of the Creed*, 5:297.

98. Perkins, *Jude*, 4:116.

Before judgment comes death, which (according to Perkins) must be considered in a double respect: (1) as it is in its own nature; and (2) as it has been changed by Christ's death.[99] Regarding the first, Perkins says that death is "a curse or forerunner of condemnation, the very gates and suburbs of hell itself."[100] It is the result of sin (Rom 6:23; Jas 1:15). The prospect of judgment at death "ought to terrify all those who live in their sins." Perkins adds, "We must think that most fearful and grievous ends may befall us, in regard of the bodily pain and torment, even then when we little fear or suspect any such thing."[101] We ought to cry with the psalmist: "So teach us to number our days, that we may apply our hearts unto wisdom" (Ps 90:12). "This consideration," says Perkins, "will be a notable means to stir up our hearts either to begin or renew our repentance."[102]

Regarding the second, death in Christ is not to be considered a curse but a blessing. For believers, death marks the end of all miseries, freedom from all dangers, a short passage unto joy, an entrance into everlasting life, and a quiet sleep.[103] The grave becomes a "resting chamber," and a "bed perfumed by the death of Christ."[104] The bodies of the elect, on the resurrection day, "shall be admitted and received into the presence of God in heaven."[105] With this in mind, Perkins exhorts his readers to bear with comfort the pangs of death and labor to die in the faith. This is achieved by constantly laying hold of "the promise of God touching forgiveness of sins and everlasting life by Christ."[106]

By calling to mind the merciful promises of God in Christ and applying them to the heart by faith, believers are comforted in life and death, whatever trials, temptations, tribulations, and afflictions may come. Perkins writes, "When it shall please God to bring unto us a cup of affliction and bid us drink a draught thereof to the bottom, the meditation of life eternal must be as sugar in our pockets to sweeten the cup withal." It is sweetened as we remember that (1) we have occasion to show our subjection and obedience to God who calls out of this world; (2) all our sin is abolished in death and

---

99. Perkins, *First Book of the Cases of Conscience*, 8:191.
100. Perkins, *First Book of the Cases of Conscience*, 8:191.
101. Perkins, *Treatise of Man's Imaginations*, 9:251.
102. Perkins, *Treatise of Man's Imaginations*, 9:251.
103. Perkins, *First Book of the Cases of Conscience*, 8:191.
104. Perkins, *First Book of the Cases of Conscience*, 8:191.
105. Perkins, *First Book of the Cases of Conscience*, 8:191.
106. Perkins, *First Book of the Cases of Conscience*, 8:192.

will no longer offend God; (3) we will be brought into a better condition than anything we experienced on earth; and (4) our soul will receive passage "to rest, life, and celestial glory, in which [we] shall see God as He is, perfectly know Him, and praise His name forever, keeping without remission an eternal Sabbath."[107]

## The Assurance of Heaven

Christ declares to his disciples, "I go to prepare a place for you. And if I go and prepare a place for you, I will come again, and receive you unto myself; that where I am, there ye may be also" (John 14:2–3). Perkins asks, "Is Christ gone to heaven beforehand to prepare a place for you? Then practice that which Paul teaches. Have your conversation 'in heaven.'"[108]

Perkins recognizes the dilemma believers face on earth; namely, at present we are "separated from our Head, and consequently from that happy and glorious fellowship which we shall enjoy with Him and all the saints, our fellow-members, in the kingdom of heaven."[109] For Perkins, the problem is solved through meditation: "We must exercise ourselves in the frequent meditation of the blessed estate of God's chosen in the kingdom of glory."[110] For Perkins, all our cares, duties, affairs, and doings must be in heaven. Although we are on earth, if we are united to Christ, our citizenship is in heaven, and, therefore, our conversation is to be in heaven too. Perkins explains, "We must converse in heaven not in body but in heart. And therefore, though our bodies be on earth, yet our heart's joy and comfort and all our meditation must be in heaven. Thus must we behave ourselves like good free men in God's house. It must be far from us to have our joy and our hearts set on the things of this world."[111]

Believers must have an eschatological framework for meditation in this life. The glorious promises of God are to occupy the mind and heart. Perkins exhorts his readers to meditate upon the reality of being "translated out of this life into the bosom of Abraham," to be "fully and perfectly freed from sin, Satan, from vanity and misery," to have "all tears wiped from their eyes," to "behold the face of God" in the beatific vision, to be made "like

---

107. Perkins, *Salve for a Sick Man*, 10:456.
108. Perkins, *Exposition of the Creed*, 5:266.
109. Perkins, *First Book of the Cases of Conscience*, 8:188–89.
110. Perkins, *First Book of the Cases of Conscience*, 8:189.
111. Perkins, *Exposition of the Creed*, 5:266.

unto Christ in holiness and honor," and to "inherit the kingdom prepared for them from the foundations of the world."[112] Meditation upon the eternal rewards promised in Christ will cause us "to use [the world] as if we used it not, to have our conversation in heaven, to think with Paul, that to be loosed and be with Christ is best of all for us, to have a true and lively taste of the joys of the world to come, and accordingly with Abraham, Isaac, and Jacob, to look for a city that has foundations, whose builder and maker is God."[113]

## *The Benefits of Meditation*

For Perkins, eschatological glory is the believer's ultimate hope. He enumerates the blessings as follows. (1) By Adam, we lost all things; by Christ, all things are restored to us. (2) By Adam, we are dead; by Christ, we are made alive. (3) By Adam, we are slaves of the devil and children of wrath; by Christ, we are the children of God. (4) By Adam, we are "worse than a toad and more detestable before God"; by Christ, we are above the angels, for we "are joined unto Him and made bone of His bone mystically." (5) By Adam, sin and Satan have ruled over us and lead us captive; by Christ, the Spirit of God dwells in us. (6) By Adam, death came to us, and "it is an entrance to hell"; by Christ, though death remains, it is only "a passage unto life." (7) By Adam, we are poor, blind, and miserable; by Christ, we are "rich and glorious," we are kings of heaven and earth, we are fellow heirs with him, and we will "as surely be partakers of it as He is even now."[114]

Perkins is convinced that meditation upon this eschatological glory is of tremendous benefit to believers. For starters, it stirs them up to pursue a heavenly and spiritual life, for the ultimate purpose of being formed into the likeness of Jesus Christ.[115] In addition, it serves as a powerful tool to combat

---

112. Perkins, *First Book of the Cases of Conscience*, 8:189.

113. Perkins, *First Book of the Cases of Conscience*, 8:189.

114. Perkins, *Estate of Damnation or in the Estate of Grace*, 8:505. Other benefits mentioned by Perkins to be meditated upon are: "(1) Through Adam, you are condemned to hell; by Christ, you are delivered from it. (2) Through Adam, you have transgressed the whole law; in Christ, you have fulfilled it. (3) Through Adam, you are before God a vile and loathsome sinner; through Christ, you do appear glorious in His eyes. (4) By Adam, every little cross is the punishment of your sin and a token of God's wrath; by Christ, the greatest crosses are easy, profitable, and tokens of God's mercy." Perkins, *Estate of Damnation or in the Estate of Grace*, 8:505.

115. Perkins, *Galatians*, 2:264. Perkins adds, "We must seek His kingdom above all

sin and to wean us from the cares of the world. According to Perkins, when we meditate upon eschatological glory, we are moved to kill sin and pursue Christ-likeness. "Meditating daily on God's promises and believing them and relying on them and applying the generals to our own selves and practicing faith by making conscience of sin and inuring ourselves to patience and long suffering."[116] When we lift our hearts to God in holy meditation, we by necessity draw ourselves away from the world. "If the mind should be always pressed down with worldly cares," writes Perkins, "it could never attain to heaven's joys. He that has not conscience on the Lord's Day to lift up his heart to heaven by prayer and hearing God's Word with meditation thereon cannot possibly have any soundness in religion nor his heart firmly settled on heavenly things."[117] By setting the mind upon eternity, we live at present in gratitude to God. Perkins writes, "Now we must show this high respect to heaven and to life eternal above that we have to this world and temporal life by heavenly meditations and by spiritual desires, joy and delight, for if heaven be our treasure, then must our delight be drawn from worldly things, and set on heaven."[118]

## The Aim of Ministry

As eschatological glory is central to Perkins's practice of biblical meditation, so too it is central to his method of pastoral ministry. He believes all ministers must seek to furnish and equip themselves that "they may bring serious and weighty matter unto God's people, and deliver the same with that convenient boldness and authority, which beseems God's Word."[119] This is accomplished by means of shepherding God's people and preaching God's Word. Central to Perkins's preaching is the hope of eschatological glory. This hope is rooted in faith in Christ. "If you would be saved by your

---

things, and take His yoke on us. It will be said, what must we do that Christ my live in us? *Answer.* We must use the means appointed: meditation of the word, prayer, sacraments" (2:138).

116. Perkins, *Cloud of Faithful Witnesses*, 3:146. See also Perkins, *Cloud of Faithful Witnesses*, 3:177.

117. Perkins, *Cloud of Faithful Witnesses*, 3:405.

118. Perkins, *Sermon on the Mount*, 1:535.

119. Perkins, *Sermon on the Mount*, 1:178.

faith in Christ after death," declares Perkins, "you must live by it here before death."[120]

Faith in Christ is that which gives believers the direction to stay the course and run the race set before them. It reminds God's people that his truth cannot be discerned by sense and reason. God promises a future resurrection to his people, yet our bodies decay and decompose in the grave. God declares that his people are blessed, yet so many are overcome with miseries and afflictions. God promises an abundant life to his people, yet many are hungry and thirsty. God promises never to leave nor forsake his people, yet oftentimes he seems distant and deaf to the cries of his people. In light of these things, Perkins declares, "Now, then comes faith, which is the substance of things hoped for, and it makes us lift our minds above the whole world to apprehend the invisible and unspeakable things of God which He has revealed and promised to us."[121]

Perkins, therefore, continually directs his people beyond this life and this world. In his preaching he leads his people beyond what their eyes can see and directs their hearts to things above, where Christ sits at the right hand of God (Col 3:1). "For when all temporal things fail us, even to the very skin and life," says Perkins, "faith preserves within us an affiance of the grace and mercy of God, and the hope of everlasting life."[122]

Perkins's preaching is to a great extent eschatological.[123] He was convinced that preaching was God's ordained means through which he revealed

---

120. Perkins, *How to Live*, 10:3.

121. Perkins, *How to Live*, 10:4.

122. Perkins, *How to Live*, 10:3.

123. Joseph Pipa notes that, prior to the Reformation, there were two forms of sermon structures: the "ancient" and the "modern" form. Pipa, "William Perkins," 32. The "ancient form" came from the homilies of the Fathers and did not elaborate on any arrangement scheme in particular but focused on a singular idea and application of any given text. The "modern form" was the product of university schools and showed the influence of Aristotelian logic and broke from the ancient form. Pipa, "William Perkins," 32. Pipa says that the Reformers, being "concerned to communicate the message of the Scripture to the people," sought to "simplify the sermon structure," and, therefore, "discarded the "elaborate 'modern' form and used more simple methods of construction." Pipa, "William Perkins," 32. Perkins was "the chief instrument" for the new Reformed method of preaching within seventeenth-century Puritanism. Pipa, "William Perkins," i. *The Art of Prophesying* was the first homiletical book written by a Protestant and centered upon this simple method of preaching. In summarizing this method, Perkins writes, (1) "read the text distinctly out of the canonical Scriptures"; (2) "give the sense and understanding of it"; (3) "collect a few and profitable points of doctrine out of the natural sense"; and (4) apply the "doctrines rightly collected to the life and manners of men in a

himself, imparted grace to his people, and united believers to Christ by the Holy Spirit.[124] Likewise, preaching was the mechanism for accomplishing God's full redemption whereby he brings many sons to glory (Heb 2:10). For Perkins, this has immediate significance for the minister, method, and message.

## *The Minister*

For Perkins, it is unimaginable that a preacher would step into the pulpit with "unclean feet to handle the holy things of God with unwashed hands."[125] Just as the priests cleansed themselves before offering sacrifices on behalf of the people (Lev 16:1–6), ministers are to sanctify themselves before preaching to the gathered assembly. Perkins writes,

> A minister is to declare the reconciliation between God and man, and is he himself not reconciled? Dare he present another man to God's mercy for pardon, and never yet [have] presented himself? Can he commend the state of grace to another, and never [have] felt the sweetness thereof in his own soul? Dare he come to preach sanctification with polluted lips, and out of an unsanctified heart? ... Dare any man presume to come into this most high and holy presence of the Lord, until he has mortified his corruptions and cast off the unruliness of his affections?[126]

---

plain and simple speech." Perkins, *Art of Prophesying*, 10:356. From this simple method of preaching, and Perkins's ability to powerfully communicate the Scriptures, Pipa writes that this placed him at "the forefront of those interested in pastoral reform of the church." Pipa, "William Perkins," 85. Concerning Perkins's preaching to be eschatological, Andrew Ballitch points out that while Perkins "did point individuals toward themselves in his preaching," and "was committed to particularism in the atonement," he also "pointed doubters to Christ and gospel promises for assurance." Ballitch, "Not to Behold Faith," 445. For more resources on the significance of Perkins's preaching see Ballitch, *Gloss and the Text*; Ballitch, "True Happiness," 49–69; Baumlin, "William Perkins's 'Art of Prophesying,'" 66–71; Blacketer, *Rhetoric of Reform*, 215–36; Beeke, "William Perkins on Predestination," 183–213. Breward, "William Perkins and the Ideal of the Ministry," 73–84; Hargrove, "Implication and Application in Exposition," 25–41; Hulse, "William Perkins," 176–94; Kuivenhoven, "Condemning Coldness and Sleepy Dullness," 180–200; McKim, "Functions of Ramism," 503–17; Yuille, "Simple Method," 215–30; Yuille, "Ready to Receive," 91–106.

124. Yuille, "Simple Method," 224.
125. Perkins, *Calling of the Ministry*, 10:252.
126. Perkins, *Calling of the Ministry*, 10:209.

Perkins acknowledges, "In many places of our land, there is by God's blessing much teaching, yet there is little reformation in the lives of the most."[127] Many ministers were presumptuous enough to exercise the high and holy function of preaching while remaining in their sin. "A minister who is wicked either openly or secretly," declares Perkins, "is not worthy to stand before the face of the most holy and the almighty God."[128]

For preachers to honor God and rightly fulfill their ministry, they must first "sanctify themselves, and cleanse their hearts by repentance."[129] According to Perkins, this "sanctifying" includes the cultivation of (1) a good conscience, (2) an inward feeling of the doctrine being delivered, (3) a fear and reverence for God's majesty, (4) a love for God's people, and (5) a constant, grave, and honest life, both in public and private.[130] It is the glory of a church to have their "doctrine powerful and effectual for the winning of souls," but more importantly and above all else, they must see that their ministers "be godly men as well as good scholars, and their lives inoffensive as well as their doctrine sound, or else they will find in woeful experience that they pull down as much with one hand as they build up with the other."[131] This echoes Paul's exhortation to Timothy: "Take heed unto thyself, and unto the doctrine; continue in them: for in doing this thou shalt both save thyself, and them that hear thee" (1 Tim 4:16). For Perkins, no man is "more honorable than a learned and holy minister." However, to the contrary, no man is more contemptible and miserable in this world "than he who (by his loose and lewd life) does scandalize his doctrine."[132]

The source of this reverential fear of God and holiness of life is an awareness that they will give an account. Christ proclaimed that "every idle word that men shall speak, they shall give account thereof in the day of judgment" (Matt 12:36). When God's Word is rightly preached and the sacraments are rightly administered, God manifests his presence and draws nearer than at any other time.[133] Perkins declares that there is coming a day

---

127. Perkins, *Calling of the Ministry*, 10:253.
128. Perkins, *Art of Prophesying*, 10:352.
129. Perkins, *Calling of the Ministry*, 10:254.
130. Perkins, *Art of Prophesying*, 10:352–53.
131. Perkins, *Calling of the Ministry*, 10:254.
132. Perkins, *Calling of the Ministry*, 10:254.
133. Perkins, *Calling of the Ministry*, 10:251. He points to other ways God's presence is experienced. (1) When one thinks of God in the conscience. (2) When one names God, or hears him named by others. These, says Perkins, are "the farthest off." Perkins, *Calling of the Ministry*, 10:251.

when there will be "a most apparent and sensible presence of God."[134] This will be the last judgment—the day when "all men shall stand before Him in His immediate presence, to receive their judgment."[135] This was the fuel that propelled Perkins's pastoral ministry. He was called to shepherd the flock of God that had been assigned to him. He was commanded to feed the flock of God and he was aware that he would give an account (1 Pet 5:2–4). He was assured that God would pay his wage, "an eternal weight of comfort here and of glory in heaven."[136]

Ungodly ministers will be "hauled into the presence of God's glory at the last day... to receive [their] just sentence of condemnation."[137] And so, "in fear and trembling and always in repentance," Perkins exhorts ministers to "lift up their heads, and say to the holy angels, and all the powers of heaven, help us and hasten us to come into the glorious presence of our God and Savior."[138]

## *The Method*

Perkins defines preaching (or prophesying) as "a public and solemn speech of the prophet, pertaining to the worship of God and to the salvation of our neighbor."[139] More specifically, the preaching the Word of God is "prophesying in the name and room of Christ, whereby men are called to the state of grace, and conserved in it."[140] The gift of prophecy is the greatest gift that God bestows upon his church for her edification, because it carries with it the greatest use of all other callings. It serves to (1) "collect the church and accomplish the number of the elect," and (2) to "drive away the wolves from the fold of the Lord."[141] Preaching, according to Perkins, is the instrument God uses "to redeem a penitent man from hell and damnation... and to pronounce his safety and deliverance" from judgment and damnation.[142] This is one of the chief reasons Perkins's preaching is eschatological. It is not

---

134. Perkins, *Calling of the Ministry*, 10:251.
135. Perkins, *Calling of the Ministry*, 10:251.
136. Perkins, *Calling of the Ministry*, 10:280.
137. Perkins, *Calling of the Ministry*, 10:253–54.
138. Perkins, *Calling of the Ministry*, 10:255.
139. Perkins, *Art of Prophesying*, 10:289.
140. Perkins, *Art of Prophesying*, 10:290.
141. Perkins, *Art of Prophesying*, 10:285.
142. Perkins, *Calling of the Ministry*, 10:226.

only the instrument through which God redeems people in this present life, but it is the only instrument through which God preserves them in faith unto everlasting life.

Perkins's view is that preaching carries God's people to an intended destination—eschatological glory. The "plain commission" of delivering a man from the power of hell, transferring him into the state of God's children, and making him an heir of heaven, constitutes the highest calling.[143] "This is indeed a high commission," says Perkins, "and so high as this was never granted out of the court of heaven to any creature but to ministers."[144] The magnitude of this calling necessitates faithful preparation, proclamation, and application.

## Preparation

The minister needs to be sanctified, and so too does his sermon. The preacher is called to be a "divine interpreter"; that is, an interpreter of God's message.[145] The means whereby the minister becomes a divine interpreter is threefold. (1) He is furnished with his learning; in other words, he has the resources for study and the environment that allows him to study.[146] (2) He is instructed by other learned and gifted men in the science of divinity. (3) He is "inwardly learned and taught by the Spirit of God."[147] For Perkins, a preacher is not only to have "divine things flowing into his brain," but it must be "engraven in his heart" and "printed in his soul" by the finger of God.[148] The preacher must pursue the first two with all diligence; however, they are only truly useful when God grants the third. Until the Holy Spirit pierces the heart with the truth of God's Word, the preacher cannot be a divine interpreter of spiritual things.

Having been prepared by the Holy Spirit, the preacher is now able to speak in the demonstration of the Holy Spirit's power. As the apostle Paul writes, "For our gospel came not unto you in word only, but also in power,

---

143. Perkins, *Calling of the Ministry*, 10:226.
144. Perkins, *Calling of the Ministry*, 10:228.
145. Perkins, *Calling of the Ministry*, 10:209.
146. Perkins was a strong proponent of Christian schools and seminaries being established and supported for the propagation and expansion of the Christian faith. See Perkins, *Calling of the Ministry*, 10:213; Perkins, *Galatians*, 2:46; Perkins, *Jude*, 4:176; Perkins, *Lord's Prayer*, 5:446.
147. Perkins, *Calling of the Ministry*, 10:208.
148. Perkins, *Calling of the Ministry*, 10:209.

and in the Holy Ghost" (1 Thess 1:5). For Perkins, the demonstration of the Holy Spirit's power in preaching comes through simple speech whereby "the capacities of the simplest may perceive not man but God teaching them in that plainness, and the consciences of the mightiest may feel not man but God reprove them in that powerfulness."[149] Perkins believed that the minister was not only to demonstrate his ability to teach God's Word, but to speak with all authority as "the ambassador of the great Jehovah," possessing great zeal, "whereby being most desirous of God's glory he does endeavor to fulfill and execute the decree of election concerning the salvation of men by his ministry."[150]

## Proclamation

As the minister proclaims the blessed hope of Christ, he enters "the holy of holies."[151] He stands in the room of Christ, bearing his office. His message is "the eternal law of the Old Testament and the everlasting gospel of the New."[152] Central to this message is eschatological glory. The minister is charged "to open and explain the covenant of grace, and rightly lay down the means how this reconciliation is wrought."[153] It entails union with the resurrected and glorified Christ, along with all his salvific benefits and rewards in future glory. Therefore, the contents of the covenant of grace are foundational to Perkins's preaching of Christ.

The first component of this preaching is repentance—that "which a man must perform to God, whom he has grievously offended by his sins."[154] Perkins explains,

> All faithful ministers must here learn the true way of comforting troubled and distressed consciences, namely, first to draw him unto a sight of some particular sins, then to summon him into God's presence, and there to arraign him for those sins until the view of the foulness of his sins and the glory of God's justice have

---

149. Perkins, *Calling of the Ministry*, 10:206.
150. Perkins, *Art of Prophesying*, 10:353.
151. Perkins, *Calling of the Ministry*, 10:212.
152. Perkins, *Calling of the Ministry*, 10:212.
153. Perkins, *Calling of the Ministry*, 10:207. As a reminder, Perkins defines the covenant of grace as "that whereby God, freely promising Christ and His benefits, exacts again of man that he would by faith receive Christ and repent of his sins." Perkins, *Golden Chain*, 6:153.
154. Perkins, *Calling of the Ministry*, 10:217.

sufficiently humbled him, and then to labor to persuade his conscience upon good grounds of the pardon of those sins by Christ Jesus.[155]

Second, the minister is to preach faith in Christ, forgiveness, and the perfect salvation found in Christ. If fear comes by the knowledge of sin, then all true comfort comes from the knowledge of the forgiveness of sins in Christ by means of the covenant of grace.

Third, the minister is to proclaim free justification before God by faith in Christ alone.[156] Justification is not only central to salvation but is fundamental to the believer's eschatological hope. "Justification," declares Perkins, "is a part of spiritual life because it is the acceptation of a sinner to eternal life."[157] Therefore, the proclamation of salvation in Christ is the means by which we are carried to eternal glory. Perkins says that the promises of eschatological glory are to be preached continually to God's people. They are to be reviewed, renewed, and received time and time again. This is accomplished partly by preaching (the invisible Word) and partly by the sacraments (the visible Word).[158] For Perkins, if the preaching of God's Word does not elevate believers beyond this present world, to establish their minds and hearts on all that awaits them in glory, then the message has fallen short of its intended purpose.

## Application

The consummation of the sermon is found in its application. Perkins sees a "great and glorious account" when God's ministers truly teach and rightly apply the Word of God to his people, because God "ties a blessing unto it."[159] This blessing comes from the promises of God.[160] Perkins believes God speaks to his people through the minister's exposition, and he believes God works in his people through the minister's application. The efficacy of the blessing comes because the Holy Spirit is adjoined to it.[161] These blessings are precisely what God's Word promises. The believer truly possesses

---

155. Perkins, *Calling of the Ministry*, 10:268.
156. Perkins, *Calling of the Ministry*, 10:217–18.
157. Perkins, *How to Live*, 10:5.
158. Perkins, *Galatians*, 2:160.
159. Perkins, *Calling of the Ministry*, 10:222.
160. Perkins, *Calling of the Ministry*, 10:224.
161. Perkins, *Art of Prophesying*, 10:334.

them when they are applied by faith. Drawing from Matthew 18:18,[162] Perkins gives the following example:

> A true minister sees a sinner burdened in his sins, and still rebelling against the will of God. He, therefore, declares unto him his unrighteousness and his sin, and denounces unto him the miseries and curses of God's justice as [are] due unto him for the same. Here he binds on earth, here he retains on earth. This man's sins are likewise bound and retained in heaven. On the other side, he sees a penitent and believing man. He pronounces forgiveness of sins and happiness unto him for the same. He looses him from the band of his sins by declaring unto him his righteousness. This man's sins are likewise loosed and remitted in heaven, and God Himself does pronounce him clear in heaven when the minister does on earth. Thus, God confirms the word of His servants, and performs the counsel of His messengers.[163]

What the minister promises and provides on earth from God's Word are the promises made and given by God in heaven. That is why Perkins recognizes that the ministry is a high and excellent calling—because the minister possesses the power of the keys, the promises and threats (rightly applied) are to be seen "as from God" and we are "to submit to them accordingly."[164] Application becomes critical in Perkins's preaching because by it "God Himself ratifies and makes good."[165] Perkins says, "It is all one as though God from heaven had said so unto you"[166] The promises of God are to be trusted and therefore applied. When rightly applied they become the believer's prized possession.

In sum, the minister is to proclaim and apply God's Word, but unless it is received personally by faith there is no blessing. "No man can receive pardon of sins and eternal life but for himself."[167] Holding to the promises of the gospel produces hope.

---

162. "Verily I say unto you, Whatsoever ye shall bind on earth shall be bound in heaven: and whatsoever ye shall loose on earth shall be loosed in heaven."
163. Perkins, *Calling of the Ministry*, 10:223.
164. Perkins, *Calling of the Ministry*, 10:223.
165. Perkins, *Calling of the Ministry*, 10:224.
166. Perkins, *Calling of the Ministry*, 10:224.
167. Perkins, *How to Live*, 10:26.

## *The Message*

The apostle Paul writes, "For we through the Spirit wait for the hope of righteousness by faith. For in Jesus Christ neither circumcision availeth any thing, nor uncircumcision; but faith which worketh by love" (Gal 5:5–6). Perkins notes that faith apprehends "the promise" and thereby "brings forth hope. And faith by means of hope makes them that believe to wait."[168] In other words, hope is a by-product of faith, yet it is also a means to sustain faith. Paul declares that Christ's second coming is "that blessed hope" (Titus 2:13). It is "the hope of righteousness," which Perkins identifies as "salvation or life eternal."[169] Although the righteousness of Christ is imputed to us when we first believe, "the fruition and the full revelation thereof is reserved to the life to come when Christ our righteousness shall appear and . . . be accomplished in us."[170] The sealing of the Holy Spirit gives unto the elect "evident assurance that the promise of life belongs to them."[171] Now they must "wait for the full revelation of their imputed righteousness and for everlasting life."[172] Paul describes this as the glorious revealing of the sons of God (Rom 8:19). According to Perkins, this is the believer's hope of eschatological glory.

### THE NATURE OF HOPE

Perkins defines hope as "a gift of God whereby we wait for the mercy of Jesus Christ to eternal life."[173] He believes it is fixed on six objects: (1) justification and the remission of sins; (2) sanctification in this life; (3) the accomplishment of sanctification at the end of this life; (4) the resurrection of the body and its reunification with the soul; (5) the glorification of body and soul; and (6) life everlasting in heaven.[174] No one has seen these things with his eyes, yet the believer hopes for them. It is faith, explains Perkins, that gives unto believers "such a certain assurance of them that they seem

---

168. Perkins, *Galatians*, 2:329.
169. Perkins, *Galatians*, 2:329.
170. Perkins, *Galatians*, 2:329.
171. Perkins, *Discourse of Conscience*, 8:63.
172. Perkins, *Galatians*, 2:329.
173. Perkins, *Jude*, 4:237.
174. Perkins, *Cloud of Faithful Witnesses*, 3:7.

present unto us, and we seem presently to enjoy them."[175] While we cannot enjoy them fully at present, faith has the power to give them a "present being in our hearts and us such a real possession of them as greatly delights a Christian soul, insomuch as the feeling of the sweetness of this glory, though it be to come, overwhelms the feeling of a worldly misery, thought it be present."[176]

"Life everlasting is a thing to be hoped for," writes Perkins.[177] While we cannot see it with the physical eye, faith presents it to the eye of the soul, which apprehends and enjoys it now, making that which is absent and invisible truly present and visible. Perkins says, "Yet if a man have grace certainly to believe the promises of God, these things shall have a being to his soul, in that both his judgment knows assuredly they shall come to pass, and his soul in most lively and joyful representations seems to enjoy them."[178] Therefore, seeing our perfection of sanctification, resurrection, and glorification with the eye of the soul now is a sustaining hope that one day we will walk by a sight of the eye in glorious immortality (2 Cor 5:7).

### The Object of Hope

Ultimately, this hope is fixed on a person—Jesus Christ. He has purchased (and, therefore, ensures) every promise. He who made them is faithful to bring them to pass (1 Thess 5:24). Therefore, we "must be certain without doubting."[179] This means that we must hope against hope (Rom 4:18), hoping "against all human hope, reason, sense, and whatsoever may be grounded upon these."[180] Also, we must be patient. "Otherwise," says Perkins, "the thing hoped for deferred makes our waiting painful and tedious."[181] Lastly, we must be grounded in the Word. Perkins comments, "The ground and anchor of our hope is made not only the promise but the oath of God, who cannot lie, although He should not swear, 'that we might hold fast the hope that is set before us' (Heb 6:18)."[182]

---

175. Perkins, *Cloud of Faithful Witnesses*, 3:7.
176. Perkins, *Cloud of Faithful Witnesses*, 3:7.
177. Perkins, *Cloud of Faithful Witnesses*, 3:8.
178. Perkins, *Cloud of Faithful Witnesses*, 3:8.
179. Perkins, *Jude*, 4:237.
180. Perkins, *Jude*, 4:237.
181. Perkins, *Jude*, 4:237.
182. Perkins, *Jude*, 4:237.

## The Content of Hope

Perkins makes it clear that we wait "not for gold, silver, honors, pleasures, but only for the mercy of God in Christ unto life eternal."[183] This mercy concerns not only that which we enjoy at present, but "the full measure and accomplishment of God's mercies hereafter to be enjoyed."[184] As Paul says, "Even we ourselves groan within ourselves, waiting for the adoption, to wit, the redemption of our body" (Rom 8:23).

## The Fruit of Hope

This waiting, proclaims Perkins, "shall bring us unto and set us in the possession of [eternal] life."[185] This teaches us seven important lessons. (1) We must learn to "rest upon Christ and quiet our hearts in him."[186] (2) We must learn to wait "for life everlasting even to death."[187] (3) "We must abide in the Lord's leisure," meaning we learn to present all our petitions to God.[188] (4) We must learn to depend wholly upon Christ. (5) We must learn that this hope never deceives nor disappoints. Hope in Christ never "deceives a man in time of need, no, not in death itself."[189] (6) We must believe our own perseverance in grace, "for where this hope is such a man cannot fall wholly from Christ."[190] (7) We must learn that this hope "brings us to the beginnings of this happiness even in this life."[191]

This fruit stirs up the hearts of all who exercise them unto "daily repentance and reformation of life."[192] In closing, Perkins declares,

> It stands us then in hand to try the truth of this hope within ourselves and manifest the truth of it unto others, and both these by this note—namely, that we find it to purge our hearts and lives and that it conform us unto Christ. For if we hope to be like Him after

---

183. Perkins, *Jude*, 4:237.
184. Perkins, *Jude*, 4:238.
185. Perkins, *Jude*, 4:238.
186. Perkins, *Jude*, 4:238.
187. Perkins, *Jude*, 4:239.
188. Perkins, *Jude*, 4:239.
189. Perkins, *Jude*, 4:240.
190. Perkins, *Jude*, 4:240.
191. Perkins, *Jude*, 4:240.
192. Perkins, *Jude*, 4:240.

this life, we must labor to resemble Him even in this life by being in some measure pure, holy, innocent, meek, loving, etc., even as He was. For otherwise if our lives are not in some reformation of ourselves and conformity to our Head, suitable to the profession of our hope, it is but pretense of hope and will make men in the end ashamed.[193]

Eschatological hope, that comes through the proclamation of Christ's glorious promises, produces a present and unflinching resolve. According to Perkins, it "makes a man bold in God's presence, and desirous rather than afraid to behold God's glory, which shall be most apparent at the last day."[194] This causes believers to be "bold before God... [and] makes [them] draw near unto God and to rejoice in His presence."[195] Therefore, declares Perkins, "Let all men here learn the way to true courage and boldness before God." It includes (1) repenting daily of sin and (2) laboring to grow in true holiness.[196] In doing so, "you shall rejoice in God's presence in this world, and delight to think of God, to speak of God, to pray unto Him, to meet Him in His Word and sacraments, and at the last day you shall stand with confidence before the throne of His glory."[197]

## The Fuel for Holiness

Third, Perkins's concept of eschatological glory is central to his pursuit of holiness. The apostle Paul writes, "Having therefore these promises, dearly beloved, let us cleanse ourselves from all filthiness of the flesh and spirit, perfecting holiness in the fear of God" (2 Cor 7:1). Eschatological glory (the "promises") is to shape the believer's present existence, in that it provides the motive and means to sanctification. Perkins remarks, "Therefore, let us now diligently endeavor to be that in this life which we desire to be found of God in the day of judgment."[198] One of the most notable effects of sanctification is the "desire and love [for] Christ's coming and the day of judgment, [and] that an end may be made of the days of sin."[199]

193. Perkins, *Jude*, 4:240–41.
194. Perkins, *Calling of the Ministry*, 10:257.
195. Perkins, *Calling of the Ministry*, 10:257.
196. Perkins, *Calling of the Ministry*, 10:257.
197. Perkins, *Calling of the Ministry*, 10:257.
198. Perkins, *True Gain*, 9:56.
199. Perkins, *Golden Chain*, 6:263.

Having received the first degree of eternal life, believers are to "endeavor to come to perfection."[200] Christ commands his followers: "Be ye perfect as your heavenly Father is perfect" (Matt 5:48). Perkins laments that many grow weary of the gospel, fail to profit from it, and fall away from it because they do not consider the call of the gospel upon their lives. He urges his readers to remember "three caveats," so as to "make good proceedings in our religion."[201] The first is to endeavor to "see and feel" the smallness of one's faith, repentance, fear of God, etc., and the corruption that remains in the flesh. The second is to remember "things past, and go on to do more good."[202] "We must live in this world as pilgrim's and strangers," says Perkins, "even in the midst of all our peace and prosperity, of all our liberty, riches, lands, and possessions, yea, of all our worldly friends and acquaintance."[203] The third is to "set before us the crown of eternal glory, and to seek to apprehend it."[204]

This "crown of eternal glory" is found in Christ alone. For this reason, Perkins exhorts believers to find their "all" in Christ, to come to him by faith, and to cleave to him with their whole heart. Consideration of Christ should "excite" us in "every way to draw near to Him as much as possible."[205] Perkins adds, "For when [Christ] was incarnate, He came near unto us by taking our nature upon Him, that we again, whatsoever we are, might come near unto Him by taking unto us His divine nature."[206] Christ became bone of our bone and flesh of our flesh, and therefore we must labor to become bone of his bone and flesh of his flesh. Meditating upon the realities of Christ's incarnation and our union with him "should be a spur to prick us forward still more and more to come to Christ."[207] This, in turn, will compel us to lay aside all pride and self-serving and to practice all duties of humility and self-giving. We purge "our hands and hearts of all our sins," labor to "become conformable unto Him in holiness of life and to become new creatures," and seek to be "plentiful in all good works."[208] Believers labor

---

200. Perkins, *Galatians*, 2:49.
201. Perkins, *Galatians*, 2:50.
202. Perkins, *Galatians*, 2:50.
203. Perkins, *Cloud of Faithful Witnesses*, 3:147.
204. Perkins, *Galatians*, 2:50.
205. Perkins, *Exposition of the Creed*, 5:122.
206. Perkins, *Exposition of the Creed*, 5:122.
207. Perkins, *Exposition of the Creed*, 5:122.
208. Perkins, *Exposition of the Creed*, 5:371.

until death, when they will be crowned with the "glorious qualities" that Christ received after his resurrection.[209]

All of this means that, for Perkins, death is not to be feared. No one knows the time, place, or manner of their death, and, therefore, they always ought to seek "to enter into [their] habitation and true resting place."[210] "While we are on this earth," proclaims Perkins, "we must wait for heaven and look and long after it. There must our joy and our affections be."[211] The means whereby we are aided in this are as follows.

First, we are to endeavor to be ready to enter our heavenly habitation. "Yea, our whole conversation must be in heaven," says Perkins, "while [we] ourselves are upon the earth."[212] We must be aware of the "strait account and reckoning of all our thoughts and words, and actions, which we must make unto God at the last day of judgment."[213]

Second, we are to love the assemblies of God's people and unite in "the holy use of the Word and sacraments, whereby we draw near unto heaven itself."[214] All the assemblies of God, says Perkins, "are the doors and gates of heaven itself, yea, the very entry into it."[215]

Third, we are to wean our affections from our earthly inheritance and fix them upon the sure habitation of heaven. Perkins explains that all will give an account to God, and this should move us to a "daily forehand reckoning with God in the practice of true repentance," and to "employ the good gifts and blessings" we have received from God unto the "best advantage of His glory."[216]

Fourth, we are to "address and prepare" ourselves for death, seeing it as "a means to bring us home to this habitation."[217] This requires serious consideration of our present estate before God, whether it is a state of sin or grace. And, therefore, Perkins calls upon his readers to avail themselves of the means of grace and find the seals of adoption in them (true faith and repentance). In doing so, "the comfort whereof will be so precious unto our

---

209. Perkins, *Exposition of the Creed*, 5:125.
210. Perkins, *Jude*, 4:122. See also Perkins, *Treatise of Man's Imaginations*, 9:250–51.
211. Perkins, *Cloud of Faithful Witnesses*, 3:157.
212. Perkins, *Jude*, 4:123.
213. Perkins, *Treatise of Man's Imaginations*, 9:251.
214. Perkins, *Jude*, 4:123.
215. Perkins, *Jude*, 4:123.
216. Perkins, *Treatise of Man's Imaginations*, 9:251. See also Perkins, *Jude*, 4:123.
217. Perkins, *Jude*, 4:124.

soul that we shall abhor to admit such wicked imaginations into our mind as any way tend to deprive us of it."[218]

Fifth, we are to be content "to leave and forsake goods, friends, native country, and all for assurance of inheritance in this our country."[219] For Christ himself says, "Verily I say unto you, There is no man that hath left house, or parents, or brethren, or wife, or children, for the kingdom of God's sake, Who shall not receive manifold more in this present time, and I the world to come life everlasting" (Luke 18:29–30).

These are the means by which believers die well, that is, die in the full assurance of faith. The death of a Christian, "which is the gate of glory," is to die in faith, and he who dies in faith "is he that receives the crown."[220]

> Oh then, what joyful news must this be unto all repentant and sorrowful sinners, when the King of heaven and earth comes unto them by death and bids them lay their bodies as ragged and patched garments, and prepare themselves to put on the princely robe of immortality? No tongue is able to express the excellency of this most blessed and happy estate.[221]

In Christ, believers receive all things necessary for life and godliness. Yet not all things are for this present life alone but are for the life to come. All the graces and gifts in Christ are given now, in order that the elect will "endure to everlasting life."[222] The grace of perseverance, gifted to the elect by Christ, produces in them a present and continual hope. It is a sure and everlasting hope because it is founded upon sure and everlasting promises: the promise of salvation, the promise of resurrection, and the promise of glorification. Perkins concludes,

> These be, as Saint Peter calls them, "great and precious promises" (2 Peter 1:4). And surely it must be a great and precious faith that can constantly believe these. No better helps of our faith can there be than often and seriously to consider of the mercy and power of Him that made them. If He be willing and able, what can let the performance of them? Let us therefore often say with holy Paul, "Faithful is he which hath promised, who will also do

---

218. Perkins, *Treatise of Man's Imaginations*, 9:252.
219. Perkins, *Jude*, 4:124.
220. Perkins, *Cloud of Faithful Witnesses*, 3:191, 193.
221. Perkins, *Salve for a Sick Man*, 10:436–37.
222. Perkins, *Jude*, 4:37.

it" (1 Thess 5:4), and with Sarah here, "We judge him faithful which hath promised."[223]

## The Anchor in Suffering

"Being confident of this very thing, that he which hath begun a good work in you will perform it until the day of Jesus Christ" (Phil 1:6). Here Paul conveys the reality that the believer's salvation is not yet complete, but that Christ will bring it to completion. The salvation of the elect has been purchased by the perfect work of Christ. They have been united to his body, filled with his Spirit, forgiven of their sins, and counted as righteous before God. Yet the revealing of the sons of God in glory is future (Rom 8:19). Christ says, "But he that shall endure unto the end, the same shall be saved" (Matt 24:13). The question, therefore, is this: How does one endure to the end?

For Perkins, perseverance is rooted in the eschatological promises of God in Christ. "He that has begun the work will bring it to completion," as Paul said (Phil 1:6). God's people have a pre-determined destination, and it ought always to be in the forefront of their minds. For Perkins, it must be central to all doctrines concerning man and his salvation. God has promised to preserve and perfect the work he has started in his people. Perseverance, therefore, rests on God's promise of eschatological glory. As in the pursuit of personal holiness, the promises of God become the means whereby perseverance is accomplished in the believer.

"After we have received the grace of renovation," writes Perkins, "we do also receive a will to persevere constantly in that good which we can do."[224] Like all that is given to the believer in Christ, perseverance is a gift of grace. According to Perkins, perseverance is contingent upon (1) the power to persevere and (2) the will to persevere.[225] Both are God's gifts. Those who truly believe "have received of God both power to persevere in grace if they will and also will to do that which they have power to do."[226] In other words, by his sovereign grace, God powerfully turns the individual's will, thereby making him (who was once unwilling) willing. Perkins writes, "The people of God that are turned and guided by the free Spirit of God must be

---

223. Perkins, *Cloud of Faithful Witnesses*, 3:180.
224. Perkins, *Manner and Order of Predestination*, 6:374.
225. Perkins, *God's Free Grace and Man's Free Will*, 6:427.
226. Perkins, *Manner and Order of Predestination*, 6:374.

a voluntary people and with all alacrity and cheerfulness do the duties that pertain to them of a ready mind, even as if there were neither heaven nor hell, judge nor judgment after this life."[227]

The grace of perseverance, for Perkins, is something that must be proclaimed as much as any other gift (i.e., justification and sanctification).[228] It is a gift that will accomplish exactly what it sets out to do—to ensure that believers are brought before the throne of God to behold his glory in the face of Christ. The foundation for perseverance, therefore, consists of the promises of God in Christ. Perkins links perseverance to the covenant of redemption and the promises made to Christ in eternity. "For the office of Christ to which He is set apart," expounds Perkins, "is to receive the promise of God for us and to apply it unto us."[229] These promises are ultimately perfect and complete redemption in Christ, the crown of glory.

In the covenant of redemption, Christ is given a people along with sure and everlasting promises. By his incarnation, Christ establishes the covenant of grace. He then mediates those benefits, rewards, and promises to all who are one with him. These promises include, not only the declarative status that we are sons of God, but also the reality that we will be fully transformed into the perfect image of the Son of God. And so, for Perkins, along with the gifts of faith, calling, justification, and sanctification is "joined inseparably the grace of perseverance unto the end."[230] This is grounded in God's election, God's promises in the covenant of grace, the offices of Christ, and the quality of grace "whose nature is to endure to life everlasting."[231]

Perseverance, therefore, is the necessary outcome of the gifts found in Christ. It is also the fuel by which the believer completes the race set before him. "For when a man is supported by the power of Christ," exhorts Perkins, "he may be able to bear many crosses patiently with a contented mind, and persevere in bearing of it howsoever long the cross endures."[232] Perkins urges believers to avail themselves of the means of grace (Word and sacrament), and to lay hold of all the promises of eschatological glory in Christ. All who are found faithful will overcome and endure to the end.

227. Perkins, *God's Free Grace and Man's Free Will*, 6:428.
228. Perkins, *Art of Prophesying*, 10:340.
229. Perkins, *Galatians*, 2:190.
230. Perkins, *Jude*, 4:37.
231. Perkins, *Jude*, 4:37.
232. Perkins, *Treatise on whether a Man is in Damnation or Grace*, 8:502.

Perkins's confidence is rooted "in God, that cannot lie" (Titus 1:2). In refuting the "popish doctors" who deny that believers can be certain of their perseverance unto the end,[233] Perkins turns to the Lord's Prayer: "Lead us not into temptation." This request entails "that God would not suffer us to be wholly overcome of the devil in any temptation; and to this petition we have a promise answerable, 'That God with the temptation will give an issue' (1 Cor 10:13)."[234] Thus, Perkins remarks, "Howsoever the devil may buffet, molest, and wound the servants of God, yet shall he never be able to overcome them."[235] When a believer becomes a member of Christ, by the nature of the covenant of grace he can never be wholly cut off. Once in Christ, he can never be severed from Christ. All who fall in sin will be brought to repentance by God's grace and thereby remain in favor with God. Likewise, all who fall to persecution will not fall "wholly, because the seed of God remains in them, nor finally, because in time they shall return unto the Lord again."[236]

Perkins concludes by exhorting his readers. First, he exhorts them to remember that God's promise to preserve his people is not spoken in general to the members of Christ's body, but "in singular to every true member thereof, because they are the words of the covenant."[237] Second, he exhorts them to note "the unspeakable goodness of God," for "he not only gives a new life, but preserves it in us . . . God has restored this life again to believers, but that they might be sure of it He Himself will now keep it for them."[238] Perkins's point is to show that in regeneration God has granted eternal, not temporal, life in Christ. Because Christ has received his reward, all the elect will share in his glorious inheritance. Third, Perkins exhorts them to be "stirred up to prayer for this gift of preservation to life everlasting and reservation to Christ, hungering for grace after grace, to be strengthened in temptation, especially in this last and declining age, wherein the gospel takes little place in our hearts."[239]

---

233. Perkins, *Reformed Catholic*, 7:31.
234. Perkins, *Reformed Catholic*, 7:31.
235. Perkins, *Reformed Catholic*, 7:31.
236. Perkins, *Jude*, 4:37.
237. Perkins, *True Gain*, 9:44.
238. Perkins, *Jude*, 4:38.
239. Perkins, *Jude*, 4:38. Aiding to these exhortations, Ralph Cudworth, who supplemented and completed Perkins's *Galatians Commentary*, proclaims,

## Conclusion

Perkins was convinced that the Roman Church was the beast of John's Apocalypse. Unsurprisingly, therefore, he viewed himself as a defender of the Church of England against the threat of Rome.[240] He defined a "Reformed Catholic" as someone who "holds the same necessary heads of religion with the Roman Church, yet so as he pares off and rejects all errors in doctrine whereby the said religion is corrupted."[241] These Romish errors touch various subjects such as freewill, original sin, justification, saints, purgatory, sacraments, repentance, faith, etc. Expounding each, Perkins seeks to demonstrate "how far forth we may join with them" and "how far forth and wherein we must dissent and depart from them."[242]

Once we have determined Rome's departure from the truth, we must take Revelation 18:4 to heart: "And I heard another voice from heaven, saying, Come out of her, my people, that ye be not partakers of her sins, and that ye receive not of her plagues." In Perkins's estimation, this departure from Rome is necessary to avoid participating in "her sins." For this reason Perkins expended much of his time and effort attempting to "stir up and kindle in the minds of [his] countrymen a further detestation and loathing of the Romish religion."[243] In sum, "All those who will be saved, must depart

> We must persevere and continue to the end, otherwise we cannot look to reap the harvest of eternal happiness. It is nothing but constancy and continuing in well doing, that does crown all our good works.... God is Alpha and Omega, and therefore requires a good end as well as a good beginning, and it is our duty not only to obey the commandment of Christ, *venite ad me*, "Come unto me" (Matt 11:28), but that also, *manete in me*, "Abide in me" (John 15:4), for he only that continues to the end shall be saved (Matt 24:13). (Cudworth, *Supplement: Or, Continuation of the Commentary upon the Sixth Chapter*, 2:507–8)

240. "Polemical theology was the order of the day . . . [for] much was at stake in the religious reforms and alignments under way after Elizabeth's accession." Paterson, *William Perkins*, 6.

241. Perkins, *Reformed Catholic*, 7:5.

242. Perkins, *Reformed Catholic*, 7:12. His purpose is threefold. (1) "To confute all such politics as hold and maintain that our religion and that of the Roman Church differ not in substance, and consequently that they may be reconciled." (2) "That the papists which think so basely of our religion may be won to a better liking of it when they shall see how near we come unto them in sundry points." (3) "That the common Protestant might in some part see and conceive the points of difference between us and the Church of Rome and know in what manner and how far forth we condemn the opinions of said church." Perkins, *Reformed Catholic*, 7:5.

243. Perkins, *Warning Against the Idolatry*, 7:415.

and separate themselves from the faith and religion of this present Church of Rome."[244]

One dogma that particularly vexed Perkins was that of purgatory. In his argument against this dogma, he quotes Augustine's assertion that, after death, "there remains no compunction or satisfaction."[245] He also quotes Cyril: "They which are once dead can add nothing to the things which they have done, but shall remain as they were left, and wait for the time of judgment."[246] For Perkins, there is no such thing as purgatory (in the Roman Catholic sense of the word). But there is another kind of purgatory: "Nothing can free us from the least punishment of the smallest sin but the sufferings of Christ—and purge us from the least taint of corruption, saving the blood of Christ."[247] As Scripture declares, Christ "hath purged our sins by Himself" (Heb 1:3). Appealing to this text, Perkins holds to a "Christian purgatory" that takes place in this life. It consists of "the afflictions of God's children."[248] They are the means through which God's people are "cleansed from their corruption, as gold from the dross by the fire,"[249] thereby preparing them for eschatological glory.

It is this hope that resides at the heart of Perkins's spirituality. As demonstrated in this chapter, it shaped his practice of biblical meditation, method of pastoral ministry, pursuit of personal holiness, and approach to personal suffering. For Perkins, "The price and crown for which we run is everlasting glory.... The judge of the runners is the Lord Himself, who has appointed this race unto every Christian in this life, who also will give the reward to everyone that runs well."[250] This means that we must heed the apostle's admonition: "Let us run with patience the race that is set before us" (Heb 12:1).

---

244. Perkins, *Reformed Catholic*, 7:12.
245. Perkins, *Reformed Catholic*, 7:127.
246. Perkins, *Reformed Catholic*, 7:127.
247. Perkins, *Reformed Catholic*, 7:127.
248. Perkins, *Reformed Catholic*, 7:126.
249. Perkins, *Reformed Catholic*, 7:126.
250. Perkins, *Cloud of Faithful Witnesses*, 3:410.

# Conclusion

WILLIAM PERKINS BEGINS HIS famous work, *A Golden Chain*, with these words: "Theology is the science of living blessedly forever. Blessed life arises from the knowledge of God."[1] This statement is at the heart of his spirituality. Without question, the knowledge of God begins in the mind, but Perkins was careful to explain that it does not remain there but descends to the heart and manifests itself in all of life. It is the key, therefore, to "living blessedly forever." Central to this knowledge of God is the hope of eschatological glory as found in Jesus Christ. The aim of this book has been to account for this conviction in Perkins, while demonstrating how it shaped his spirituality.

To that end, chapter 2 communicated what Perkins believes concerning the relationship between the believer's blessed hope and the beatific vision. He stands in a long tradition of those who affirm that, while believers will enjoy the sight of the soul at death, their real hope is the sight of the eye at the resurrection, when they will behold the glory of God in the face of Jesus Christ.

Chapters 3–5 demonstrated how Perkins's eschatological hope is related to his convictions concerning God's eternal covenant ("God to us"), God's sending of his Son to become one with us in our humanity ("God with us"), and God's sending of his Spirit by whom we are made one with Christ ("God in us"). In brief, God created man with a specific end in view—the enjoyment of him. Christ has secured this (as our Prophet, Priest, and King) by his death, burial, and resurrection. All that he accomplishes in his

---

1. Perkins, *Golden Chain*, 6:11.

life, and receives at his glorification, constitutes the inheritance believers will receive in glory. For this to happen, they are united to Christ through faith. Everything accrues to them through the covenant of grace, but they enter this covenant through union with Christ. Because they are one with him, they enjoy the blessings of justification, adoption, sanctification, and glorification.

This hope is foundational to Perkins's life and ministry. Chapter 6 was devoted to an analysis of this reality. His hope of eschatological glory was the subject of his meditation, the aim of his ministry, the fuel of his holiness, and the anchor in his suffering. In short, Perkins believed that an appreciation of who we are in Christ, and what we will be in Christ, changes everything. When this future hope becomes a present reality, it shapes all of life.

Each of these subjects could be a book in their own right—Perkins's practice of meditation, method of ministry, pursuit of holiness, and approach to suffering. This work has established the close relationship between these facets of Perkins's spiritual life and his conviction concerning eschatological glory. It remains to others to develop these in greater detail.

Without question, Perkins was a towering figure in his day, as his influence extended well beyond the confines of Cambridge. Centuries later, he still has much to say to the church. Among the many lessons we can learn from him stands his assertion that the hope of glory is the believer's greatest need. In a day in which so many seem preoccupied with the material and temporal, Perkins's conviction might seem sorely out of touch. Yet it is this very response that makes his message so necessary. As the apostle Paul penned centuries ago, "Our conversation is in heaven; from whence also we look for the Saviour, the Lord Jesus Christ: Who shall change our vile body, that it may be fashioned like unto his glorious body, according to the working whereby he is able even to subdue all things unto himself" (Phil 3:20–21).

Perkins was convinced of this. In sum, when we die, our bodies will be placed in the grave where they will decay, but our renewed souls will enter heaven to be with Christ. We will behold him with the eye of the soul, and it will be glorious. But this is not the end of the story. When Christ returns in glory, he will bring our renewed souls with him, and he will raise our decayed bodies from the grave. At that moment, our bodies and souls will be reunited, and we will behold God's glory in the face of Christ. We will be glorious in soul; we will be partakers of the divine nature, that is, divine virtues and qualities (2 Pet 1:4). We will also be glorious in body; we will have glorified bodies like Christ's.

It is this eschatological hope that gives ballast amid life's many storms—strength in the face of temptation and fortitude in the fire of persecution. It is this eschatological hope that enables believers to navigate life's manifold perils and pitfalls. It is this eschatological hope that compels believers to live for the glory of God during their earthly sojourn. In sum, for Perkins, it is this future hope (what it will mean to be crowned with immortal glory), that determines the course of the believer's life at present.

# APPENDIX 1

## The Book of Revelation

THE PURPOSE OF THIS appendix is to understand Perkins in the broader context of his contemporaries' interpretation of the book of Revelation. Crawford Gribben acknowledges that "eschatology was not something Puritans studied so much as something in which they believed themselves to be involved."[1] They saw themselves as living out John's apocalyptic vision. They were convinced that much of the book had been fulfilled, and yet some elements were still to be fulfilled before Christ's return. They believed they were seeing John's vision unfold before their eyes.[2] Like most of his contemporaries, Perkins believed that the time line of Revelation fell between the two advents of Christ and, therefore, spanned the entire history of the church. Believing that John penned his vision during the reign of Domitian (AD 81–96),[3] Perkins writes, "This prophecy concerns the present and future state of the church,"[4] and its purpose is "to make known and manifest things to come"[5] for "the great good and comfort of [God's] children to the end of the world."[6]

Perkins's historicist interpretation was the popular view among Protestants in the sixteenth and seventeenth centuries.[7] Peter Toon describes

---

1. Gribben, *Puritan Millennium*, 13–14.
2. Beeke and Jones, *Puritan Theology*, 774–75.
3. Perkins, *Revelation*, 4:361–62.
4. Perkins, *Revelation*, 4:318.
5. Perkins, *Revelation*, 4:312.
6. Perkins, *Revelation*, 4:308.
7. Other views include Preterism, Futurism, and Idealism. For an overview of these, see Gregg, *Revelation, Four Views*.

APPENDIX 1

this interpretive model as the "modified Augustinian historicist approach."[8] In his debate with the Chiliasts/Millenarists,[9] Augustine recognized two possible interpretations of the millennium. First, it might refer to "what remains of the thousand years that make up the 'sixth day.'"[10] Second, it might refer to "the entire course of time this world has still to go" between the first and second comings of Christ.[11] The second interpretation became more most widely accepted than the first. The Puritans "modified" Augustine's view in two ways. (1) They affirmed that there would be a great conversion of Jews prior to Christ's return. They developed this view based on their interpretation of Romans 11. Ian Murray identifies this expectation as the

---

8. Toon, *Puritans*, 6.

9. *Millenarianism* (Latin: one thousand) or *Chiliasm* (Greek: one thousand). Estévao Bettencourt gives a compendium of chiliastic thought in Christian theology: "(i) the second coming of Christ, in majesty; (ii) the first resurrection, that of the just only; (iii) a general judgment, of the nations as a whole, not of individuals; (iv) a messianic kingdom lasting a thousand years; (v) the second resurrection, that of all men; (vi) last judgment, of all persons individually; (vii) the eternal destiny, reward or punishment." Hill, *Regnum Caelorum*, 5. See also Shedd, *History of Christian Doctrine*, 2:389–98; Cross and Livingstone, *Oxford Dictionary of the Christian Church*, s.v. "millienarianism."

10. Regarding the first interpretation, "this event is to take place in the sixth and last millennium (the sixth 'day'), the latter span of which is now passing, and that when St. John spoke of the last part of this millennium as 'a thousand years' he was using, figuratively, the whole to indicate a part. (After this 'sixth day' will come the 'sabbath' that has no evening, namely, the endless repose of the blessed)." Augustine, *City of God*, 269. Perkins rejects this view, writing, "You do abuse the place of Scripture which is in St. Peter [cf. 2 Peter 3:8]. For his meaning is this: that the greatest time and the smallest differ not in respect of God, to whom all times are present." Perkins, *Fruitful Dialogue*, 6:460. Perkins also refutes this view in Perkins, *Exposition of the Creed*, 5:287–88.

11. Pertaining to the second interpretation, Augustine writes,

> The "thousand years" stand for all the years of the Christian era, a perfect number being used to indicate the "fullness of time." For the number one thousand is the cube of ten. Ten times ten equals one hundred, which is already a square, but still a plane, figure; to give it depth and make it a cube, one hundred is further multiplied by ten to make a thousand. Now, it is true that the number one hundred is sometimes made to stand for "all." Thus, our Lord promised to anyone leaving all things to follow Him: "He shall receive a hundredfold." One may say that St. Paul explains this in the words, "As having nothing yet possessing all things," taken in connection with an earlier text: "All the world's riches belong to the man of faith." How much more properly, then, does the number one thousand stand for the whole, since it is the cube, whereas one hundred is only the square, of ten? (Augustine, *City of God*, 266)

impetus for Puritan post-millennialism.[12] (2) They held that the millennium was a literal one thousand years that spans Christ's two advents.

Perkins believed that the book of Revelation was a "prophetical history" concerning the church from the time of John to the end of the world.[13] Even though an analysis of that history can be elicited from Perkins's works, there is not a dedicated treatise on that thought. The closest summary is found in *A Digest or Harmony of the Books of the Old and New Testament*. In contrast, several of his contemporaries provided detailed explanations of "modified Augustinian historicism."[14]

## *Robert Hill*

In 1596, Robert Hill produced *The Contents of Scripture: Containing the sum of every Book and chapter of the old and new Testament*, in which he lays out a succinct description of each chapter in Revelation.[15] In 1604, Hill wrote the prescript to Perkins's *A Godly and Learned Exposition or Commentary Upon the Three First Chapters of the Revelation*. His prescript includes a summary of Revelation.

Hill held a historicist view, believing John's vision describes "things to fall out after [Christ's] ascension."[16] John provides "Christ's history" in his gospel account, and "the church's history" in his apocalypse.[17] Chapters 1–3 describe the church in John's time. Chapters 4 and 5 describe the authors of the revelation: God the Father and His Son Jesus Christ. Chapters 6–9 provide an overview of world history. Here John speaks of the miseries that come upon the world (chap. 6), the preservation of God's elect from those miseries (chap. 7), and the judgment of God upon sinners (chaps. 8–9).[18]

---

12  Toon, *Puritans*, 6. See Murray, *Puritan Hope*, 45–46.

13. Perkins, *Art of Prophesying*, 10:296.

14. These contemporaries are Robert Hill (d. 1623), George Gifford (1548–1620), and Thomas Brightman (1556–1607). The criteria for choosing these three theologians are as follows. (1) They are English Protestants. (2) They are Perkins's contemporaries. (3) They wrote on John's Apocalypse during Perkins's lifetime. (4) They provided a concise analysis of Revelation. For a brief biography of Robert Hill, see Beeke and Pederson, *Meet the Puritans*. For George Gifford and Thomas Brightman, see Brook, *Lives of the Puritans*.

15. See appendix 2.

16. Hill, *Contents of Scripture*, 507.

17. Hill, "Dedication Epistle," in Perkins, *Revelation*, 4:291.

18. Hill, *Contents of Scripture*, 510.

According to Hill, the last is a "prediction of things to come."[19] Chapters 10–20 describe the church of Christ. Their events occur concurrently with those of chapters 6–9. Hill is convinced, therefore, that John explains history from two perspectives: the world's (chaps. 6–9) and the church's (chaps. 10–20). John "proceedeth to foretell the future estate of the Church, beginning first with the prophets and teachers of the Church, and so commeth to speak of the body thereof."[20] The church's preachers and teachers fight against its enemies (chap. 11).[21] This struggle begins with "Church of the Jews," which was "assaulted by the Dragon" (chap. 12).[22] It continues with the "Christian Church."[23] Christ defends the church through "preaching" (chap. 14), as it faces threats (chap. 15) and judgments (chap. 16). Eventually, the church is victorious over the whore (chaps. 17–18), the beast (chap. 19), and the dragon (chap. 20).[24] Chapters 21–22 provide a description of "the glory of the church, wherein it perpetually triumpheth, and shall triumph in the heavenly Jerusalem."[25]

## *George Gifford*

In 1599, George Gifford[26] published *Sermons upon the Whole Booke of the Revelation*.[27] He declares that Revelation "is a prophecy which openeth the state of things to come in the world from the time that it was given to John, even to the great day of the general judgement."[28] Like Hill, he believes chapters 1–3 pertain to the time of John with "no opening or foreshadowing

---

19. Hill, "Dedication Epistle," 4:292.

20. Hill, *Contents of Scripture*, 511.

21. These enemies, according to Hill, are the flesh, the world, the devil, the antichrist (the pope), the Turks (Islam), and the wicked. See Hill, *Christ's Prayer Expounded*.

22. Hill, *Contents of Scripture*, 511. This may be taken as John speaking of the early church (Acts 1–10), the entire record of the early church (Acts 1–28,) or the first three hundred years of the church.

23. Hill, *Contents of Scripture*, 512.

24. These are the Church of Rome, the Roman Empire, and the devil.

25. Hill, "Dedication Epistle," 4:293.

26. For more on Gifford, see McGinnis, *George Gifford*.

27. See appendix 3.

28. Gifford, *Sermons upon the Revelation*. Gifford holds to a late date (AD 96) and sees three main visions in Revelation: chaps. 1–3; chaps. 4–11; chaps. 12–22.

of things to come."²⁹ Chapters 4–11 provide a "very brief and dark"³⁰ summary of the entire prophecy from John's time to the general judgment.³¹ The summary begins with a "glorious vision, which setteth forth the majesty, the glory and praise of the most high God" (chap. 4).³² Christ alone is worthy to open the seals (chaps. 5–6). The first seal is Christ's conquest by the gospel over the nations of the world. The second, third, and fourth seals are the plagues and judgments sent upon the "wicked world for despising and abusing the holy and precious gospel."³³ The fifth seal describes "the happy rest of the souls of those which were murdered by the tyrants [persecuting emperors], and cruel rage of the people for the testimony of Jesus."³⁴ The sixth seal contains the "most fearful and horrible tokens of God's displeasure upon the wicked world,"³⁵ and "a spiritual plague of God upon the world, even the staying of the course of the holy gospel."³⁶

Chapter 7 provides a vision of God's protection of His elect on the earth. They endure "great assaults, even in the time of the Antichrist," yet are as "safe as the martyrs in heaven."³⁷ Chapter 8 describes the opening of the seventh seal, which leads to the seven trumpets. The first trumpet marks the coming of the "kingdom of the great Antichrist,"³⁸ while the seventh trumpet marks "the last judgement" (chaps. 8–11).³⁹ More specifically, the first trumpet is the beginning of the "errors, lies, and strong delusions" that come upon the visible church. The second trumpet represents the great

---

29. Gifford, *Sermons upon the Revelation*.
30. Gifford, *Sermons upon the Revelation*.
31. Chaps. 4–6 deal with the first one thousand years of the church; chap. 7 is a transition and exhortation to believers; chaps. 8–11 are events from AD 1000 to the final judgment and Christ's return.
32. Gifford, *Sermons upon the Revelation*.
33. Gifford, *Sermons upon the Revelation*.
34. Gifford, *Sermons upon the Revelation*.
35. Gifford, *Sermons upon the Revelation*, 138.
36. Gifford, *Sermons upon the Revelation*.
37. Gifford, *Sermons upon the Revelation*, 142.
38. Gifford writes, "Thus it is to be understood that popery is the kingdom of the beast, the pope is antichrist." Gifford, "Sermon I," in *Sermons upon the Revelation*. For Gifford, this "coming" began around AD 998 with Pope Sylvester II (998–1003), who Gifford says "was in league with the devil," or Pope Hildebrand (Gregory VII 1073–85), who Gifford describes as a "most horrible wicked Pope, who had also familiarity with the devil and wrought exceeding much mischief." Gifford, *Sermons upon the Revelation*.
39. Gifford, *Sermons upon the Revelation*.

APPENDIX 1

apostasy as professing believers fall from the truth into the kingdom of antichrist. The third trumpet marks the "fall and decline" of pastors within the church who "corrupt the pure doctrine." The fourth trumpet signals the gradual decline of the church because of corrupt teachers. With the fifth trumpet, the "Bishops of Rome" decline to such a degree that they "become the great antichrist."[40] They receive the key to open the door and let in "devilish doctrine, ignorance of the truth, darkness, idolatry, superstition, and all wicked errors."[41] For Gifford, this trumpet is "most undoubtedly certain, and without all controversy, a description of antichrist's full exaltation."[42]

The sounding of the sixth trumpet (chaps. 9–13) introduces another major threat to the church; namely, "the Turks."[43] Gifford writes, "No man of any judgment, as I suppose, can doubt, that this revelation revealing and describing all the greatest calamities and plagues that should come upon men in the world, should not set forth the kingdom of the Turks."[44] The Roman Church and Turkish Empire were seen as posing the greatest threat to the true church. Toon remarks, "References to the Turkish Empire appear in virtually every commentary on the Apocalypse of John which was produced by English Puritans, Independents, Presbyterians and Baptists."[45] Thus, as the Reformation advances, the church faces two great enemies: the "Papists" in the western church and the "Turks" in the eastern church.

The vision of chapter 10 is "joyful" for "after the dark kingdom of antichrist, and that horrible murdering army of the Turks, a mighty angel commeth down from heaven and relieveth the poor Church, and to be avenged

---

40. Gifford, *Sermons upon the Revelation*, 165.

41. Gifford proceeds to declare that "man's devises and superstition greatly increased, the clear light of the most pure doctrine was much dimmed, and so by little and little Antichrist was exalted: and when he was come to his full strength, the pit of hell being opened, that Satan might send forth what strong delusion he would, the case is far more miserable then before." Gifford, *Sermons upon the Revelation*, 165.

42. Gifford, *Sermons upon the Revelation*, 166.

43. Gifford, *Sermons upon the Revelation*. He provides a history of Islam from Mohammad (591) to the fall of Constantinople (1453).

44. Gifford, *Sermons upon the Revelation*, 173. Toon writes, "The year 1300 was believed to have great significance for it was at that time that the Turk became a threat to European civilization. In fact by 1280 the Ottoman Turks were established in northwestern Asia Minor and from this base they expanded their lands by absorbing the decaying Byzantine Empire. In 1450 the great part of the Balkans was conquered and in 1453 Constantinople fell to them." Toon, *Puritans*, 20.

45. Toon, *Puritans*, 19.

of those cruel enemies."[46] It is at this juncture, according to Gifford, that the events of Revelation become current to day: "[God] sendeth forth the gospel again, dispelling the darkness and errors which came by . . . reforming his Church, and gathering great multitudes of his saints together. This vision is fulfilled, or at least begun to be fulfilled in our days: for we live under the opening of the seventh seal, and under the sounding of the sixth trumpet."[47] The "little book" (the Scriptures) is now opened and placed in the hands of "thousand thousands, and ten thousand thousands of God's people, which out of it do learn to know God, and to worship him aright in spirit and in truth." They are delivered from the Papists and Turks. Gifford identified the ministers of his day as those who would "preach the truth for the throwing down of antichrist."[48] They will see "what indignation and grief it worketh when it is known and digested, to see it despised, to see error, falsehood and abominable wickedness exalted and magnified."[49]

Chapter 11 introduces the two witnesses,[50] the third woe,[51] and the seventh trumpet. These presage the recovery, reform, and restoration of the true church which will ultimately destroy the antichrist. It culminates in

---

46. Gifford, *Sermons upon the Revelation*, 181.

47. Gifford, *Sermons upon the Revelation*, 181. Gifford also believed this trumpet was "sounded long," because the "little book" (10:2) was opened and began to give light in 1516/1517 when "Martin Luther began to call some matters into question touching the popery." Gifford, *Sermons upon the Revelation*.

48. Gifford, *Sermons upon the Revelation*, 186.

49. Gifford, *Sermons upon the Revelation*, 187. Perkins has a similar interpretation:

> When we learn that all God's ministers and those which prepare themselves to the work of the ministry are diligently to read and study the holy Scriptures and to meditate therein. . . . And Saint John likewise is commanded "to eat up the little book" (Rev. 10:9-10), which thing he did—all which strongly enforce the former duty, showing that God's servant in the ministry must as it were eat up God's Book, that in judgment and understanding he may digest as far as possible the deep things of God and the hardest places of the Scripture. (Perkins, *Cloud of Faithful Witnesses*, 3:207)

50. For Gifford, the two witnesses are true and worthy servants who teach the Word of God: Heinrich Bullinger (1573), John Napier (1593), Robert Hill (1596), Arthur Dent (1607), Hugh Broughton (1610), James Brocard (1610), Thomas Brightman (1616).

51. In Rev 8:13, John pronounces three "woes" that are announced at the blowing of the fifth, sixth, and seventh trumpets. For Gifford, the first "woe" (9:12) is the rise and defeat of the Roman Church. The second "woe" (11:14) is the rise and defeat of the Turks. And the third "woe" (11:14) is the final judgement at Christ's return.

APPENDIX 1

the "woe of eternal judgment and vengeance," which ends in "the reward of the good and the destruction of the bad."[52]

Chapters 12–22 provide "large and plain descriptions, which open the former things more clearly."[53] Chapter 12 portrays the church militant. Christ casts down the devil from heaven to earth. The devil then wages war against the church. The first beast represents the Roman emperors, while the second beast is the antichrist (the Roman bishop) (chap. 13). Christ preserves and protects His people, the church militant, in the days of antichrist (chap. 14). Chapters 15–16 describe the seven vials and seven plagues poured out upon antichrist and his kingdom. This culminates in Christ's second coming. Chapter 17 describes Babylon (the whore) as the city of Rome, the seat of Antichrist who falls by the "light of the gospel" (chap. 18). Chapter 19 describes "the rejoicing, the triumph, and praising, and the magnifying of the name of God by the heavenly companies of angels and of blessed souls, and by all the faithful upon the earth."[54] The light of the gospel is "carried and spread swiftly over the large dominions of Antichrist, and discloseth all his errors and filthy abominations, and so overcometh and destroyeth the beast."[55] Chapter 20 is the history of how the devil deceived the nations prior to the coming of Christ. The devil was bound and the church flourished for one thousand years. At the end of this time, Satan was loosed and began to seduce the nations by antichrist (the beast) and the Turk (the false prophet). Finally, Gog and Magog (the Papist and the Turk) along with the devil are cast into eternal fire.

Chapters 21–22 describe "the eternal felicity and blessed estate of the Church." Gifford concludes with these words:

> If men do but observe this general course of this prophecy, and studiously observe the handling of matters, they shall find no such darkness as is feared, much less shall it be found so obscure as the Papists do bear in hand, when they would drive men from the

---

52. Gifford, *Sermons upon the Revelation*, 209.

53. Gifford, *Sermons upon the Revelation*. Gifford adds, "There be no new matters (for all things were contained in the book sealed with seven seals, all which seals are opened, and the secrets disclosed, in the brief and dark manner) but here we shall have some of the same things, even the chief and principle which have been so briefly, and so darkly uttered in the opening of the seals, more largely and more clearly for our better instruction, painted out." Gifford, *Sermons upon the Revelation*.

54. Gifford, *Sermons upon the Revelation*, 365.

55. Gifford, *Sermons upon the Revelation*, 377.

reading and study of it, because it painteth out great Babel, that Romish harlot. Farewell in Christ.[56]

## Thomas Brightman

In 1616, Thomas Brightman's *The Revelation of S. John illustrated with an Analysis and scholions. Wherein the sense is opened by the Scripture, and the event of things fore-told, shewed by Histories* was published.[57] He declares that "the matters [of the prophecy] should be begun by and by, and should flow from thence with a perpetual course without interruption, although the final consummation should be afterward for many ages."[58] While the book is addressed to seven churches in John's day, they are representative of seven ages of church history from the time of the apostles to the present day. The church at Ephesus is the age "from the preaching of the apostles to Constantine the great" (1–300).[59] The church at Smyrna is the age from Constantine to Gratian (300–382), when Arianism began to assault the church.[60] The church of Pergamos marks the rise of papal power (380–1300).[61] The church of Thyatira signifies the true church and its struggle against the Roman Church (1300–1520).[62] The last three churches correspond to the first three generation of Reformers. The church of Sardis points to Martin Luther.[63] The church of Philadelphia represents the Reformed churches of "Helvtia, Svevia, Geneva, France, Holland, Scotland."[64] The church at Laodicea is the Church of England (1534 to Brightman's day).[65] The Church of England was not cold "in as much as it doth profess the sound, pure, and sincere doctrine of salvation, by which we have renounced that Antichrist of Rome," but neither was it hot, for its "outward

---

56. Gifford, *Sermons upon the Revelation*.

57. The 1616 edition of this particular work is the third edition of Brightman's commentary. It was originally published in Latin in 1609 (posthumously), and then translated in English in 1615. See appendix 4.

58. Brightman, *Revelation of S. John*, 8.

59. Brightman, *Revelation of S. John*, 52.

60. Brightman, *Revelation of S. John*, 74, 76.

61. Brightman, *Revelation of S. John*, 84, 86.

62. Brightman, *Revelation of S. John*, 97.

63. Brightman, *Revelation of S. John*, 118, 126.

64. Brightman, *Revelation of S. John*, 139. Helvtia is Switzerland, and Svevia is Sweden.

65. Brightman, *Revelation of S. John*, 159.

regiment is as yet for the greatest part Antichristian and Romish." "We stand," writes Brightman, "just in the middle between cold and hot, between the Romish and the Reformed church."[66]

The seven seals of chapters 4–7 take place between John (98) and Constantine (313). The first six represent a Roman emperor who persecuted the church but was overcome by the truth of the gospel.[67] The seventh seal was broken by Constantine, when "the happiness of the faithful grew great."[68] The seven trumpets of chapters 8–11 begin with Constantine and end with the crowning of Elizabeth I in 1558.

The two beasts of chapter 13 point to the development of the papacy, while chapter 14 corresponds to the early Reformers (1300–1556): John Wycliffe, John Huss, Jerome of Prague, Martin Luther, Fredrick of Saxony, Thomas Cromwell, and Thomas Cranmer. The seven vials of chapters 15–16 represent God's wrath upon the papacy and Islam. The first vial was Elizabeth I, who cast out the remaining Roman bishops who denied "due allegiance to their lawful princess."[69] The second was Martin Chemnitz who published *Examination of the Council of Trent*.[70] The third was William Cecil who passed legislation to suppress Jesuits in England. The fourth represents the spread of the gospel throughout the world, so that there was a "more clear opening of the Scriptures, whereby the man of sin may be more vehemently scorched."[71] The fifth was poured out upon the "throne of the Beast," which is the demise of the "Popish Kingdom."[72] The sixth marks the conversion of ethnic Jews. They return to Jerusalem

> to make the goodness of God shine forth to all the world, when they shall see him give to that nation (which is now and hath

---

66. Brightman, *Revelation of S. John*, 168.

67. Seven Seals: [1st] Trajan (98–117)—Antonius (138–161). Beast 1: Quadratus of Athens, Aristides of Athens, Justin Marty. [2nd] Marcus Aurelius (161–180). Beast 2: Justin Martyr, Melito of Sardis, Apollinaris Claudius. [3rd] Septimius Severus (193–211). Beast 3: Tertullian. [4th] Decius (249–251). Beast 4: Cyprian. [5th] Quintillus (270)—Aurelian (270–275)—Diocletian (284–303). During this period was an intermission of public persecutions. [6th] Diocletian (303–305)—Maximian (285–310). It was from 305–310 that these two "raged against the church." [7th] Peace that was brought about by Constantine (312–337). Brightman, *Revelation of S. John*.

68. Brightman, *Revelation of S. Iohn*.

69. Brightman, *Revelation of S. John*, 664.

70. Brightman, *Revelation of S. John*, 670.

71. Brightman, *Revelation of S. John*, 681.

72. Brightman, *Revelation of S. John*, 684.

been for many ages scattered thoroughout the whole world, and inhabiteth nowhere but by leave and entreaty) their own habitations where their fathers dwelt, wherein they shall worship Christ purely, and sincerely according to his will, and commandment alone.[73]

The seventh vial brings "a most grievous calamity" upon the entire kingdom of the devil.[74] This includes the final destruction of the papacy and Islam. All of Christ's enemies are subjugated under His feet and His kingdom is consummated.

Chapters 17–18 provide another account of the demise of the papacy. Chapter 19 records the saints' celebration. Chapters 21–22 depict the victory of the church over all Christ's enemies. The glory of God fills the earth and shines forth in the church.[75]

---

73. Brightman, *Revelation of S. John*, 689.

74. Brightman, *Revelation of S. John*, 699.

75. Toon writes, "To this world Christ will come and so the Revelation ends with the prayer 'So be it. Come Lord Jesus.' With the Second Coming of Christ the last acts of the whole drama of salvation and judgment take place. The dead are raised, all men are judged and allotted to their eternal homes, heaven or hell." Toon, *Puritans*, 30.

# APPENDIX 2

## Robert Hill

THIS FIGURE IN THIS appendix shows Robert Hill's unfolding interpretation of Revelation. The figure gives a chapter-by-chapter layout of Hill's understanding and unfolding of John's apocalypse with highlights from his commentary.

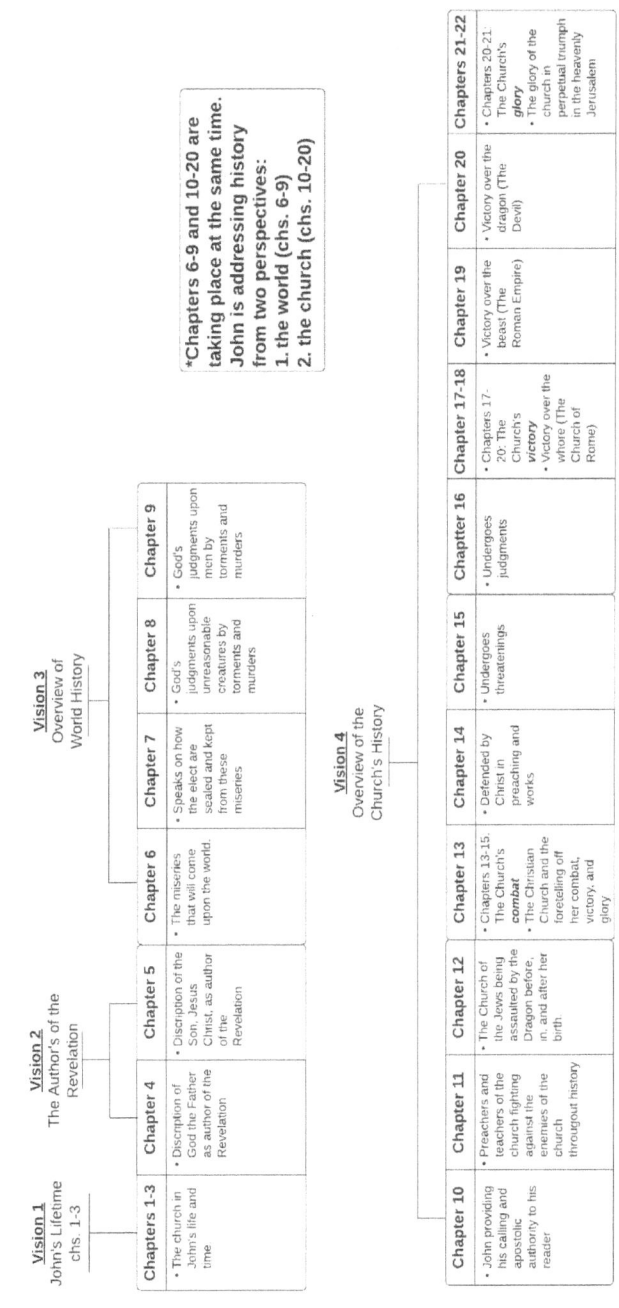

Figure A1. Robert Hill's interpretation of Revelation

# APPENDIX 3

## George Gifford

THIS APPENDIX SHOWS GEORGE Gifford's unfolding interpretation of Revelation. The figure gives a chapter-by-chapter layout of Gifford's understanding and unfolding of John's apocalypse with highlights from his commentary.

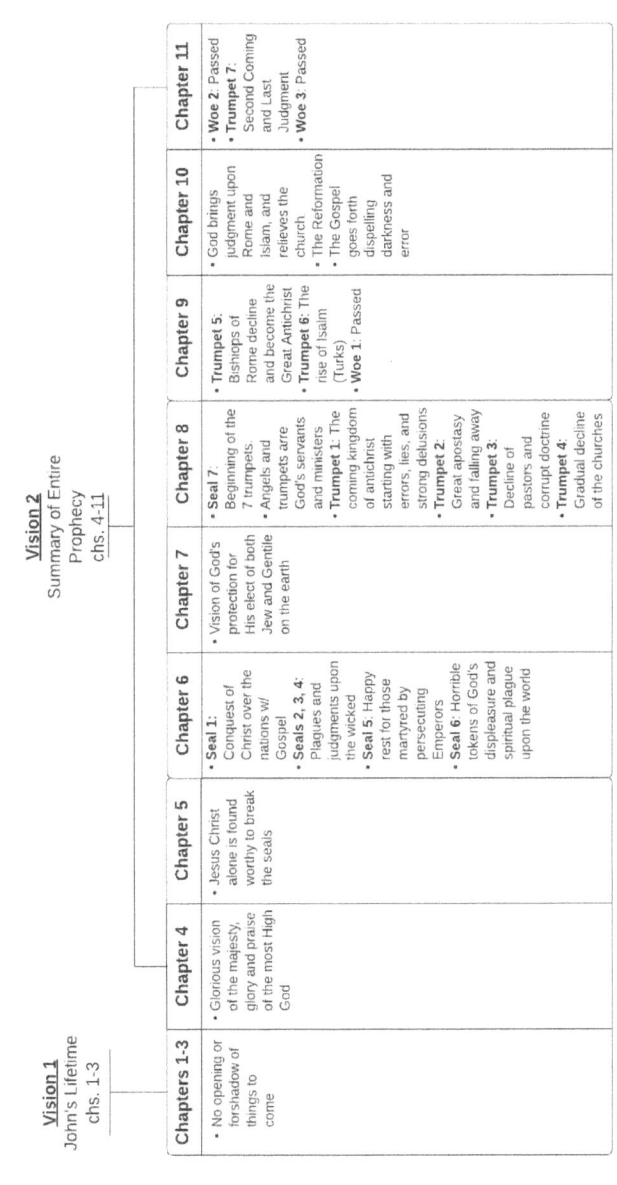

Figure A2. George Gifford's interpretation of Revelation

APPENDIX 3

**Vision 3**
Large and Plain Descriptions
which Open the Former (Vis. 2)
More Clearly
chs. 12-22

| Chapter 12 | Chapter 13 | Chapter 14 | Chapter 15 | Chapter 16 | Chapter 17 | Chapter 18 | Chapter 19 | Chapter 20 | Chs. 21 & 22 |
|---|---|---|---|---|---|---|---|---|---|
| • Church Militant on earth that brings forth the Messiah<br>• Messiah casts the Devil to the earth<br>• Devil wages ware on the church on earth | • Chief instruments used by Satan to torment the church<br>• Persecuting Emerors of Rome<br>• The Roman Church and Papacy (The Great Antichrist) | • Christ preserving the church militant<br>• Fall of Antichrist through the preaching of the gospel | • **Seven angels with seven vials**: Ministers of God's wrath and vengence upon Antichrist and the wicked | • Vials 1-6<br>• Vial 7: Second Coming of Christ and eternal judgment | • Babylon (the Harlot) the city of Rome is the seat of the Antichrist and the Beast (Papacy) | • The Fall of Antichrist by the light of the gospel | • Vison of the Marriage of Christ to His Triumphant Church and the rejoicing with the hosts of heaven for the destruction of the Roman church at Papacy | • History of Satan deceiving the nations prior to the Incarnation<br>• Incarnation/Start of the Millennium<br>• Millennium ended and Satan begins to seduce the nations by Antichrist (beast) and the Turks (false prophet)<br>• Gog and Magog (Papacy and Islam) are destroyed and thrown into the Lake of Fire | • The eternal felicity and blessed estate of the Church. |

Figure A2. George Gifford's interpretation of Revelation (continued)

# APPENDIX 4

## Thomas Brightman

This appendix shows Thomas Brightman's unfolding interpretation of *Revelation*. The figure gives a chapter-by-chapter layout of Brightman's understanding and unfolding of John's apocalypse with highlights from his commentary

APPENDIX 4

Figure A3. Thomas Brightman's interpretation of Revelation

| Chapter 12 | Chapter 13 | Chapter 14 | Chapter 15 | Chapter 16 | Chapter 17 | Chapter 18 | Chapter 19 | Chapter 20 | Chapter 21-22 |
|---|---|---|---|---|---|---|---|---|---|
| • The history of the Dragon of things done by him on earth from AD 98-313<br>• The Dragon is the Devil and men as instruments to do his fury<br>• The Woman (the church) travails for a child to deliver her from persecutions<br>• The child/ Michael (Constantine) ruled the nations with a rod of iron and kept down all his enemies | • Two beasts are two states of development of the Papcy<br>• First beast came in AD 325<br>• Second beast was the Papacy's rise in power by Pepin (AD 751-768) and Charlemagne (AD 800-814) | • Taking place from 1300-1556<br>• God raises up men to preach the gospel and battle against Antichrist (Rome)<br>• These are men such as John Wycliffe, John Huss, Jerome of Prague, Martin Luther, Fredrick of Saxony, Thomas Cromwell and Thomas Cranmer | • Chapters 15-16 are God's wrath upon the Roman Catholic Church, the Papacy, and Islam<br>• Chapter 15 begins in AD 1558<br>• Brightman believed that the first three vials had been fulfilled in his lifetime | • Vial 1: Elizabeth I casing Roman Bishops out of their Bishoprics<br>• Vial 2: Martin Chemintz writing against and rebutting the council of Trent (AD 1565-1573)<br>• Vial 3: William Cecil passing legislation to suppress Jesuits in England<br>• Vial 4: The spread and expanse of the Gospel in the world<br>• Vial 5: The demise of the Popish Kingdom<br>• Vial 6: The mass conversion of Jews to the Christian faith<br>• Vial 7: The final and absolute destruction upon the Papacy and the Turks (Islam)<br>• Ushering in the final consummation of Christ's Kingdom | • Chapters 17-18 a zoomed in view of the fifth vial and the destruction of the Papacy<br>• The first execution of the vial | • The second execution of the vial on the Roman Catholic Church and the Papacy | • The joy of the saints that come from the destruction of the Roman Church<br>• Verses 1, 10 is the the sixth vial and the calling and conversion of the Jews<br>• The chapater ends with the seventh vial being opened and the destructio not the false prophet (Islam) and the beast (Pope of Rome) | • Two literal Millennial periods<br>• First Millennial period (AD 300-1300)<br>• Second Millennial period halfway through in Brightman's day (AD 1300-2300) | • The last part of the seventh vial<br>• The happiness of the church over all of Christ's enemies<br>• The glory of God filling the earth and shining through the one church (Jew and Gentile) |

**Figure A3.** Thomas Brightman's interpretation of Revelation (continued)

# APPENDIX 5

## William Perkins's Ocular Catechism

The figure in this appendix is William Perkins's "Ocular Catechism," which shows his understanding of man's end from predestination to life eternal or death eternal in hell. Perkins constructed this chart for those who could not read, wherein they could point and trace the main points of the faith within their proper order.

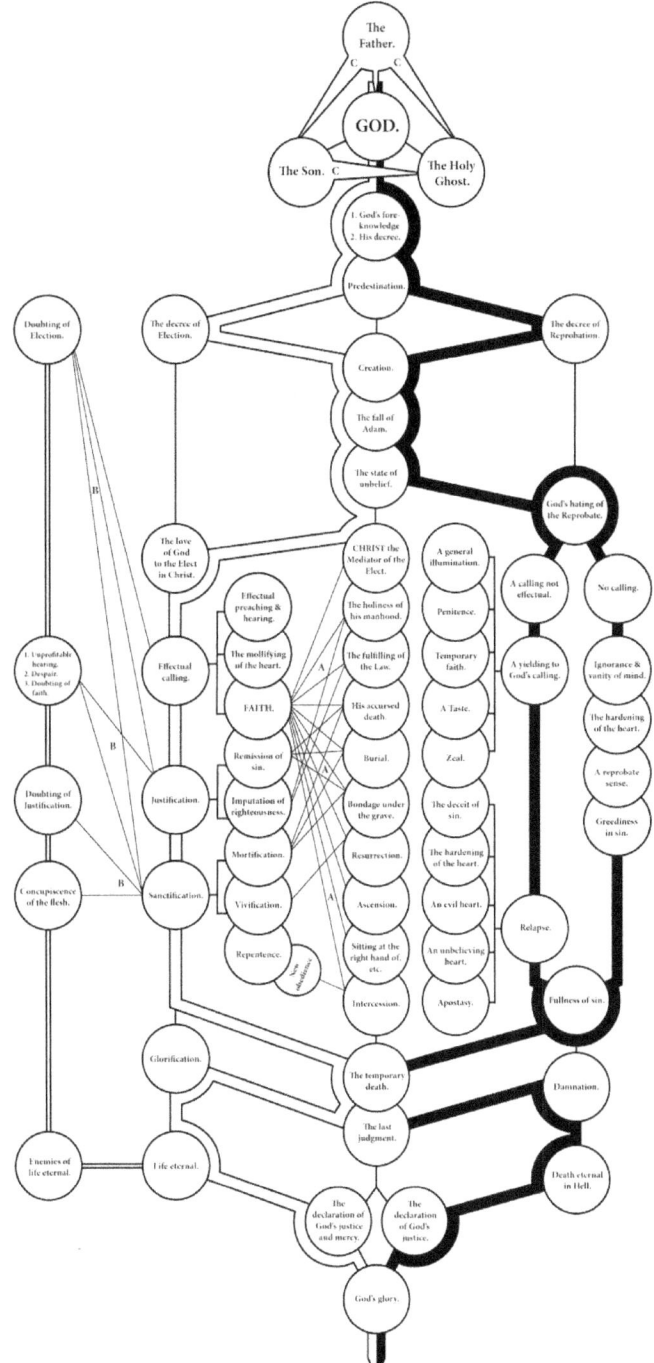

Figure A4. William Perkins's "Ocular Catechism"

# Bibliography

Ambrose, Isaac. *Looking unto Jesus, As carrying on the Great Work of Man's Salvation*. In *The Complete Works of That Eminent Minister of God's Word Mr. Isaac Ambrose*, 371–814. Dundee: Galbraith, 1759.

———. *Prima, Media, et Ultima, or, The First, Middle, and Last Things*. In *The Complete Works of That Eminent Minister of God's Word Mr. Isaac Ambrose*, 1–361. Dundee: Galbraith, 1759

Ames, William. *The Marrow of Theology*. Edited and translated by John Dykstra Eusden. Grand Rapids: Baker, 1997.

Aquinas, Thomas. *Summa Theologica*. Translated by the Fathers of the English Dominican Province. 22 vols. London: Burns Oates & Washbourne, n.d. Logos Bible Software.

Augustine of Hippo. *The City of God, Books XVII–XXII*. In *The Fathers of the Church*, edited by Hermigild Dressler, translated by Gerald G. Walsh and Daniel J. Honan, 24:83–182. Washington, DC: The Catholic University of America Press, 1954.

Baarsel, Jan Jacobus van. *William Perkins: Eene Bijdrage tot de Kennis der Religieuse Ontwikkeling in Engeland ten Tijde, van Koningin Elisabeth*. 's-Gravenhage: De Swart & Zoon, 1912.

Bale, John. *The Image of both Churches, after the most wonderful and heavenly Revelation of saint John the Evangelist, containing a very fruitful exposition or Paraphrase upon the same*. London, 1570.

Ball, Bryan W. *A Great Expectation: Eschatological Thought in English Protestantism to 1660*. Leiden: Brill, 1975.

Ballitch, Andrew S. *The Gloss and the Text: William Perkins on Interpreting Scripture with Scripture*. Bellingham, WA: Lexham, 2020.

———. "God the Son in the Theology of William Perkins." *Puritan Reformed Journal* 9 (2017) 147–64.

———. "'Not to Behold Faith, but the Object of Faith': The Effect of William Perkins's Doctrine of the Atonement on His Preaching of Assurance." *Themelios* 40 (2015) 445–58.

———. "'Scripture Is Both the Glosse and the Text': Biblical Interpretation and Its Implementation in the Works of William Perkins." PhD diss., The Southern Baptist Theological Seminary, 2017.

———. "True Happiness: William Perkins's Interpretation of the Sermon on the Mount." *Puritan Reformed Journal* 8 (2016) 49–69.

Barbee, David M. "A Reformed Catholike: William Perkins' Use of the Church Fathers." PhD diss., University of Pennsylvania, 2013.

Baumlin, James S. "William Perkins's 'Art of Prophesying' and Milton's 'Two-Handed Engine': The Protestant Allegory of 'Lycidas.'" *Milton Quarterly* 33 (1999) 66–71.

Bayly, Lewis. *The Practise of Pietie: Directing a Christian How to Walke That He May Please God*. London, 1613.

Beeke, Joel R. *How Can I Practice Christian Meditation?* Grand Rapids: Reformation Heritage, 2016.

———. *Puritan Reformed Spirituality: A Practical Theological Study from Our Reformed and Puritan Heritage*. Webster, NY: Evangelical, 2006.

———. "William Perkins and His Greatest Case of Conscience: 'How a Man May Know Whether He Be the Child of God, or No.'" *Calvin Theological Journal* 41 (2006) 255–78.

———. "William Perkins on Predestination, Preaching, and Conversion." In *The Practical Calvinist: An Introduction to the Presbyterian and Reformed Heritage*, edited by Peter A. Lillback, 183–213. Fearn: Christian Focus, 2002.

Beeke, Joel R., and Mark Jones, eds. *A Puritan Theology: Doctrine for Life*. Grand Rapids: Reformation Heritage, 2012.

Beeke, Joel R., and Randall J. Pederson. *Meet the Puritans: With a Guide to Modern Reprints*. Grand Rapids: Reformation Heritage, 2006.

Beeke, Joel R., and Greg Salazar. *William Perkins: Architect of Puritanism*. Grand Rapids: Reformation Heritage, 2019.

Beeke, Joel R., and Derek W. H. Thomas. "General Preface." In *The Works of William Perkins*, edited by J. Stephen Yuille, 1:vii–viii. Grand Rapids: Reformation Heritage, 2014.

Beeke, Joel R., and J. Stephen Yuille. "Biographical Preface: William Perkins, the 'Father of Puritanism.'" In *The Works of William Perkins*, edited by J. Stephen Yuille, 1:ix–xxxii. Grand Rapids: Reformation Heritage, 2014.

———. *William Perkins*. Welwyn Garden City: EP, 2015.

Berkhof, Louis. *Systematic Theology*. Grand Rapids: Eerdmans, 1996.

Blacketer, Raymond A. "The Rhetoric of Reform: William Perkins on Preaching and the Purification of the Church." In *Scholasticism Reformed: Essays in Honour of Willem J. van Asselt*, edited by Maarten Wisee et al., 215–36. Leiden: Brill, 2010.

———. "William Perkins (1558–1602)." In *The Pietist Theologians*, edited by Carter Lindberg, 38–51. Malden, MA: Blackwell, 2005.

Boersma, Hans. *Seeing God: The Beatific Vision in Christian Tradition*. Grand Rapids: Eerdmans, 2018.

Brakel, Wilhelmus à. *The Christian's Reasonable Service*. Vol. 1, *God, Man, and Christ*. Edited by Joel R. Beeke. Grand Rapids: Reformation Heritage, 2017.

Brannan, Rick, ed. *Historic Creeds and Confessions*. Bellingham, WA: Lexham, 2001.

Breward, Ian. "The Life and Theology of William Perkins." PhD diss., University of Manchester, 1963.

———. "The Significance of William Perkins." *Journal of Religious History* 4 (1966) 113–28.

———. "William Perkins and the Ideal of the Ministry in the Elizabethan Church." *Reformed Theological Review* 24 (1963) 73–84.

———. "William Perkins and the Origins of Reformed Casuistry." *Evangelical Quarterly* 1 (1968) 3–20.

———. *The Work of William Perkins*. Edited by Ian Breward. Abingdon: Sutton Courtenay, 1970.

Brightman, Thomas. *The Revelation of S. John illustrated with Analysis and scholions. Wherein the sense is opened by the Scripture, and the event of thins fore-told, shewed by Histories.* Leyden, 1616.
Brocard, James. *The Revelation of Saint John revealed. Opening by Conference of time and place many points very necessary for the time present. Especially against the Papacy.* London, 1610.
Brook, Benjamin. *The Lives of the Puritans.* Vol. 2. London: Black, 1813.
Broughton, Hugh. *A Revelation of the Holy Apocalypse.* London, 1610.
Bruhn, Karen. "Pastoral Polemic: William Perkins, the Godly Evangelicals, and the Shaping of a Protestant Community in Early Modern England." *Anglican and Episcopal History* 72 (2003) 102–27.
Bullinger, Henry. *A Hundred Sermons Upon the Apocalypse of Jesus Christ, revealed by the angel of the Lord: but seen or received and written by the holy Apostle and Evangelist S. John.* London, 1573.
Calamy, Edmund. *The Art of Divine Meditation. Or, A Discourse of the Nature, Necessity, and Excellency thereof. With Motives to, and Rules for the better performance of that most Important Christian Duty.* London, 1680.
Calvin, John. *Commentaries on the Epistle of Paul the Apostle to the Romans.* Edited and translated by John Owen. Calvin's Commentaries 19. Grand Rapids: Baker, 2009.
———. *Commentary on a Harmony of the Evangelists: Matthew, Mark, and Luke.* Vol. 1. Translated by William Pringle. Calvin's Commentaries 16. Grand Rapids: Baker, 2009.
———. *Institutes of the Christian Religion.* Edited by John T. McNeill. Translated by Ford Lewis Battles. Philadelphia: Westminster, 1960.
Chalker, William H. "Calvin and Some Seventeenth Century English Calvinists." PhD diss., Duke University, 1961.
Cho, Youngchun. "A Study of Puritan Covenant Theology." *Puritan Reformed Journal* 9 (2017) 191–210.
Clarke, Samuel. *The Marrow of Ecclesiastical History Contained in the Lives of the Fathers and Other Learned Men and Famous Divines Which Have Flourished in the Church Since Christ's Time to this Present Age.* London: Dugard, 1650.
Cross, F. L., and Elizabeth A. Livingstone, eds. *The Oxford Dictionary of the Christian Church.* Oxford: Oxford University Press, 2005.
Cudworth, Ralph. *The Supplement: Or, Continuation of the Commentary upon the Sixth Chapter.* In *The Works of William Perkins,* edited by Paul M. Smalley, 2:395–575. Grand Rapids: Reformation Heritage, 2015.
Cushing, Douglas D. "The Inspiration of Scripture in the Theologies of William Perkins and John Calvin." MA thesis, Trinity Evangelical Divinity School, 1993.
Davies, Horton, ed. *Studies of the Church in History.* Eugene, OR: Pickwick, 1983.
———. *Worship and Theology in England: From Cranmer to Baxter and Fox, 1534–1690.* Grand Rapids: Eerdmans, 1996.
*A Declaration of the Faith and Order Owned and Practiced in the Congregational Churches in England: Agreed Upon and Consented unto by their Elders and Messengers in Their Meeting at the Savoy, October 12, 1658.* London, 1659.
Deios, Laurence. *That The Pope is That Antichrist: And An answer to the Objections of Sectaries, which condemne this Church of England.* London, 1590.
Dent, Arthur. *The Ruin of Rome. Or An Exposition upon the whole Revelation.* London, 1607.

Ditzenberger, Christopher S. "William Perkins and Seventeenth-Century Conception of Pastoral Theology with Special Consideration of George Herbert and Richard Baxter." MA thesis, Gordon-Conwell Theological Seminary, 1994.

Dixon, Leif. *Practical Predestinarians in England, c. 1590–1640.* New York: Routledge, 2016.

———. "William Perkins, 'Atheisme,' and the Crises of England's Long Reformation." *Journal of British Studies* 50 (2011) 790–812.

Fenner, Dudley. *Sacra theologia, sive, Veritas quæ est secundum pietatem ad vnicæ & versæ methodi leges descripta & in decem libros per Dudleium Fennerum digesta.* Vignon, 1585.

Fesko, J. V. *The Covenant of Works: The Origins, Development, and Reception of the Doctrine.* Oxford: Oxford University Press, 2020.

———. *The Trinity and the Covenant of Redemption.* 2016. Reprint, Glasgow: Mentor, 2021.

———. "William Perkins on Union with Christ and Justification." *Mid-America Journal of Theology* 21 (2010) 21–34.

Firth, Katharine R. *The Apocalyptic Tradition in Reformation Britain, 1530–1645.* Oxford: Oxford University Press, 1979.

Flavel, John. *Sermon X: Revel. 3:20, If any man hear my voice, and open the door, [I will come into him, and sup with him.].* In *The Whole Works of the Reverend John Flavel*, 4:211–35. London, 1820.

———. *The Tenth Meditation: Upon John 6:55, For my flesh is meat indeed, and my blood is drink indeed.* In *The Whole Works of the Reverend John Flavel*, 6:444–50. London, 1820.

Foord, John. *Apocalypsis Iesu Christi, reuelata per angelum Domini, excepta atque conscripta à Ioanne Apostolo & Euangeliographo.* London, 1597.

Forbes, Patrick. *An Exquisite Commentary Upon The Revelation of Saint John: Wherein, Both The course of the whole Booke, as also the more abstruse and hard places thereof not heretofore opened; are now at last most clearly and evidently explained.* London, 1613.

Ford, Coleman M. "'Everywhere, Always, by All': William Perkins and James Ussher on the Constructive Use of the Fathers." *Puritan Reformed Journal* 7 (2015) 95–111.

Foxe, John. *Acts And Monuments of matters must special and memorable, happening in the Church, with an universal history of the same.* London, 1596.

Frost, R. N. *Richard Sibbes: God's Spreading Goodness.* Vancouver, WA: Cor Deo, 2012.

Fulke, William. *Praelections upon the Sacred and holy Revelation of S. John.* London, 1573.

Fuller, Thomas. *Abel Redevivus: or, The Dead Yet Speaking. The Lives and Deaths of the Modern Divines.* London, 1651.

Gaine, Simon. "Thomas Aquinas and John Owen on the Beatific Vision: A Reply to Suzanne McDonald." *New Blackfriars* 97 (2016) 432–46.

Gatiss, Lee, ed. *Pilgrims, Warriors, and Servants: Puritan Wisdom for Today's Church.* London: Latimer Trust, 2010.

Gentry, Kenneth L., Jr. *He Shall Have Dominion: A Postmillennial Eschatology.* 3rd ed. Draper, VA: Apologetics Group, 2009.

Gevitz, Norman. "Practical Divinity and Medical Ethics: Lawful versus Unlawful Medicine in the Writings of William Perkins." *Journal of the History of Medicine and Allied Sciences* 68 (2012) 198–226.

Gifford, George. *Sermons Upon the Whole Booke of the Revelation*. London: Field and Kingston, 1599.
Gleason, Randall C., and Kelly M. Kapic, eds. *The Devoted Life: An Invitation to the Puritan Classics*. Downers Grove, IL: InterVarsity, 2004.
Gregg, Steve. *Revelation, Four Views: A Parallel Commentary*. Rev. ed. Nashville: Nelson, 2013.
Greve, Lionel. "Freedom and Discipline in the Theology of John Calvin, William Perkins, and John Wesley: An Examination of the Origin and Nature of Pietism." PhD diss., Hartford Seminary Foundation, 1976.
Gribben, Crawford. *The Puritan Millennium: Literature and Theology, 1550–1682*. Rev. ed. Eugene, OR: Wipf & Stock, 2008.
Grimes, Dee A. "God's Imposition: The Centrality of Vocation in the Spirituality of William Perkins." PhD diss., The Southern Baptist Theological Seminary, 2021.
Hall, David D. *The Puritans: A Transatlantic History*. Princeton: Princeton University Press, 2019.
Hall, Joseph. *The Arte of Divine Meditation: Profitable for all Christians to knowe and practises*. London, 1605.
Hancock, Maxine. "Meditation." In *Dictionary of Christian Spirituality*, edited by Glen G. Scorgie, 606–8. Grand Rapids: Zondervan, 2011.
Hargrove, Carl A. "Implication and Application in Exposition, Part 3: Four Historical Examples of Application—John Calvin, William Perkins, Charles Simeon, D. Martyn-Lloyd Jones." *The Master's Seminary Journal* 31 (2020) 25–41.
Herbert, James C. "William Perkins's 'A Reformed Catholic': A Psycho-Cultural Interpretation." *Church History* 51 (1982) 7–23.
Hill, Charles E. *Regnum Caelorum: Patterns of Millennial Thought in Early Christianity*. 2nd ed. Grand Rapids: Eerdmans, 2001.
Hill, Robert. *Christ's prayer expounded, A Christian Directed, and a Communicant prepared*. London, 1606.
———. *The Contents of Scripture: Containing the sum of every Book and chapter of the old and new Testament*. London, 1596.
Hulse, Erroll. "William Perkins: Application in Preaching." In *The Pure Flame of Devotion: The History of Spirituality*, edited by G. Stephen Weaver Jr. and Ian Hugh Clary, 177–96. Ontario: Joshua, 2013.
Jones, Hywel R. *Transfiguration and Transformation*. Carlisle, PA: Banner of Truth, 2021.
Jones, R. Tudur. "Union with Christ: The Existential Nerve of Puritan Piety." *Tyndale Bulletin* 41 (1990) 186–208.
Junius, Franciscus. *The Revelation of Saint Iohn the Apostle and Evangelist, with a briefe and learned Commentarie*. London, 1594.
Kaufmann, U. Milo. *The Pilgrim's Progress and Traditions in Puritan Meditation*. New Haven: Yale University Press, 1966.
Kendall, R. T. "The Nature of Saving Faith from William Perkins (d. 1602) to the Westminster Assembly (1643–1649)." PhD diss., University of Oxford, 1976.
Kuivenhoven, Maarten. "Condemning Coldness and Sleepy Dullness: The Concept of Urgency in the Preaching Models of Richard Baxter and William Perkins." *Puritan Reformed Journal* 4 (2012) 180–200.
Lee, Hansang. "Trinitarian Theology and Piety: The Attributes of God in the Thought of Stephen Charnock (1628–1680) and William Perkins (1558–1602)." PhD diss., University of Edinburgh, 2009.

Lee, Jon English. "An Examination of the Origins of English Puritan Sabbatarianism." *Puritan Reformed Journal* 7 (2015) 103–19.
Letham, Robert W. A. "Saving Faith and Assurance in Reformed Theology: Zwingli to the Synod of Dort." 2 vols. PhD diss., University of Aberdeen, 1979.
Lightfoot, R. David. "William Perkins' View of Sanctification." ThM thesis, Dallas Theological Seminary, 1984.
Lillback, Peter A. *The Practical Calvinist: An Introduction to the Presbyterian & Reformed Heritage*. Fearn: Christian Focus, 2002.
Machielsen, Jan, ed. *The Science of Demons: Early Modern Authors Facing Witchcraft and the Devil*. New York: Routledge, 2020.
MacLean, Donald John. *"Ours Is a True Church of God": William Perkins and the Reformed Doctrine of the Church*. London: Latimer Trust, 2019.
Manton, Thomas. *The Transfiguration of Christ: Sermon II*. In *The Complete Works of Thomas Manton*, 1:347–58. 1870. Reprint, Homewood, AL: Solid Ground Christian, 2008.
Markham, C. C. "William Perkins' Understanding of the Function of Conscience." PhD diss., Vanderbilt University, 1967.
McDonald, Suzanne. "Beholding the Glory of God in the Face of Jesus Christ: John Owen and the 'Reforming' of the Beatific Vision." In *The Ashgate Research Companion to John Owen's Theology*, edited by Kelly M. Kapic and Mark Jones, 141–58. Burlington, VT: Ashgate, 2012.
McGiffert, Michael. "The Perkinsian Moment of Federal Theology." *Calvin Theological Journal* 29 (1994) 117–48.
McGinnis, Timothy Scott. *George Gifford and the Reformation of the Common Sort: Puritan Priorities in Elizabethan Religious Life*. Kriksville, MO: Truman State University Press, 2004.
McKim, Donald K. "The Functions of Ramism in William Perkins' Theology." *The Sixteenth Century Journal* 16 (1985) 503–17.
———. "Ramism in William Perkins." PhD diss., University of Pittsburgh, 1980.
———. "William Perkins and the Theology of the Covenant." In *Studies of the Church in History: Essays Honoring Robert S. Paul on His Sixty-Fifth Birthday*, edited by Horton Davies, 85–102. Eugene, OR: Pickwick, 1983.
Medders, J. A. "Grazing and Gazing: Meditation and Contemplation in Puritan Spirituality." *Journal of Spiritual Formation & Soul Care* 15 (2022) 30–43.
Moore, Jonathan D. "Predestination and Evangelism in the Life and Thought of William Perkins." The Evangelical Library Annual Lecture 2008. http://www.evangelical-library.org.uk/articles/EL_Annual_Lecture_2008.pdf.
Morison, Samuel. *The Intellectual Life of Colonial New England*. 2nd ed. New York: New York University Press, 1956.
Mosser, Carl. "The Gospel's End and Our Highest Good: Deification in the Reformed Tradition." In *With All the Fullness of God: Deification in Christian Tradition*, edited by Jared Ortiz, 83–108. Lanham, MD: Lexington, 2021.
———. "Recovering the Reformation's Ecumenical Vision of Redemption as Deification and Beatific Vision." *Perichoresis* 18 (2020) 3–24.
Muller, Richard A. *Calvin and the Reformed Tradition: On the Work of Christ and the Order of Salvation*. Grand Rapids: Baker, 2012.
———. *Christ and the Decree: Christology and Predestination in Reformed Theology from Calvin to Perkins*. Grand Rapids: Baker, 2008.

———. *Dictionary of Latin and Greek Theological Terms: Drawn Principally from Protestant Scholastic Theology.* 2nd ed. Grand Rapids: Baker, 2017.

———. *Grace and Freedom: William Perkins and the Early Modern Reformed Understanding of Free Choice and Divine Grace.* Oxford: Oxford University Press, 2020.

———. "Perkins' *A Golden Chaine*: Predestinarian System or Schematized Ordo Salutis?" *The Sixteenth Century Journal* 9 (1978) 68–81.

———. "Predestination and Christology in Sixteenth-Century Reformed Theology." PhD diss., Duke University, 1976.

———. "Toward the *Pactum Salutis*: Locating the Origins of a Concept." *Mid-America Journal of Theology* 18 (2007) 11–65.

Munson, Charles Robert. "William Perkins: Theologian of Transition." PhD diss., Case Western Reserve, 1971.

Murray, Iain. *The Puritan Hope: Revival and the Interpretation of Prophecy.* Carlisle, PA: Banner of Truth, 1975.

Napier, John. *A Plain Discovery of the whole Revelation of Saint John: set down in two treatises: The one searching and proving the true interpretation thereof: The other applying the same paraphrastically and Historically to the text.* Edinburgh, 1593.

Op't Hof, Willem Jan. *Engelse Piëtistische Geschriften in het Nederlands, 1598-1622.* Rotterdam: Lindenberg, 1987.

Ortlund, Gavin. "Will We See God's Essence? A Defence of a Thomistic Account of the Beatific Vision." *Scottish Journal of Theology* 74 (2011) 323–32.

Owen, John. *A Declaration of the Glorious Mystery of the Person of Christ.* In *The Works of John Owen*, edited by William H. Goold, 1:29–272. Carlisle, PA: Banner of Truth, 2013.

Packer, J. I. "An Anglican to Remember—William Perkins: Puritan Popularizer." In *Pilgrims, Warriors, and Servants: Puritan Wisdom for Today's Church*, edited by Lee Gatiss, 141–68. London: Latimer Trust, 2010.

———. *Concise Theology: A Guide to Historic Christian Beliefs.* Carol Stream, IL: Tyndale, 1993.

———. *A Quest for Godliness: The Puritan Vision of the Christian Life.* Wheaton, IL: Crossway, 1990.

Paterson, W. B. *William Perkins and the Making of a Protestant England.* Oxford: Oxford University Press, 2014.

———. "William Perkins as Apologist for the Church of England." *Journal of Ecclesiastical History* 57 (2006) 252–69.

Perkins, Harrison. *Catholicity and the Covenant of Works: James Ussher and the Reformed Tradition.* Oxford: Oxford University Press, 2020.

Perkins, William. *The Art of Prophesying: Or A Treatise Concerning the Sacred and Only True Manner and Method of Preaching.* In *The Works of William Perkins*, edited by Joseph A. Pipa and J. Stephen Yuille, 10:281–356. Grand Rapids: Reformation Heritage, 2020.

———. *A Case of Conscience, The greatest that ever was: How a man may know whether he is the child of God or not.* In *The Works of William Perkins*, edited by J. Stephen Yuille, 8:595–637. Grand Rapids: Reformation Heritage, 2019.

———. *A Christian and Plain Treatise of the Manner and Order of Predestination, and of the largeness of God's grace.* In *The Works of William Perkins*, edited by Joel R. Beeke and Greg A. Salazar, 6:273–384. Grand Rapids: Reformation Heritage, 2018.

———. *Christian Oeconomie, or, A Short Survey of the Right Manner of Erecting and Ordering a Family, According to the Scriptures.* In *The Works of William Perkins*, edited by Joseph A. Pipa and J. Stephen Yuille, 10:109–94. Grand Rapids: Reformation Heritage, 2020.

———. *A Cloud of Faithful Witnesses, Leading To The Heavenly Canaan: Or, A Commentary upon the 11th Chapter to the Hebrews.* In *The Works of William Perkins*, edited by Randall J. Pederson and Ryan Hurd, 3:1–411. Grand Rapids: Reformation Heritage, 2017.

———. *The Combat between Christ and the Devil Displayed: or A Commentary upon the Temptations of Christ.* In *The Works of William Perkins*, edited by J. Stephen Yuille, 1:71–165. Grand Rapids: Reformation Heritage, 2014.

———. *The Combat of the Flesh and Spirit.* In *The Works of William Perkins*, edited by J. Stephen Yuille, 9:169–81. Grand Rapids: Reformation Heritage, 2020.

———. *A Commentary, or, Exposition Upon the five first Chapters of the Epistle to the Galatians.* In *The Works of William Perkins*, edited by Paul M. Smalley, 2:1–575. Grand Rapids: Reformation Heritage, 2015.

———. *A Declaration of the True Manner of Knowing Christ Crucified.* In *The Works of William Perkins*, edited by J. Stephen Yuille, 9:1–78. Grand Rapids: Reformation Heritage, 2020.

———. *A Digest or Harmony of the Books of the Old and New Testament.* In *The Works of William Perkins*, edited by J. Stephen Yuille, 1:1–70. Grand Rapids: Reformation Heritage, 2014.

———. *A Discourse of Conscience: Wherein is set down the nature, properties, and differences thereof, as also the way to get and keep a good conscience.* In *The Works of William Perkins*, edited by J. Stephen Yuille, 8:1–94. Grand Rapids: Reformation Heritage, 2019.

———. *A Discourse of the Damned Art of Witchcraft: So far forth as it is revealed in the Scriptures, and manifested by true experience.* In *The Works of William Perkins*, edited by J. Stephen Yuille, 9:293–403. Grand Rapids: Reformation Heritage, 2020.

———. *An Exposition of the Lord's Prayer In the Way of Catechism: Serving for ignorant people.* In *The Works of William Perkins*, edited by Ryan Hurd, 5:423–69. Grand Rapids: Reformation Heritage, 2017.

———. *An Exposition of the Symbol, or Creed of the Apostles: According to the tenor of the Scripture, and the consent of Orthodox Fathers of the Church.* In *The Works of William Perkins*, edited by Ryan Hurd, 5:1–416. Grand Rapids: Reformation Heritage, 2017.

———. *A Faithful and Plain Exposition Upon Zephaniah 2:1–2: Containing a powerful exhortation to repentance, as also the manner how men in repentance are to search themselves.* In *The Works of William Perkins*, edited by J. Stephen Yuille, 9:79–122. Grand Rapids: Reformation Heritage, 2020.

———. *The First Book of the Cases of Conscience: Concerning man as he stands in relation to himself.* In *The Works of William Perkins*, edited by J. Stephen Yuille, 8:113–218. Grand Rapids: Reformation Heritage, 2019.

———. *The Foundation of Christian Religion Gathered into six Principles.* In *The Works of William Perkins*, edited by Ryan Hurd, 5:481–509. Grand Rapids: Reformation Heritage, 2017.

———. *A Fruitful Dialogue between the Christian and the Worldling, Concerning the End of the World.* In *The Works of William Perkins*, edited by Joel R. Beeke and Greg A. Salazar, 6:445–74. Grand Rapids: Reformation Heritage, 2018.

———. *A Godly and Learned Exposition of Christ's Sermon on the Mount*. In *The Works of William Perkins*, edited by J. Stephen Yuille, 1:167–734. Grand Rapids: Reformation Heritage, 2014.

———. *A Godly and Learned Exposition, or, Commentary Upon the First Three Chapters of Revelation*. In *The Works of William Perkins*, edited by J. Stephen Yuille, 4:287–626. Grand Rapids: Reformation Heritage, 2017.

———. *A Godly and Learned Exposition Upon the Whole Epistle of Jude*. In *The Works of William Perkins*, edited by J. Stephen Yuille, 4:1–285. Grand Rapids: Reformation Heritage, 2017.

———. *A Golden Chain, Or, The Description of Theology: Containing the order of the causes of Salvation and Damnation, According to God's Word*. In *The Works of William Perkins*, edited by Joel R. Beeke and Greg A. Salazar, 6:1–265. Grand Rapids: Reformation Heritage, 2018.

———. *A Grain of Mustard Seed, or, The least measure of grace that is, or can be, effectual to salvation*. In *The Works of William Perkins*, edited by J. Stephen Yuille, 8:639–58. Grand Rapids: Reformation Heritage, 2019.

———. *How to Live, and That Well In all estates and times, especially when helps and comforts fail*. In *The Works of William Perkins*, edited by Joseph A. Pipa and J. Stephen Yuille, 10:1–29. Grand Rapids: Reformation Heritage, 2020.

———. *A Reformed Catholic, or, A Declaration Showing how never we may come to the present Church of Rome in sundry points of Religion, and wherein we must forever depart from them, With an Advertisement to all favorers of the Roman religion, showing that the said religion is against the catholic principles and grounds of the catechism*. In *The Works of William Perkins*, edited by Shawn D. Wright and Andrew S. Ballitch, 7:1–167. Grand Rapids: Reformation Heritage, 2019.

———. *A Resolution to the Country Man: Proving It Utterly Unlawful to Buy or Use Our Yearly Prognostications*. In *The Works of William Perkins*, edited by J. Stephen Yuille, 9:405–38. Grand Rapids: Reformation Heritage, 2020.

———. *A Salve for a Sick Man, or, A Treatise Containing the Nature, Differences, and Kinds of Death, as also the Right Manner of Dying Well*. In *The Works of William Perkins*, edited by Joseph A. Pipa and J. Stephen Yuille, 10:399–458. Grand Rapids: Reformation Heritage, 2020.

———. *The Second Book of The Cases of Conscience: Concerning man as he stands in relation to God*. In *The Works of William Perkins*, edited by J. Stephen Yuille, 8:219–358. Grand Rapids: Reformation Heritage, 2019.

———. *A Treatise on God's Free Grace and Man's Free Will*. In *The Works of William Perkins*, edited by Joel R. Beeke and Greg A. Salazar, 6:358–443. Grand Rapids: Reformation Heritage, 2018.

———. *A Treatise of Man's Imaginations: Showing His natural evil thoughts, His want of good thoughts, The way to reform them*. In *The Works of William Perkins*, edited by J. Stephen Yuille, 9:181–252. Grand Rapids: Reformation Heritage, 2020.

———. *A Treatise Tending unto a Declaration whether a Man is in the Estate of Damnation or in the Estate of Grace. And if he is in the first, how he may in the time come out of it; if in the second, how he may discern it and persevere in the same to the end*. In *The Works of William Perkins*, edited by J. Stephen Yuille, 8:441–94. Grand Rapids: Reformation Heritage, 2019.

———. *The True Gain: More in Worth than All the Goods in the World.* In *The Works of William Perkins*, edited by J. Stephen Yuille, 9:23–78. Grand Rapids: Reformation Heritage, 2020.

———. *A Warning Against the Idolatry of the Last Times and An Instruction Touching Religious or Divine Worship.* In *The Works of William Perkins*, edited by Shawn D. Wright and Andrew S. Ballitch, 7:411–514. Grand Rapids: Reformation Heritage, 2019.

———. *The Whole Treatise of The Cases of Conscience: Distinguished into three books. The first whereof is revised and corrected in sundry places, and the other two annexed.* In *The Works of William Perkins*, edited by J. Stephen Yuille, 8:94–440. Grand Rapids: Reformation Heritage, 2019.

Pickering, Thomas. "Epistle Dedicatory." In *The Works of William Perkins*, edited by J. Stephen Yuille, 9:295–302. Grand Rapids: Reformation Heritage, 2020.

Pipa, Joseph A. "William Perkins and the Development of Puritan Preaching." PhD diss., Westminster Theological Seminary, 1985.

Porter, Harry C. *Reformation and Reaction in Tudor Cambridge.* Cambridge: Cambridge University Press, 1958.

Priebe, Victor Lewis. "The Covenant Theology of William Perkins." PhD diss., Drew University, 1967.

Reeves, Stan. *Confessing the Faith: The 1689 Baptist Confession for the 21st Century.* Cape Coral, FL: Founders, 2012.

Rohr, John von. *The Covenant of Grace in Puritan Thought.* Eugene, OR: Wipf & Stock, 1986.

Ryken, Leland. *Worldly Saints: The Puritans as They Really Were.* Grand Rapids: Zondervan, 1990.

Saxton, David W. *God's Battle Plan for the Mind: The Puritan Practice of Biblical Meditation.* Grand Rapids: Reformation Heritage, 2015.

Schaefer, Paul R., Jr. "The Spiritual Brotherhood on the Habits of the Heart: Cambridge Protestants and the Doctrine of Sanctification from William Perkins to Thomas Shepard." PhD diss., Keble College, Oxford University, 1994.

———. *The Spiritual Brotherhood: Cambridge Puritans and the Nature of Christian Piety.* Grand Rapids: Reformation Heritage, 2011.

Schwanda, Tom. *Soul Recreation: The Contemplative-Mystical Piety of Puritanism.* Eugene, OR: Pickwick, 2012.

Shaw, Mark R. "Drama in the Meeting House: The Concept of Conversion in the Theology of William Perkins." *Westminster Theological Journal* 45 (1983) 41–72.

———. "The Marrow of Practical Divinity: A Study in the Theology of William Perkins." PhD diss., Westminster Theological Seminary, 1981.

Shedd, William G. T. *A History of Christian Doctrine.* Vol. 2. Eugene, OR: Wipf & Stock, 1999.

Sisson, Rosemary. "William Perkins." MA thesis, University of Cambridge, 1952.

———. "William Perkins, Apologist for the Elizabethan Church of England." *Modern Language Review* 47 (1952) 495–502.

Sommerville, C. J. "Conversion, Sacrament, and Assurance in the Puritan Covenant of Grace to 1650." MA thesis, University of Kansas, 1963.

Song, Timothy Young-Jae. "Theology and Piety in the Reformed Federal Thought of William Perkins and John Preston." PhD diss., Westminster Theological Seminary, 1998.

Spinks, Bryan D. *Two Faces of Elizabethan Anglican Theology: Sacraments and Salvation in the Thought of William Perkins and Richard Hooker*. Lanham, MD: Scarecrow, 1999.

Sprunger, Keith L. "English and Dutch Sabbatarianism and the Development of Puritan Social Theology (1600–1660)." *Church History* 51 (1982) 24–38.

Strobel, Kyle. "Jonathan Edwards' Reformed Doctrine of the Beatific Vision." In *Jonathan Edwards and Scotland*, edited by Kenneth P. Minkema et al., 171–88. Edinburgh: Dunedin Academic Press, 2011.

Sullivan, Erin. "Doctrinal Doubleness and the Meaning of Despair in William Perkins's 'Table' and Nathaniel Woodes's *The Conflict of Conscience*." *Studies of Philology* 110 (2013) 533–61.

Thomas, W. H. Griffith. *The Principles of Theology: An Introduction to The Thirty-Nine Articles*. Eugene, OR: Wipf & Stock, 2005.

Tipson, Lynn Baird, Jr. "The Development of a Puritan Understanding of Conversion." PhD diss., Yale University, 1972.

Toon, Peter, ed. *Puritans, the Millennium, and the Future of Israel: Puritan Eschatology, 1600–1660*. London: Clark, 1970.

Torrance, T. F. *Scottish Theology: From John Knox to John McLeod Campbell*. Edinburgh: T. & T. Clark, 1996.

Tufft, J. R. "William Perkins, 1558–1602: His Thought and Activity." PhD diss., University of Edinburgh, 1952.

Tuke, Thomas. "Dedication Epistle." In *The Works of William Perkins*, edited by Joel R. Beeke and Greg A. Salazar, 6:277–302. Grand Rapids: Reformation Heritage, 2018.

Ussher, James. *A Body of Divinity: Or, The Sum and Substance of Christian Religion*. Edited by Michael Nevarr. Birmingham, AL: Solid Ground Christian, 2007.

Vos, Geerhardus. *The Pauline Eschatology*. Phillipsburg, NJ: P&R, 1994.

Watson, Thomas. *The Beatitudes: An Exposition of Matthew 5:1–12*. Carlisle, PA: Banner of Truth, 2000.

*The Way to True Happiness: Leading to the Gate of Knowledge*. London, 1613.

Weaver, Stephen G., Jr., and Ian Hugh Clary, eds. *The Pure Flame of Devotion: The History of Christian Spirituality*. Ontario: Joshua, 2013.

Westbury, Joshua R., ed. "The Lexham Figurative Language of the New Testament Dataset." In *Lexham Figurative Language of the Bible Glossary*. Bellingham, WA: Faithlife, 2016.

*The Westminster Confession of Faith*. Oak Harbor, WA: Logos, 1996.

White, Thomas. *A Method and Instructions for the Art of Divine Meditation, with Instances of the several Kindes of Solemne Meditation*. London, 1672.

Wilcox, William G. "New England Covenant Theology: Its Precursors and Early American Exponents." PhD diss., Duke University, 1959.

Wilken, Robert Louis. *The Spirit of Early Christian Thought: Seeking the Face of God*. New Haven: Yale University Press, 2003.

Williams, James Eugene, Jr. "An Evaluation of William Perkins' Doctrine of Predestination in the Light of John Calvin's Writings." ThM thesis, Dallas Theological Seminary, 1986.

Wisse, Maarten, et al., eds. *Scholasticism Reformed: Essays in Honour of Willem J. van Asselt*. Leiden: Brill, 2010.

Woolsey, Andrew A. *Unity and Continuity in Covenantal Thought: A Study in the Reformed Tradition to the Westminster Assembly*. Grand Rapids: Reformation Heritage, 2012.

Wright, Louis B. "William Perkins: Elizabethan Apostle of 'Practical Divinity.'" *Huntington Library Quarterly* 3 (1940) 171–96.

Yuille, J. Stephen. "'Blessedness' in the Piety of William Perkins: Objective Reality or Subjective Experience?" *Puritan Reformed Journal* 2 (2009) 155–69.

———. "Conversing with God's Word: Scripture Meditation in the Piety of George Swinnock." *Journal of Spiritual Formation & Soul Care* 5 (2012) 35–55.

———. *Great Spoil: Thomas Manton's Spirituality of the Word*. Grand Rapids: Reformation Heritage, 2019.

———. *Living Blessedly Forever: The Sermon on the Mount and the Puritan Piety of William Perkins*. Grand Rapids: Reformation Heritage, 2012.

———. "A Puritan, Spiritual Household: William Perkins and the 'Right Ordering' of a Family." *Puritan Reformed Journal* 8 (2016) 158–79.

———. *Puritan Spirituality: The Fear of God in the Affective Theology of George Swinnock*. Eugene, OR: Wipf & Stock, 2007.

———. "Ready to Receive: Humbling and Softening in William Perkins's Preparation of the Heart." *Puritan Reformed Journal* 5 (2013) 91–106.

———. "'A Simple Method': William Perkins and the Shaping of the Protestant Pulpit." *Puritan Reformed Journal* 9 (2017) 215–30.

———. "William Perkins, Part One—Puritan Pastors and Influential Figures." *Vimeo*. https://vimeo.com/ondemand/puritan/472296598.

# Index

## OLD TESTAMENT

*Genesis*

| | |
|---|---|
| 1:26–27 | 29 |
| 1:28 | 33 |
| 1:31 | 30 |
| 2:15 | 31, 32 |
| 2:17 | 33, 37, 38, 39n84 |
| 3:15 | 42 |
| 3:24 | 33 |
| 12:3 | 16 |

*Leviticus*

| | |
|---|---|
| 16:1–6 | 116 |
| 18:5 | 39n84 |

*Numbers*

| | |
|---|---|
| 24:17 | 103n60 |

*1 Samuel*

| | |
|---|---|
| 16 | 65n89 |

*2 Samuel*

| | |
|---|---|
| 5 | 65n89 |

*Psalms*

| | |
|---|---|
| | 5 |
| 2:12 | 67 |
| 8:5 | 31 |
| 16:11 | 26 |
| 90:12 | 111 |

*Ecclesiastes*

| | |
|---|---|
| 5:4 | 77 |

*Isaiah*

| | |
|---|---|
| 49:8 | 51 |
| 53:2–3 | 66 |
| 65:17 | 60 |

*Jeremiah*

| | |
|---|---|
| 23:29 | 83 |

*Daniel*

| | |
|---|---|
| 12:3 | 64 |

*Malachi*

| | |
|---|---|
| 3:1 | 51 |

## NEW TESTAMENT

*Matthew*

| | |
|---|---|
| 5:48 | 127 |
| 10:32 | 104 |
| 11:28 | 133n239 |
| 12:36 | 117 |
| 17:1–13 | 63 |
| 18:18 | 122 |
| 19:28 | 15n19 |
| 24:13 | 130, 133n239 |
| 24:30 | 16 |
| 24:31 | 17 |
| 25:21 | 99 |
| 25:32 | 18 |

## INDEX

### Matthew (continued)

| | |
|---|---|
| 25:34 | 19, 99 |
| 25:41 | 19 |
| 25:46 | 19 |
| 28:18 | 67 |
| 28:19 | 49 |

### Mark

| | |
|---|---|
| 9:1–13 | 63 |
| 12:29–30 | 93 |

### Luke

| | |
|---|---|
| 9:28–36 | 63 |
| 10:28 | 39n84 |
| 18:29–30 | 129 |
| 21:25 | 16 |
| 24:50 | 65 |

### John

| | |
|---|---|
| 1:4 | 98n32 |
| 1:16 | 71 |
| 1:18 | 23 |
| 3:5 | 73 |
| 11 | 87 |
| 14:2–3 | 112 |
| 14:9 | 23 |
| 15:1 | 81 |
| 15:4 | 133n239 |
| 15:19 | 83 |
| 20:17 | 64 |

### Acts

| | |
|---|---|
| 1–10 | 142n22 |
| 1–28 | 142n22 |
| 2:15–17 | 10 |
| 22:16 | 77 |

### Romans

| | |
|---|---|
| 3:23 | 80 |
| 5 | 37, 45 |
| 6:3 | 77 |
| 6:3–4 | 76 |
| 6:5 | 61, 80, 97n27 |
| 6:12 | 76 |
| 6:23 | 80, 111 |
| 8:3 | 56 |
| 8:9 | 75 |
| 8:19 | 123, 130 |
| 8:23 | 125 |
| 8:29 | 93 |
| 11 | 140 |

### 1 Corinthians

| | |
|---|---|
| 1:30 | 52 |
| 3:16 | 75 |
| 3:21 | 82 |
| 10:3 | 43 |
| 10:11 | 11 |
| 10:13 | 132 |
| 13:12 | 26 |
| 15 | 45 |
| 15:13–17 | 61 |
| 15:42–51 | 62 |
| 15:44 | 101 |

### 2 Corinthians

| | |
|---|---|
| 3:18 | 21, 21n60 |
| 4:6 | 21 |
| 5:7 | 124 |
| 5:10 | 18 |
| 5:17 | 60 |
| 7:1 | 126 |

### Galatians

| | |
|---|---|
| 2:16 | 39 |
| 2:20 | 80 |
| 3:8 | 16 |
| 3:20 | 39 |
| 3:24 | 39n84 |
| 4:4 | 11 |
| 4:24–25 | 39 |
| 5:5–6 | 123 |
| 5:16–24 | 76 |

### Ephesians

| | |
|---|---|
| 1:3 | 65, 92 |
| 2:8–9 | 48 |
| 4:1 | 7 |
| 4:8 | 20n55 |
| 4:11 | 59 |
| 4:24 | 93 |

## Philippians

| | |
|---|---|
| 1:6 | 130 |
| 1:21 | 94 |
| 2:7–8 | 56 |
| 3:9 | 81 |
| 3:11–14 | 98 |
| 3:20–21 | 136 |
| 3:21 | 101 |
| 4:8 | 106 |

## Colossians

| | |
|---|---|
| 1:15 | 23 |
| 2:3 | 23, 71, 109 |
| 3:1 | 115 |
| 3:10 | 93 |

## 1 Thessalonians

| | |
|---|---|
| 1:5 | 120 |
| 4:16 | 17 |
| 5:2 | 11 |
| 5:4 | 130 |
| 5:24 | 124 |

## 2 Thessalonians

| | |
|---|---|
| 2 | 13, 14n19 |
| 2:3 | 13n13 |
| 2:3–4 | 13 |
| 2:6 | 13 |
| 2:8 | 13n13 |

## 1 Timothy

| | |
|---|---|
| 4:1 | 10 |
| 4:16 | 117 |
| 6:16 | 23 |

## 2 Timothy

| | |
|---|---|
| 3:1 | 10 |
| 3:1–5 | 15, 15n25 |

## Titus

| | |
|---|---|
| 1:2 | 132 |
| 2:13 | 11, 123 |

## Hebrews

| | |
|---|---|
| 1:2 | 10 |
| 1:3 | 23, 134 |
| 2:10 | 80, 116 |
| 6:18 | 124 |
| 8:6 | 53 |
| 9:27 | 110 |
| 11:10 | 26, 26n94 |
| 11:40 | 98 |
| 12:1 | 134 |
| 12:24 | 53 |

## James

| | |
|---|---|
| 1:15 | 111 |
| 5:3 | 10 |

## 1 Peter

| | |
|---|---|
| 1:20 | 10 |
| 3:21 | 76, 77 |
| 4:11 | 93 |
| 5:2–4 | 118 |

## 2 Peter

| | |
|---|---|
| 1:4 | 92, 129, 137 |
| 3:3 | 10 |
| 3:10 | 17 |

## 1 John

| | |
|---|---|
| 2:18 | 10 |
| 3:1 | 102 |
| 3:2 | 102 |
| 3:3 | 25 |

## Jude

| | |
|---|---|
| 25 | 66 |

## Revelation

| | |
|---|---|
| | 25, 95, 139–57 |
| 1 | 156 |
| 1–3 | 141, 142, 142n28, 151, 153, 156 |
| 2 | 156 |
| 2–3 | 95 |
| 2:7 | 96, 99 |
| 2:10 | 100n41 |
| 2:11 | 96 |
| 2:17 | 96, 100 |
| 2:26 | 96 |
| 2:26–28 | 102 |

## INDEX

*Revelation (continued)*

| | |
|---|---|
| 3 | 156 |
| 3:5 | 96, 103 |
| 3:12 | 96, 104 |
| 3:21 | 96, 105, 106 |
| 4 | 141, 143, 151, 153, 156 |
| 4–6 | 143n31 |
| 4–7 | 148, 156 |
| 4–11 | 142n28, 143, 153 |
| 5 | 141, 151, 153, 156 |
| 5–6 | 143 |
| 6 | 14, 151, 153, 156 |
| 6–9 | 141, 142, 151 |
| 7 | 14, 141, 143, 143n31, 151, 153, 156 |
| 8 | 143, 151, 153, 156 |
| 8–9 | 141 |
| 8–11 | 143, 143n31, 148, 156 |
| 8:13 | 145n51 |
| 9 | 14, 14n16, 151, 153, 156 |
| 9:12 | 145n51 |
| 9–13 | 144 |
| 9:20 | 14n16 |
| 10 | 144, 151, 153, 156 |
| 10:2 | 145n47 |
| 10:9–10 | 145n49 |
| 10–20 | 142, 151 |
| 11 | 142, 145, 151, 153, 156 |
| 11:8 | 12n10 |
| 11:14 | 145n51 |
| 12 | 142, 146, 151, 154, 157 |
| 12:17 | 14 |
| 12–22 | 142n28, 146, 154 |
| 13 | 13, 146, 148, 151, 154, 157 |
| 13:8 | 13, 14n19 |
| 13:11 | 13 |
| 13:16 | 13, 14n19 |
| 14 | 14, 142, 146, 148, 151, 154, 157 |
| 15 | 14, 142, 151, 154, 157 |
| 15–16 | 146, 148 |
| 16 | 142, 151, 154, 157 |
| 17 | 14, 146, 154, 157 |
| 17–18 | 142, 149, 151 |
| 18 | 146, 154, 157 |
| 18:4 | 133 |
| 19 | 142, 146, 149, 151, 154, 157 |
| 20 | 14, 142, 146, 151, 154, 157 |
| 20:1–8 | 13 |
| 20:5 | 13, 14n19 |
| 20:6 | 94 |
| 20:12 | 18 |
| 20:15 | 19 |
| 21 | 154 |
| 21–22 | 142, 146, 149, 151, 157 |
| 22 | 154 |

## EARLY CHRISTIAN WRITINGS

| | |
|---|---|
| Aquinas, Thomas | 34 |

*Summa Theologica*

| | |
|---|---|
| Suppl. Q. 92, a, 1 | 21n64, 22n64 |
| Suppl. Q. 92, a, 1–3 | 21n64 |
| Suppl. Q. 92, a, 2 | 22n64 |

*Augustine*

34, 63, 134, 140

*City of God*

| | |
|---|---|
| 266 | 140n11 |
| 269 | 140n10 |

| | |
|---|---|
| "Sermon de. Temp" | 63n76 |
| Cyril | 134 |
| Irenaeus of Lyons | 34 |
| Tertullian | 34 |

www.ingramcontent.com/pod-product-compliance
Lightning Source LLC
Chambersburg PA
CBHW062047220426
43662CB00010B/1681